CAN A WOMAN PREACH

JOSEPH BRICE

Copyright

Dedication

To my lovely wife, Janet, thank you for your love, support, and sacrifices. You are the one. I am so proud of you for taking the steps for Theological Studies and passing with honors. I'm impressed with your knowledge of the scriptures and even more so with your dedicated prayer life and vision of "The Wailing Women." "Keep fighting the good fight of faith."

To the youngest of my girls, Cianilyz "CiCi" and Briche', I want you to know that I firmly believe I was born for a time such as this, to fight for you and break down barriers that man has put in place so that you can walk in the path God has chosen for you. Always remember, God knew you before you came into this world. Keep Him first above all else, and you will never be last.

To my beloved daughters, Eboni, Latara, Jada, Ajia, Azaria, and Promise, know that God knew you before your father and mother even—thought of meeting. It was crucial for you to be here in this world that nothing and no one could stop the divine plan, regardless of situations and circumstances.

Now that you are here, be aware of your purpose. I

want you to know that you are part of a generation of women witnessing and will continue to see historic changes in the world toward gender equality. As a father, I would never want you to experience any injustice or discrimination because of your gender."Equal work for equal pay." Initially, I didn't understand why God blessed me with so many daughters, but now it's becoming more apparent.

I have a personal and vested interest in fighting for good women's rights. You all give me hope for the future, showing that only good women can change our society positively. Always remember who you are and what you stand for in this world and the next. You have already achieved so much. Keep fighting for justice and truth. Continue to be a positive force in our society. Overall, keep God first.

I sincerely thank Howard, Geneva Cottman, and the Kingdom Rights Family for their invaluable help and support. This project would not have been possible without their contribution. Elder Howard, your spiritual growth is evident and commendable. You have come a long way, and your dedication for two decades now goes without scrutiny.

Evangelist Geneva, I am so proud of you as a woman and woman of God. Congratulations on graduating from the 2024 Metamorphosis Experience Program. You pressed your way and are so faithful. Shout out to Women of

Stamina for the great job they do.

To my dear brother Louis White, I want to express my sincere gratitude for the invaluable lessons you have taught me. During a challenging time in my life, you spoke words of wisdom that still resonate with me today. You said, "Remember who you are; you are better than to succumb to the enemy." Your inspiring words gave me the strength to keep moving forward, no matter what life throws at me. No matter the opinions of flesh, you are spirit and touched by the hands of YHWH… No one can take that away from you. Always remember your true identity and hold onto the light that shines within you.

Hey, my Brother Joe Carter, I had to give you a shout-out because you're an awesome brother with an incredible testimony. It's unbelievable how our paths have crossed, and I believe it's all part of a more excellent plan God ordained for us. Trust me; this isn't a coincidence. It's not what it looks like, and I'm confident we're headed for something big. So let's prepare for more incredible things, Brother. We've got this.

Hey Jaiden, I hear you have your ride now; that's what's up. I'm glad for you. Remember to put God first; I would like you to take the seven-minute prayer God challenge. Give God 7 minutes when you start your day, and watch what God will do in your life. Peace, be sure to take care of Mom.

* * *

To mother Schries Carter, the last couple of years have been a journey, but look how God has been with you to bring you out and look good! Keep the faith, and your laboring is not in vain. Peace and blessings.

To my neighbors, Brother Robert and Sister Shirley, you guys are so faithful. I admire how you press your way and continue to support your church, no matter what is going on… awesome! Great is your reward; keep the faith.

Brother Cortney Fraizer. You're in the kingdom now! You are working so hard, and your efforts will surely pay off. Remember to keep praying and prioritize God in your life. You will soon realize nothing surprises God, who is always with you, even when walking alone.

Prophetess Hurline McGee, you are wise beyond your years. Don't count it strange that as the daughter of the Most High, you have been set apart, and in due season, the words he has placed in your mouth shall be released.

Prophetess Llisa Dorsey, With all that you have gone through, you are like a sword that has been beaten, shaped, and put in the fire, but when it's finished, it is the weapon of protection and defense. Be confident in the God who knew you and has chosen you. Rise and Shine, Woman of God.

* * *

Evangelist Bernice Sanders, Since the beginning, our spirits have been kindred. Thank you for being the woman of God and giving yourself unselfishly to the cause of Kingdom Rights Vision. May God continue to keep and Bless you.

To Joni and the Lovely Lady Center, I had to give you a shout-out. The ladies there do tremendous work, and I commend your hard work and passion in serving one another. It was a pleasure to speak at the center and share the word of God, along with my testimony of how God set me free so many years ago, and I am still free. What the Holy Spirit can do and how He can deliver and reveal is fantastic. May God continue to bless and lead you. The church has so much work we need to do. Peace and Blessings to you all.

To Tamara Lowe, Zack, Julian, and the entire Kingdom Builders Academy family—words cannot fully express my gratitude for the wisdom, guidance, and inspiration you have poured into my life. The lessons I've gained from each of you are truly invaluable, and I am committed to continuing this journey of growth, seeking deeper understanding of the Kingdom and God's divine purpose for His people.

A special shoutout to Coach Cindy Nash—you are a true inspiration! I deeply appreciate the way you challenge me to reach higher and strive for greater. Thank you all!

'Do the right things, in the right way, in the right order!'

This book is a tribute to all the women, past and present, who have devoted their lives to answering the call of God and spreading the message of Jesus Christ. Your commitment and dedication to this noble cause is truly inspiring. We honor your unwavering faith in the face of the many challenges and sacrifices you have endured. We recognize the many obstacles you have overcome, including discrimination, persecution, and often isolation. Despite these challenges, you have persisted, and your work has touched the lives of countless people. We are grateful for your selflessness and your tireless efforts to make the world a better place. This book is a testament to your achievements and a reminder of the vital role that women have played in shaping the history of Christians everywhere.

For those daughters who have had to make the difficult decision to leave their homes due to unfavorable circumstances, it is essential to acknowledge the strength and courage it takes. It is likely that such decisions were made with great thought and consideration and that you have worked tirelessly to secure a place for yourself in this world. We have been endowed with a unique portion of divine providence; you are no exception. However, life can be unpredictable, and it is not uncommon for one abusive situation to be traded for another that is even direr. Trusting in God is the key to a fulfilling life.

Keep in mind that He knew you even before you knew yourself. Let His voice be your guide, and don't ignore the small voice inside you that agrees with His plan. Remember that seeking help is not a sign of weakness but strength. You are never alone. Jesus is always there with you, and everything happens for a reason. You have overcome so much since your childhood. Surrendering your heart to Him will reveal the purpose over time.

The fact that you are reading this proves you can overcome any obstacle. When God calls for you, answer with an open heart and mind. Your life will be forever changed for the better. You cannot know how great you are until you give Jesus the wheel and let Him be your driver through life.

We are praying for you,

Joseph Brice and Kingdom Rights

Testimonial

Saved by Grace: A Journey from Addiction to Salvation

Description: In the darkest depths of addiction, salvation found me in the most unexpected way. My life was spiraling out of control—three days high and intoxicated, yearning for peace and sleep that eluded me. On an early Easter morning, I felt a divine nudge, a voice whispering, "Today is the day of salvation." Desperate and frightened, I heeded the call, despite not having stepped inside a church for over a decade.

Guided to my mother's church, I encountered an old acquaintance who had been clean for over three years—a beacon of hope. Inside, the woman pastor proclaimed that God had changed her message: "Today is the day of salvation." These words, echoing what I had already heard twice that morning, pierced my heart.

The pastor's sermon on God's immense love, Jesus' sacrifice, and the cleansing power of His blood stirred a powerful conviction within me. At the altar, I confessed my sins and gave my life to the Lord. Through her prayer, I was set free, born again, and filled with the Holy Spirit. That transformative moment occurred over thirty years ago, and I have remained free from drugs and alcohol ever since.

Reflecting on that pivotal day, I recognize the vital role of women in ministry. Had this woman pastor succumbed to the opposition against her calling, I might have died in my sins. Jesus faced opposition and criticism but persisted, proclaiming His eternal authority.

I am profoundly grateful that this woman answered God's call to preach. Her obedience saved me from destruction and taught me about the love of Jesus Christ. My story stands as a testament to the power of women in ministry. Jesus said, "You are witnesses of me; go preach the gospel of the kingdom." Women of God, stand firm in your calling. You have the authority to preach and the power to overcome the enemy. PREACH, WOMAN!

Introduction

Know this and understand: **God is your Father. You are His daughter, a citizen of His Kingdom, and a joint heir with Jesus Christ.**

You are not a bystander—you are an **owner** in His Kingdom. It's time to rise, walk in your divine authority, and represent your Father's house with confidence and power!

When God chooses you, it's not something you can explain; it has to be experienced. Although God is the same and will never change, the experience of the one chosen is quite different and unique, having its own character stemming from Him. God has called and chosen you, so you are an original, not a copy of who you may admire and be tempted to compete against.

God is the Original, who has called you, ultimately choosing you, so don't accept your calling and then get trapped into trying to be a duplicate of what has already been done. We must build on those before us who have proven God chose them. Each person God determines has their spiritual fingerprint and footprint for life's journey. Whatever we do on earth is temporary for us but not for those whose lives we have touched and chosen to be impactful to bring about necessary change.

* * *

When God has chosen you to do something, be something, or say something, there is a constant nag at your spirit concerning what you are called to do. Where most of us fail at answering the call or being fulfilled by walking in the call, we are too concerned about what others may think or say about us. We seek affirmation from people far more than confirmation from God, who created us. We worship and esteem the creature more than we do the creator in many cases.

The selection by God is often accompanied by the breaking of established norms and standard procedures. It remains a puzzle why chosen individuals often engage in conflict with one another. One must recall the arduous nature of the journey towards fulfilling God's will and how it commenced. To be selected by God, it is essential to avoid relationships with individuals who prioritize money, as this invariably leads to a rift. Such individuals tend to worship money and finding harmony or complete concordance with them is unfeasible. Just as one made the decision to choose God after realizing His choice, one's peers must do likewise. This book serves as a testament to my loyalty to God and my admiration for Him.

I have been chosen by God to share the revelations and content of this book. I have been an ordained minister and pastor for over two decades and have experience with what goes on behind the scenes of the church. My confidence comes from my experience with God, knowing His voice, and therefore, I speak with authority because I am sent from the highest authority. I had to pay a high price to write this book, but God challenged me to put Him first. Through hardship and humility, I discovered that God's grace and mercy are boundless. This message is from God, and the next generation must thrive. You are not alone, and I am here to support you on your journey.

Many people wait for a sign from God, and this message is just that - one of many yet to come. Although natural disasters may cause fear and despair, it's important to remember that you're not alone in your struggles. Many people are searching for the original church that Jesus founded - a church of unity and love where ordinary individuals can achieve extraordinary things. You are one of His chosen ones, and your faith will guide you through the toughest of times.

For those who are not called to preach but are called to be the best woman they can be, don't allow anyone or anything to stop you from your purpose and destiny. If you are a woman and know that you are a real woman, then respect and represent her. Know that if God made you a woman, He purposely made you a game changer. There's no greater influence in this world than you besides God Himself. Bring the good to this troubling world that only you can. You have been ordained to have God's glory and favor to work alongside your anointing.

The enemy knows this and has been abusing you while recruiting you at the same time to work for his kingdom, with the understanding that you have the power to turn things around. It's a war going on in the world, and we fight the fight everywhere and every day in politics, relationships, families, marriages, churches, amongst leaders, our careers, our finances, our jobs, and above all, the war in our minds. Fight like you've never fought before the fight of faith!

We must be warriors for Christ and the right things. Warriors for your rights as a woman and a woman of God. Whatever you are supposed to do, then fight to do it! We are fighting the fight of faith because we cannot see what we are fighting, but the fight is real, and so are the defeats and or victories.

On that day, you will be surprised at who this weak devil is who you allowed to lead you and destroy your life if you don't get to know God and the gift given in the sum of Jesus Christ.

I am a warrior of Christ and the kingdom. I am looking forward to the day when I crossover to eternity and judgment, where I will be allowed to see eye to eye and fight this cowardly devil who has been hiding behind anyone and anything, manipulating circumstances, and not taking responsibility for the evils he has caused and the lives he deceived and destroyed.

In the beginning, Adam failed to protect his woman from the enemy in the garden. This was not because he didn't love her but because he lacked the necessary skills, experience, wisdom, and strength to save her.

However, the second man, Adam (Jesus Christ), defeated the enemy, he went into the wilderness to find the devil and confronted him to reclaim the authority for the man and woman. Christ laid down his life willingly and died on the cross and said, "It is finished." Another translation says, "It is completion." He was pierced in his side, through his ribcage, and out of him came blood and water, which gave birth to the church, later to be called his bride. This restored the woman to her rightful place with God and by her husband's side.

The Genesis account affirms that Eve was formed from Adam's rib and taken from his side. This is where God intended for her to be. It stands to reason that if the second Adam, Jesus, is responsible for humanity's redemption, then women should be fully reinstated and given their place and authority back. The schism between men and women originated from the sinister, but Christ has bridged the divide. The woman did not come out of the man's behind but his side; therefore, she is not required to be behind him. Instead, she can walk hand in hand with him as her partner, side by side. She is not his competition, but his completion. Together, they become one, and unity is their strength. As the word of God says, "One can chase a thousand, but two can put ten thousand to flight."

We are divided on many things; a woman preaching should not be one of them. We need all our help in these last and evil days! One of the most controversial subject matters in the church is about a woman preaching. For a long time, this has been the question that many leaders, predominantly men, say NO to a woman preaching. Many believe that women should be silent as well as not teach or have authority over men in the church according to scriptures in the Bible, "1 Corinthians 14:34, 1 Timothy 2:11-12" are the most famous quotes to address this subject.

* * *

Previously, women were not allowed to attend the temple alongside men. According to the law, women were repeatedly reminded of the sin of eating fruit from the forbidden tree and their conversation with the serpent, resulting in deception. People used to live accordingly being the seed of Abraham and by the Law of Moses. Before writing the letters that are respectfully regarded as scriptures in the New Testament, Paul communicated with the Gentile churches since the Jews rejected him. Paul's first ministry was established with the non-Jewish people.

The way certain scriptures are used can sometimes be unfair, as they may not accurately interpret the truth. This is especially evident in the context of the early church when women did not have equal rights, and the law of Moses was still prevalent. It is important to note that Paul (formerly known as Saul) was a follower of Moses but was ultimately saved by the grace of Jesus Christ. As he struggled between these two ways of salvation, he was caught between the Law and Grace, two men (Saul and Paul), two natures, and two sets of characteristics, trying to fulfill both without negating the other. This was the dilemma Paul faced, and his transformation from Saul to Paul was the evidence of his internal struggle.

The spiritual development of the apostle is not being duly recognized. Jesus is imparting to him extraordinary revelations and insights about the mysteries of the kingdom of heaven that have never been seen or heard of before in this world. These revelations shape the apostle's understanding of the divine and give him a deeper insight

into the nature of God through Jesus Christ and his
kingdom.

The problem is that when Saul was converted on the road
to Damascus, he was on assignment to persecute and kill
the very people that he became. Saul was given the
authority to kill these followers of Jesus. Now that he has
become one of them supernaturally, he has no apostle to
go to because of his reputation as a Christian killer. He's
not able to return to headquarters in Jerusalem because he
is considered a traitor, and there is a warrant for his arrest.
Now, the same authorities who tried and condemned Jesus
to death were in desperate want for Saul to make a public
example out of him because the Pharisees believed he was
forsaking the law of Moses.

Saul must escape to survive, just as believers had to run
away from him. Despite being a newly converted believer,
no one wants to believe him. He has no teacher to guide
and tell him about the testimonies and witness accounts of
Jesus' ministry and resurrection. Saul, a Jewish Pharisee,
was unaware of the significance of Pentecost and the upper
room experience where the Holy Spirit descended upon
Peter, the apostles, men, and women on that monumental
and historical day for the first church.

Why would God have women present and tarrying for the
Holy Ghost and Power, if He wanted women to be silent
and not be witnesses and preach the gospel alongside the
men? The church was a new movement from heaven
inclusive of men and women, Adam and Eve.

* * *

Before Saul's conversion, he was in a position to put that movement of church called, "The Way" to rest or death. Later after receiving his encounter with Jesus on the road to Damascus and receiving the Holy Spirit, he went into hiding, trying to escape the wrath of the Jews who were after him for abandoning his assignment of persecuting the early Christians.

Despite his situation, Saul desperately needed knowledge about Jesus and who He was. Saul found refuge among the Gentile people, whom the Jews shunned, and this allowed him to research and learn about Jesus in his own way. However, since he had no disciple or apostle(one who actually, physically walked with Jesus to guide him. He had no one who had experienced, been taught by him who understood the purpose of the church and its model. Understandably, Saul's understanding of Jesus was limited, to say the least. He had to search for understanding and secretly learn of Jesus' ministry and teachings by others who had been taught by Jesus' disciples.

Saul's notoriety as a tyrant grew amongst the believers, so he realized he needed to change his identity to avoid being caught. He changed his name to Paul, a character that would not arouse suspicion and allow him to continue his learning of Jesus and the church secretly. Despite the danger and challenges he faced, Paul was determined to spread the message of Jesus Christ to the Jews and the Gentiles, and little may he know how his teachings would continue to inspire and guide Christians around the world to this day.

The initial epistle addressed to the Thessalonians church, a congregation of Gentiles, reflects

Paul's beginnings and evolving understanding of grace. In his approach, Paul remains under the law, as is evidenced by his reference to the dead in Christ rising first. This notion is grounded in the teachings of the Tora, The Law of Moses, and the prophets, which suggest that those who die await the coming of the Messiah. However, in later teachings, Paul avers that "To be absent from the body is to be present with the Lord." This assertion affirms his belief that following Jesus' resurrection, there is no waiting period between death and life, nor the sleeping in the grave waiting for the trumpet to sound, at least not for us, this will be after the rapture and second coming of Christ. Paul began to understand there will be rewards in the kingdom of heaven, which is bestowed upon the faithful believers, and those who encounter suffering.

It is unfair to take Paul's letters to the early churches as a universal message, without understanding his position and absence of maturity in the grace of Jesus Christ at the time. He was under tremendous pressure to prove himself to the people of "The Way" (believers of Jesus) and to convince the Pharisees that Jesus was not an enemy of The Law of Moses or an impostor and false teacher. That Jesus came to fulfill the law not destroy it. Grace is the fulfillment.

After his encounter and later relationship with Christ, Paul wanted them to know that Jesus was truly the awaited Messiah of the Jews. He desperately wanted them to believe in Jesus and accept him and his followers as brothers and sisters, not enemies. However, many of the priests did not believe in Jesus, his disciples, or Paul. They were determined to kill both Paul and Saul as they did Jesus and annihilate this movement.

These popular scriptures, as we know them, were in a letter written by the Apostle Paul to the churches over the years. Saul/ Paul (a Pharisee) was a very educated and accomplished man concerning the law of Moses. However, the Apostle Paul later wrote that there is neither male nor female, for we are all one in Christ Jesus" Galatians 3:28. In one of his letters to the early church, the apostle Paul boldly stated that circumcision was not a requirement for salvation. This view was in direct opposition to the belief held by many Jewish believers at the time, who saw circumcision as an essential aspect of their faith and a necessary step towards redemption. Paul's message sparked intense debate and controversy among the Jewish Christian community, with some seeing it as a dangerous departure from traditional teachings. Despite the backlash, Paul's teachings on circumcision eventually gained wider acceptance and helped pave the way for a more inclusive and diverse Christian faith, especially among non-Jewish people, known as Gentiles.

This disobedience was the cause of the fall of humanity. God said to the serpent, because of what you have done, I will put enmity between you and the woman, your seed and her seed. The woman's seed will crush the serpent's head, and the serpent's seed will strike the seed of the woman's heel, and your husband will rule over you."

Genesis 3:13-16. When this prophecy is fulfilled, the woman will be vindicated by the pains and sorrows manifesting while carrying God's seed and giving birth to his son.

Once fulfilled, the woman will no longer be under the curse of being ruled by her husband, not in a disrespectful way, but will be restored to her original place of being by his side. Jesus came to put things back in order.

During Jesus' ministry, he broke protocols and norms like talking to the woman at the well without her husband being present, and to top it off, she was a Samarian woman and the Jews had no dealings with the Samaritan people...talking about racists! That woman went into the city preaching and telling people they needed to see this man, he had to be the long-awaited Messiah. First of all, he was not prejudiced and gave her word and love as she had never witnessed before without lust for her flesh. He touched her soul. Well, she couldn't keep that experience silent. She became an evangelist and didn't know what one was...she just became because of Jesus!

After his resurrection, Jesus restored the woman's rights by allowing her to be the first human witness to see his new glorified body and hear his voice. Jesus gives her the first message and assignment to give word from Him after rising from the grave, making her an oracle of God, one who directly carries God's word, not just a preacher. She was responsible for giving the disciples the first word from a Risen Savior and compelling them to believe Jesus was alive and well. Now, she is the speaker of the house, like it or not, sent by God!

* * *

It's a new day and movement. Her sorrows are turned into joy in an instant! Imagine how biased and sexist the men were in those times, now with all of that going on, they were challenged whether to believe a woman's message of hope or be defeated with fear and hopelessness. They chose to believe and ran down to the tomb to see if Jesus was still there. Image them feeling like, why Jesus did not appear to us men first, after all, we are his devoted followers. Remember when Jesus said, "The first shall be last and the last shall be first." Well here we are still fighting over who should preach…the man (first) or the woman who sinned in the garden (last because of the order)?

The Lord assigns her to tell his disciples that He is alive."Do not touch me," Jesus said, I have not yet ascended to my Father, tell them I ascend to my Father and your Father, and my God and your God."

Do we see how powerful, transformative, and historical this assignment was for a woman to carry in toses days? Why would Jesus give this woman such an important assignment and message if he didn't want her to preach? "Can A Woman Preach?" If so...by what authority? Jesus started the woman to message all women who have genuinely repented for their past mistakes and start anew to answer His call. He is not holding what she did in the first garden against her. Still, he has proven her restoration by his intercession in the last Garden of Gethsemane, where he sweated blood and was arrested and taken into custody to pay the price for our sins. Her restoration is in

His resurrection! As long as Jesus lives, then His message lives in you....preach!

Jesus is the first human being on record to put Satan behind him and rule over him…proving his divine authority on earth. When Jesus sacrificed his life, he paid the price for all our sins.

We are facing historically difficult and challenging times in which the anointing is not enough…we also need God's wisdom and glory. Unifying men and women of God would be the game changer.

When Mary gave birth to Jesus over two thousand years ago, it fulfilled the most significant prophecy of redemption. Sin silenced the woman, but grace restored her to speak again, to use her gift of influence and speaking to save lives, not destroy them.
As we contemplate the essence of God's heart and the spirit of the law, we must understand that God is not inclined to punish women who devote themselves to the noble cause of saving souls, preserving lives, and nourishing his flock. The scriptures indeed contain numerous references to gender roles and responsibilities. Still, it is equally valid that these references are often steeped in cultural and historical contexts that may not necessarily apply to our contemporary society.

Is the blood shed for our sins not enough to restore and save? Is there another Christ, Messiah, Cross, or blood that will be shed to regain humanity and redeem us from the curse of the law? According to the prophecy, did Mary birth the seed that would crush the serpent's head? How can the woman's seed crush anything if it is to remain silent?

In the vindication of the woman, she is a victor, not a victim. If she can not preach and proclaim the Kingdom message, give her testimony and experience of how the enemy tried to take her mind along with her innocence and pervert her for his use. She has to speak louder and more effectively than ever because the serpent wants the woman to swing from the pole. You are not Satan's employee, but in Christ, you are forever more his boss.

Did the woman come out of the man's side? Why are we so determined to put her behind the man…she did not come from the man's behind or hinder parts. She should represent the man's heart like the church is the bride of Christ. The birthplace of the woman and the church is the heart, as it was said that Jesus' side was pierced, and out of it came blood and water. Do we genuinely believe in the deepest parts of our hearts that God would hate a woman for wanting to spread the good news of the kingdom and lift Jesus so that he may draw all people to Himself?

Jesus did not come here to die for you and then tell you to shut your mouth while the enemy molests, rapes, and abuses you all in the name of God…the devil is a liar! Can't nobody tell your story the way you can? No one has two wombs like you do…the natural one and the heart, the spiritual one. Every human has a heart (spiritual womb); this is the mystery of why salvation is the work of the heart and not the works of the flesh…it's your choice to accept it. But only the woman has the natural and spiritual womb.

You are so uniquely put together. You need to begin to understand why the devil wants to use you without you knowing you're being used. He can't make it without you!

This little factoid about the devil: he wants to use your body, mind, and mouth for everything and anything else but to preach the gospel and word of God. You can be anything but a speaking spirit for God. Satan wants to use your body…your flesh for lust; on the other hand, God made you from love and wants to use your passion to save your seed and a generation. The devil didn't make you; God did. Who are you representing? You are representing something.

What kingdom are you in? You are always saying something, but you can't be a mouthpiece for God; now, who made that a universal rule? Indeed, not your God. You have been given the authority and anointing to speak this truth. The Holy Ghost won't hold His peace, so by what authority do you do what you do? Be bold and beautiful. Blow that devil up! Your voice is a powerful force.

Let the world hear you proclaim the gospel of God's kingdom and His Christ. Preach!
"How, then, will they call on him whom they have not believed? And how are they to believe in him of whom they have never heard? And how are they to hear without someone preaching? And how are they to preach unless they are sent? As it is written, "How beautiful are the feet of those who preach the good news!" But they have not all obeyed the gospel. For Isaiah says, "Lord, who has

believed what he has heard from us?" So faith comes from hearing and hearing through the word of Christ. But I ask, have they not heard?
Indeed they have, for "Their voice has gone out to all the earth, and their words to the ends of the world." Roman 10: 14-18.

She's pleading with you, telling you that God is calling her to preach and to pastor. She is afraid to say it to you because she knows your stance on a woman preaching. She sees you as a man of God and highly respects your anointing. To her surprise, you are not her confirmation; you are set on God being against a woman preaching and teaching. You tell her, "God did not tell you to pastor or preach." She is baffled because God is not the author of confusion. She has no clue that she is a servant of God, and God is indeed calling her because she trusts you, but you need her to serve you. Man we are not her God!

The Problem is that God will not stop calling her all day and night because she belongs to him. Serving you has become your high. You and your people feel so good and powerful telling the woman God did not call her to preach. But why with so much hate and sarcasm? Now, she is stuck and bound. You will give her scripture backing up what you say every chance you get. She may not know and understand that the devil quoted scriptures to Jesus, but Jesus, being the word, did not just quote scriptures but also held the revelation to His word...hidden mysteries from the foundations of the world.

The Pharisees were skilled in quoting the scriptures but

could not live the word that they quoted. The woman and other women know they are more of your servant than the Lord's. Do any of us genuinely believe that apostle Paul is hateful and mean, rejoicing at the fact that we can stop someone's joy in serving their God because of a misinterpreted letter? Paul is not dead but alive, and when women go to heaven who have preached and pastored and ask did you tell the world and every generation that by gender, they have no right to preach the gospel and word of God?

I believe with everything in me that Paul's reply would be, I am not God. I asked the early church "Is Christ divided? was Paul crucified for you? or were you baptized in the name of Paul?" 1 Corinthians 1:13. Paul didn't save you, and neither did Apollos; why are you guys so carnal-minded? Serve God, not man. So, woman of God, will you make a god out of a man, or will you give honor where honor is due, but if they cannot hear God's voice, you have to move on? Maybe they are living off of their past experiences with God, like the Pharisees but have not heard from God in a long time. God is not dead; he is still moving and still speaking.

Many leaders like pastors, bishops, and prophets have hated me for the word of God delivered to them as warnings from God. These leaders lied to me and used their positions to profane what is precious to God. Just as it was in the days of the prophets, no one can stop God! There is nothing more important to God than His people and their souls. For 24 years, God had me traveling into a place in Him that cannot be observed with a carnal mind.

* * *

Being like other pastors and preachers, I had no clue how much idolatry I had in me. Just because the majority does a thing doesn't make it right. Sometimes God will put you in a wilderness to expose what's in the heart. No of us likes being in the wilderness away from pleasure and action. But away from the familiar is where you get to know God and yourself and get the fill of the anointing. Like Abram, who, after 24 years, God changed his name from Abram to Abraham. He left his family and land behind and brought his nephew Lot with him, and we see how that turned out when people were with you for the wrong reasons. Abram still had the teachings of his culture, family, and idolatry worship in him. It took time to get these things out of him; he probably didn't think anything was wrong with it, because of traditions.

Preachers do not want to believe they can preach the word and have idolatry in them. This is why monetary gifts drive everything they do. Many have bowed down to the same devil that Jesus rebuked and said, I will worship only MY God and will serve him only." The devil has promised to give them access to the kingdoms of the world and the glory that goes with it, so many pastors have bowed. Because the church has become so worldly and canal, they think these blessings come from God. Not if you have to compromise Pastors are being glorified for what they showcase in the natural when the truth is God. They are stripped of their spiritual power.

How can a false prophet/preacher cast out Satan when everything they have, including their messages, comes from him? False prophets endorse other false prophets and their agendas, so they repeatedly do the same predictable things; the devil doesn't have any new tricks. Know this fact: when Lucifer was kicked out of heaven, God did not repossess his anointing. This is why we have anointed talented people, saved and unsaved and the in-betweens. The difference is the ungodly anointing cannot destroy yokes; it builds them. If we are not good stewards with our anointing, we will never get God's glory. Most leaders never get to the other dimension of having the anointing and God's glory.

We, as the church, have become a harlot and the preachers' prostitutes. Jesus is waiting on his true church. The first church was established on truth; it is the reason the Pharisees had Jesus killed because they were the thieves and murderers who had taken over the House of God. They were about the money. If Jesus were physically here, He would be turning over tables in the church just as he did at the temple in Jerusalem; Jesus said, "My Father's House shall be called a house of prayer, but you have turned into a den of thieves and the house of merchandise." How many conferences do we think Jesus would attend? If so, what would He say or do?

If he did attend, people would be healed and not spend all their money on disappointments. Where is the Holy Ghost and power? We have become masters of production and good entertainment; this is why food, sex, drugs, and alcohol can be the festivities, just like the world. When the sinner gets tired of the world and wants to find God, what will your answer be to him when you partied with them?

Jesus said, "Woe unto you, Pharisees, hypocrites!" "These sinners will enter into heaven before you do." As a servant-preacher, I am compelling all who can and are convicted to Repent! It's God's final offer.
I am blowing the trumpet for a new generation to repent. The older generation has died in their sins while preaching to sinners.

Do not turn the word into lasciviousness. Don't preach and get cast out into eternal darkness after leaving this world. Many of yesterday's pastors and leaders didn't see God's face when they left this world. They loved money and the glory of being a pastor more than caring for God's sheep—read Jeremiah chapter 23. They sold the word to the people and put God's name to it when it was a lie; they preached to gain people's favor and get their money.

The devil used false teachers who were anointed to bring the people to eat from the wrong tree. They were anointed but rejected by God, like King Saul. What you will learn about God is He will allow you to continue to go before His people, although your replacement has already been anointed to take your place. God will always feed His sheep, even if it is through the unworthy and unclean. Your replacement is on its way, just like all of the other false prophets before you. The wicked will see each other on the other side just like the tours of deception you did together.

Many people have seen the signs of corruption and talked about it behind closed doors. Do you not think God heard you? Judgment to you for upholding the lie and glorifying

the lying vessel. You cannot do God's will and be a friend of the world. Five things you, as a real woman and man of God, need to be aware of: Lucifer, Satan, the Devil, that Old Serpent, and the False Prophet; these are the different characteristics of evil. Just because you shared the same womb to get into this world doesn't certify that you have the same father; Satan has many children preaching for him in the church in Jesus' name. They take on the personality that fits the occasion to deceive the people, turning their hearts to vanity.
They will get the same reward as Lucifer and his followers. You will know that a true prophet has been among you. All of that preaching to find out you are cast out and down.

Women, if God has called you to preach, then live the life that goes with the calling. Never get comfortable with the gift to preach because "gifts come without repentance." Pray, fast, read, study, be faithful and dedicated to your Lord, and make no false gods out of any flesh, including your own.

You cannot afford to preach for the wrong reasons. The prosperity gospel has run its course and is over. Everyone expects God to make them rich based on how much they sow. The first church was about giving to the people and having the power to do what money could not buy, and it is about to come back to this generation. The church Jesus established had power over things money couldn't buy. Jesus chose his disciples from the streets for a reason; he did not want them from organized religious groups or secret societal gentlemen's clubs.

* * *

Women who are called do not allow the enemy to deceive and buy you and the message. Preach what God gives you, and do not be afraid of their faces. "They will fight against you but will not prevail." Woman of God, be holy; don't allow the enemy to use you as a distraction, giving you the desire to attract men to your flesh, causing him to fall. Make him go somewhere else. Lust fulfilled in any form is not your friend; it will turn on you. Guard your heart and mind; the enemy is after your mind; don't entertain him in your mind, "resist the devil, and he will flee from you."

It's crucial to differentiate between God and Lucifer, especially for leaders. Following a stranger's voice can lead us astray. It's wise to ask God for signs and confirmation so we can serve wholeheartedly. This isn't about being insubordinate; it's about being submissive to the spirit of God. If God calls you, He will continue to speak to you, hoping you'll answer Him. You can make a difference in the world by preaching His word. Women, in particular, have the power to birth offspring that will crush the serpent's head. It's time to spread the message and make the world a better place. Let God use you for His glory. Obedience to God is the key to your success as His messenger. Stay in His will and walk where He leads you. "And how shall they preach, except they are sent? as it is written, How beautiful are the feet of them that preach the gospel of peace, and bring glad tidings of good things!

"By what authority do you do these things?"…by the Authority of Jesus Christ who died for you, redeemed you, saved you and restored you!

* * *

Can a Woman Preach? Yes, she can—boldly and unapologetically —if God has called and anointed her to so and advance His kingdom...PREACH WOMAN OF GOD...PREACH!

"May YAHWAH be with you and strengthen you. May the LORD bless you, and keep you: and make his face shine upon you, and be gracious unto you: May The LORD our God King of the Universe lift up his countenance upon you, and give you peace...And you shall teach your children my name, and I will bless them...Amen." SHALOM...

CHAPTER ONE

Chosen

Chapter 1

When God chooses you, all rules and standard
protocols are broken. It's difficult to understand why
chosen people fight against each other. Do people
remember how difficult it was for them when they started
and during the process of carrying out God's calling? To be
chosen by God, it's important not to have a relationship
with anyone who loves money, as money will always
create a wedge between you and them. Money will always
be their God of choice, and it's impossible to have
harmony or total agreement with such people. Just as you
had to choose God after realizing that He chose you, your
counterparts must face the same. This book is my
testament to my allegiance to God and my respect for Him.

I don't consider myself to be a professional writer, but I
have undoubtedly been chosen and anointed to share these
revelations and content for this book. I have been an
ordained minister and pastor for over two decades, and I
have experience with what goes on behind the scenes of
the church. I do not speak to appease any human being,

but I speak the truth as ordained by God. I do not have a deceptive style of writing, nor am I politically correct. My confidence lies in my experience with God and the fact that this was not some idea I came up with to write. I speak with authority because I am sent from the highest authority. As in olden times, God puts his word in the prophet's mouth to speak to his people.

To write this book, I had to pay a high price, including money, relationships, family, children, marriages, and careers, things that we consider normal in our lives. However, God challenged me to put Him first, above all else, including myself. When you are chosen by God, you cannot tell Him how to handle what He has chosen. Everything is tailored to the purpose, time, and the one He chooses, and His will is fulfilled. I tried my best not to be a voice and vessel for Him, but God's calling was stronger than my desires. Despite having experienced all the pleasures and luxuries life could offer, I found myself unfulfilled. But my journey led me to a revelation - that God had been with me all along, even during my darkest times. Through hardship and humility, I discovered that God's grace and mercy are boundless. I now know Him personally and understand that He can sanctify all that belongs to Him. I owe everything to Him, and I am grateful for His unwavering presence in my life.

I used to feel like I didn't belong, like an outcast. I would pray and fast, seeking answers from God. But when

I received revelations, certain people who claimed to be holy were upset with me. It wasn't until later that I realized they were only pretending to be holy. As a child, I was too young to understand what was happening behind closed doors. I felt like I could never fit in the church because I didn't want to play church or with God. So I left to go to the world. For a while, it seemed exciting. It felt like a sort of freedom that I had never experienced before. However, soon enough, I realized that I had to try too hard to fit in with the world. I started indulging in things just to fit in, and it didn't work. It put me in chains of bondage. I came to understand that I would never fit in anywhere or with anyone outside of God and His Kingdom if that's where I belong. The same things are happening to you and to many others; you are my witnesses.

However, now I understand that I belong in the kingdom of God. I had to overcome my fear of losing everything to follow God, and when I did He became my everything. I am no longer alone; I am surrounded by a great cloud of witnesses. I am running with perseverance, the race set before me, casting off everything that hinders me and the sin that easily entangles me.

I understand the significance of the message that I am about to share with you. It comes from God, and it is necessary for the next generation to thrive. I know that many of you have been waiting for a sign from God, and this message is just that, one of many to come. It's not a matter of if but when disaster will strike, and I know that it can be overwhelming and frightening. It's okay to feel lost and unsure about your faith. I want you to know that you are not alone in your struggle. Many people are seeking the original church that Jesus established, where ordinary people can do extraordinary things—the church of unity and love. And you, my friend, are one of His chosen. I hope this message provides you with the comfort and guidance you seek, and I am here to support you on your journey.

When you are chosen by God, you may be misunderstood by those who are not spiritually inclined. God is sovereign and answers to no one but Himself. He is the rule and the protocol. Most of the holy people we admire have already finished their journey called life (especially the people in the Bible). Many times, we are guilty of revering the dead while dishonoring and disrespecting the living.

We often read and quote scriptures, which are God's word, but we use the letter of the law to destroy people's hopes, dreams, and callings instead of relying on the spirit of the word and the heart of God, which is there to provide a better life.

"Many are called, but few are chosen." Unfortunately, many of the called think they are called to destroy the chosen. The truth is that when you answer God's calling, you become one of the chosen. God wouldn't have called you if He had not chosen you. God is not a respecter of persons but He is a respecter of faith. It's evident that God has chosen you, so use your faith to answer His call and please Him by choosing Him back.

You may have asked God for a sign to assure you that He has called you. When people start leaving you, walking out of your life, talking bad about you, being misunderstood, hating on you for no apparent reason, and all hell begins to break loose in your life...There is your sign.

God has chosen you to preach, so keep going despite opposition and obstacles.

"As the Father has loved me, so have I loved you. Abide in my love. If you keep my commandments, you will abide in my love, just as I have kept my Father's commandments and abide in his love. These things I have spoken to you, that my joy may be in you, and that your joy may be full. "This is my commandment, that you love one another as I have loved you. Greater love has no one than this, that someone lay down his life for his friends. You are my friends if you do what I command you. No longer do I call you servants, for the servant does not know what his master is doing, but I have called you friends, for all that I have heard from my Father I have made known to you. You did not choose me, but I chose you and appointed you that you should go and bear fruit and that your fruit should remain so that whatever you ask the Father in my name,

he may give it to you. These things I command you so that you will love one another."If the world hates you, know that it has hated me before it hated you. If you were of the world, the world would love you as its own; but because you are not of the world, but I chose you out of the world; therefore the world hates you."

Remember the word that I said to you: A servant is not greater than his master.' If they persecuted me, they will also persecute you. If they kept my word, they will also keep yours. But all these things they will do to you on account of my name because they do not know him who sent me. If I had not come and spoken to them, they would not have been guilty of sin, but now they have no excuse for their sin. Whoever hates me hates my Father, too. If I had not done among them the works that no one else did, they would not be guilty of sin, but now they have seen and hated both me and my Father. But the word that is written in their Law must be fulfilled: They hated me without a cause.'

"But when the Helper comes, whom I will send to you from the Father, the Spirit of truth, who proceeds from the Father, he will bear witness about me. And you also will bear witness because you have been with me from the beginning." John 15: 9-27.

The Holy Spirit is your Helper and speaks to you, telling you to be the witness you were chosen to be. So Preach! No matter the consequences of men, God is your reward. When it is all said and done, your enemies will have to stand before God and give an account of how they abused and mistreated you.

Being chosen by God is unique and cannot be fully explained, but it must be accepted and embraced. You will never just fit in with any crowd. You have been chosen… God chose you. When God chooses someone, it means that person is an original and not a copy of someone else. God has something in particular He wants you to do. Therefore, there is no need to duplicate what has already been done. Each person chosen by God has a spiritual fingerprint and footprint that will guide them throughout their journey in life. Everything we do on earth is temporary, but it can have a lasting impact on the lives of those we touch. We have been chosen to make a difference and bring about necessary change.

When God has chosen you to do something, be something, or say something, there is a constant nag at your spirit concerning what you are called to do. Where most of us fail at answering the call or being fulfilled by walking in the call, we are too concerned about what others may think or say about us. We seek affirmation from people far more than confirmation from our God, who created us. Sometimes, we are guilty of worshiping and esteeming the creature more than we do the Creator in many cases.

Throughout history, we have on record witnesses of the cruelty and abuse of those who desire to do what they believe they were born to do. To make a difference by committing to something good rather than evil.

Time and again, we witness the pain of being misunderstood and even persecuted for doing what is right. It's astonishing how someone can be hated for doing good, for following their inner voice, even if it causes them suffering. What keeps them going when the opposition is so fierce? It's a power that cannot be explained - a faith that never wavers. Abraham had this kind of faith, and his wife Sarah proved faithful to God's call, her husband, and ultimately, God Himself. Without her acceptance and support, the covenant would not have been possible.

A few chosen women:

Sarah was the wife of Abraham, a wealthy man of Ur. Told by God to leave their home, they went to Canaan. And at 90 years old, she was blessed by God's gift of a son. Their account is found in Genesis.

In **Genesis 17:15-16**, God spoke to Abraham, saying, "You are no longer to call your wife Sarai, but her name will be Sarah. I will bless her and give you a son through her. She will become the mother of nations, and kings of peoples will come from her.

"Sarah shows us that it's never too late to receive **God's miracles**.

Mary, Mother of Jesus, Mary was a young woman chosen by God for an amazing purpose. Her story is predicted in the Book of Isaiah and is entirely told in the

Gospels.

"I am the Lord's servant,' Mary answered. 'May your word to me be fulfilled.' Then the angel left her" (Luke 1:38).

Mary shows us that we can **completely trust** in God even when we don't understand. God will never abandon his word. No matter how long, he remembers and will see you through. Many women have been encouragers behind the scenes when they needed encouragement themselves. Mary was very young when she was catapulted into her purpose and destiny. She had no clue as to her contribution to greatness and what eternal impact she would bring to humanity by what she would give birth to. You don't know what God has placed inside you.

Deborah was appointed to be a judge over Israel; Deborah instructed a warrior named Barak to go into battle. When Barak refuses to go without her, the book of Judges quotes Deborah's reprimand.

"'Certainly I will go with you,' said Deborah. 'But because of the course you are taking, the honor will not be yours, for the Lord will deliver Sisera into the hands of a woman.' So Deborah went with Barak to Kedesh" (Judges 4:9).

Miriam, The sister of Moses, led worship for the people of Israel. Because she spoke against the wife of Moses, however, she was struck with leprosy but was later healed. Her story is told in the books of Exodus and

Numbers.

"Then Miriam the prophet, Aaron's sister, took a timbrel in her hand, and all the women followed her, with timbrels and dancing" (Exodus 15:20).

Miriam shows us that **all our words matter** to God.

Rahab was a prostitute in Jericho. When Joshua sent two spies into the city, she took them in and protected them from the king. The book of Joshua tells the request she makes of them.

"Now then, please swear to me by the Lord that you will show kindness to my family because I have shown kindness to you. Give me a sure sign that you will spare the lives of my father and mother, my brothers and sisters, and all who belong to them — and that you will save us from death" (Joshua 2:12-13).

Ruth married a son of Naomi. When they both became widows, Ruth followed Naomi to her homeland. Marrying a man named Boaz, she became part of Jesus' family line. The book of Ruth tells this beautiful story.

But Ruth replied, 'Don't urge me to leave or turn back from you. Where you go, I will go, and where you stay, I will stay. Your people will be my people and your God my God" (Ruth 1:16).

Priscilla and her husband Aquilas met the Apostle Paul, working alongside him. She taught and traveled as part of her ministry. Introduced in the book of Acts, she's mentioned by Paul in his letter to the Romans.

Meanwhile, a Jew named Apollos, a native of Alexandria, came to Ephesus. He was a learned man with a thorough knowledge of the **Scripture**…When Priscilla and Aquila heard him, they invited him to their home and explained to him the way of God more adequately" (**Acts 18:24**, 26).

Pricilla shows us that we must **help each other mature** in our faith.

Mary Magdalen, This Mary, after being healed of demons by Jesus, became an integral part of His group of disciples. She appears in many Gospel accounts.

"Early on the first day of the week, while it was still dark, Mary Magdalene went to the tomb and saw that the stone had been removed from the entrance" (John 20:1).

Mary Magdalene shows us what God can do with a heart **submitted** to Him.

Rachel is a shepherdess. Rachel met Jacob when he arrived at her father's house. She later became his wife and bore him Joseph and Benjamin. Genesis shares the many twists and turns of her life.

Jacob was in love with Rachel and said, 'I'll work for you seven years in return for your younger daughter Rachel'" (Genesis 29:18).

Rachel shows us that God will give us the patience to wait for Him.

* * *

Hannah, one of Elkanah's two wives, was in despair because she was barren. 1 Samuel tells the account of her tearful vow to God in the temple and the result.

"...they brought the boy to Eli, and she said to him, 'Pardon me, my lord. As surely as you live, I am the woman who stood here beside you praying to the Lord. I prayed for this child, and the Lord has granted me what I asked of him. So now I give him to the Lord. For his whole life, he will be given over to the Lord" (1 Samuel 1:25-28).

Hannah shows us the need to be **faithful** to God.

Esther became queen and learned of a plan to destroy the Jews by one of King Xerxes' nobles. Despite great danger to herself, Esther went before the king. The book of Esther explains how she helped save God's people.

"Then Esther sent this reply to Mordecai: 'Go, gather together all the Jews who are in Susa, and fast for me. Do not eat or drink for three days, night or day. I and my attendants will fast as you do. I will go to the king when this is done, even though it is against the law. And if I perish, I perish" (Esther 4:15-16).

Esther shows us that God will grant us the **courage to be bold** for Him.

Abigail's husband's bad behavior caused King David to threaten her home, and Abigail's wisdom in bringing a peace offering to David prevented destruction. Soon, her husband died, and she became one of David's wives.

David said to Abigail, 'Praise be to the Lord, the God of

Israel, who has sent you today to meet me. May you be blessed for your good judgment and for keeping me from bloodshed this day and from avenging myself with my own hands" (1 Samuel 25:32-33).

Abigail shows us that **God will equip us with wisdom** for any situation.

Elizabeth was the cousin of Mary, Jesus' mother. Elizabeth had been barren but, by God's blessing, became pregnant. Mary soon visited her, and the Book of Luke records their great joy at what God had done.

When Elizabeth heard Mary's greeting, the baby leaped in her womb, and Elizabeth was filled with the Holy Spirit. In a loud voice, she exclaimed: 'Blessed are you among women, and blessed is the child you will bear! But why am I so favored that the mother of my Lord should come to me?'" (Luke 1:41-43).

Elizabeth shows us how to keep **a sense of awe** about God.

Mary of Bethany, Mary was one of two sisters who hosted Jesus when He came to the village. When He taught, Mary placed herself right at His feet. Later, she washed His feet with oil as a display of worship. And as the Gospels tell, she fell at His feet with grief when her brother died.

"'Martha, Martha,' the Lord answered, 'you are worried and upset about many things, but few things are needed — or indeed only one. Mary has chosen what is better, and it will not be taken away from her'" (Luke 10:41-42).

Mary shows us what it looks like to **give ourselves completely to God**.

Martha of Bethany was the other sister from Bethany. She loved Jesus, as did Mary, but displayed it differently, using her gifts to nurture Him. In the Gospel accounts, we also see a woman who held Jesus in great esteem.

"As Jesus and his disciples were on their way, he came to a village where a woman named Martha opened her home to him" (Luke 10:38).

"'Lord,' Martha said to Jesus, 'if you had been here, my brother would not have died. But I know that even now God will give you whatever you ask'" (John 11:21-22).

Martha shows us that God gifts us in **practical** as well as **spiritual ways**.

Jochebed, the birth mother of Moses, put her son in a wicker basket and placed him in the river to protect him from the king. Exodus tells how Moses was rescued, and Jochebed became his nurse.

"Now, a man of the tribe of Levi married a Levite woman, and she became pregnant and gave birth to a son. She hid him for three months when she saw he was a fine child. But when she could hide him no longer, she got a papyrus basket for him and coated it with tar and pitch. Then she placed the child in it and put it among the reeds along the bank of the Nile" (**Exodus 2:1-3**).

Jochebed shows us that we can **rest in God's care** for our loved ones.

Anna the Prophetess An old prophetess, Anna had spent her life at the temple in Jerusalem, devoted to prayer and fasting. The book of Luke describes how the sight of young Jesus led her to evangelize about Him.

"Coming up to them at that very moment, she thanked God and spoke about the child to all who were looking forward to the redemption of Jerusalem" (Luke 2:38).

Anna shows us that we must **keep watch** for and be ready to **praise God's works**.

Lydia, a cloth dealer in Thyatira, was a believer when she heard the Apostle Paul speak one Sabbath. But his words brought her to a deeper faith, and her house eventually became a meeting place for other followers.

"When she and the members of her household were baptized, she invited us to her home. 'If you consider me a believer in the Lord,' she said, 'come and stay at my house.' And she persuaded us" (Acts 16:15).

Lydia shows us that we must **grow in love** for God and others.

Rebekah, the wife of Isaac, was childless until God blessed them with twin boys, Esau and Jacob. She asked the Lord why the babies were pushing against each other inside her, and Genesis details the surprising prophecy.

The Lord said to her, 'Two nations are in your womb,

and two peoples from within you will be separated; one people will be stronger than the other, and the older will serve the younger'" (Genesis 25:23).

Rebekah shows us that God's plans are sometimes mysterious but always more significant than **we could imagine**.

Eve is a well-known character in the Bible, known for being the partner, companion, and wife of Adam. Her most prominent act was disobeying God's command not to eat from the Tree of Knowledge, Good and Evil. Unfortunately, she fell prey to the serpent's voice, who convinced her to eat the forbidden fruit, and she, in turn, persuaded her husband to do the same. This act of disobedience was the root of her sin, which was then passed on to her husband.

The serpent managed to deceive Eve by imitating the voice of God and sounding like a deity. This is how he was able to create confusion in her mind and convince her to disobey God's command. Despite her mistake, Eve showed remarkable character when confronted by God about her actions. She did not lie but instead tried to cover her sin and was afraid. This was evidence that the devil had not entered her.

This story highlights the power of the spoken word and demonstrates the importance of listening to the right voice. It also shows the consequences of disobedience and the importance of following God's commands. In conclusion, this narrative serves as an essential lesson in how one should not let others influence them in making decisions that can have severe repercussions.

Genesis 3: 8-13, "And they heard the voice of the LORD God walking in the garden in the cool of the day: and Adam and his wife hid themselves from the presence of the LORD God among the trees of the garden. 9 And the LORD God called to Adam, and said to him, Where are you? 10 And he said, I heard your voice in the garden, and I was afraid because I was naked; and I hid myself. 11 And he said, Who told you that you were naked? Have you eaten of the tree, whereof I commanded you that you should not eat? 12 And the man said, The woman whom you gave to be with me, she gave me of the tree, and I did eat. 13 And the LORD God said to the woman, What is this that you have done? And the woman said, The serpent beguiled me, and I did eat."

Adam and Eve committed a grave error, yet they abstained from compounding their guilt by misleading God. Despite their trepidation, they acknowledged their wrongdoing and refrained from dishonesty. It is common for individuals to be tempted to conceal their mistakes instead of confessing them to God. On approaching the serpent, God did not deem it necessary to inquire about the events leading to the mistake, as He was aware of the serpent's tendency towards falsehood.

* * *

Genesis 3:14 And the Lord God said to the serpent, because you have done this, you are cursed above all cattle, and above every beast of the field; on your belly shall you go, and dust shall you eat all the days of your life: And the LORD God said to the serpent, because you have done this, you are cursed above all cattle, and every beast of the field; on your belly shall you go, and dust shall you eat all the days of your life:

LISTEN TO THIS: According to the Bible, God did not curse the man or the woman, but the serpent. Instead, God made declarations of judgment against them for their disobedience. When we rebel against God's word, we bring curses upon ourselves and those we support. In verse 15, God declares a war between the serpent and the woman, not Adam, which is significant because these words hold the key to humanity's redemption through her due to her actions with the serpent.

VERSE 15 And I will put enmity between you and the woman, and between your seed and her seed; it shall bruise your head, and you shall bruise his heel.

This is a direct promise from God. The woman's seed is the lethal weapon loaded with the power and authority to crush the serpent's seed head. The woman who listened to the wrong voice and obeyed became the wrong voice to her husband, and he obeyed. Therefore, the serpent knew she had a powerful voice. His job became getting her to use her voice for him….for evil.

* * *

These accounts in scripture are loaded with information and revelation concerning why we are the way we are towards one another. Why does the sexiest and bigot community continue to rail against her and attempt to keep their foot on her neck? When God created the man and took the woman out of him, the enemy understood right then and there that God chose her. Therefore, understanding that the enemy always covets everything that God chooses. This is the reason he goes after what God values and twist it to degrade, molest, rape, abuse, use and strip her physically and spiritually of her full potential in hopes of destroying her confidence to do what she was created to do. Whatever that might be.

Let's take a look at verse 16: *To the woman, he said, "I will surely multiply your pain in childbearing; in pain, you shall bring forth children. Your desire shall be contrary to your husband, but he shall rule over you."*

This is the part of the judgment from God that the world and religion are holding on to. Men are afraid of losing the "rule over you" part, and women are being "contrary" when we are supposed to be in agreement working this thing called life together…in harmony.

In our arrogance and possible ignorance, we are bound by the law, curse, and judgment of past sins. These sins originated from the Garden of Eden, and they are responsible for triggering divorce, separations, divisions, and the restriction of women from being leaders or pastors in our churches and organizations. Fear drives most of these actions- fear of losing control, respect, and possibly the man's place in society. When Eve was created for Adam, she was meant to be his partner and helper in fulfilling his purpose and destiny. In turn, she would also reach her full potential and purpose. They were created to be one. If the woman is under judgment, then the man is also under judgment.

Listen to what God had to say to Adam. *And to Adam, he said, "Because you have listened to the voice of your wife and have eaten of the tree of which I commanded you, 'You shall not eat of it,' cursed is the ground because of you; in pain, you shall eat of it all the days of your life; thorns and thistles it shall bring forth for you; and you shall eat the plants of the field. By the sweat of your face, you shall eat bread till you return to the ground, for out of it you were taken; for you are dust, and to dust you shall return."*

In the story of Adam and Eve, it is said that Eve was deceived into disobeying God, and Adam disobeyed God because he loved Eve more than God. The image of Adam blaming Eve for their alienation from God and being put out of paradise is a common one. Now, Adam has to work hard to take care of his family. As he sweats, he can't stop thinking about what Eve did instead of focusing on what they both did wrong.

* * *

God did not tell Eve to shut her mouth! Her silence is a badge of defeat, not victory. The enemy knows she is the key to the destruction of his seed and his kingdom. But if he can now deceive the man in this dispensation into believing the woman doesn't have the right to lead, speak, or have a voice and influence being restricted by the men, then the enemy will not have to worry about the crushing of his head. I'm not talking about rebellion, I'm talking about total submission and recognition of God being in control and us doing his will.

The enemy's latest tactic is to use men to manipulate women into working for his kingdom. If we don't protect and support women, they may end up nurturing and protecting the enemy's offspring instead of destroying them. If women were able to walk with God and fulfill their calling with the help of appointed and anointed men of God, Satan's kingdom would stand no chance. The woman was chosen before she was revealed, but as soon as she was exposed and vulnerable, she became prey to the enemy. Adam lacked experience and didn't know how to protect his woman from the enemy, even though he loved her.

Through Christ, she has been set free. We all have been set free from the first Adam to the last Adam, from the Garden of Eden to the Garden of Gethsemane. Adam cannot point the finger, and neither can Eve; we are to look at the work Jesus did at Calvary. That curse to the ground was nailed to the cross. We are redeemed if we believe. Jesus became the curse for our sakes.

Not only is the woman of God anointed to preach, but she's also justified and glorified to do this,

"And we know that all things work together for good to them that love God, to them who are the called according to his purpose. For whom he did foreknow, he also did predestinate to be conformed to the image of his Son, that he might be the firstborn among many brethren. Moreover whom he did predestinate, them he also called: and whom he called, them he also justified: and whom he justified, them he also glorified.

What shall we then say to these things? If God be for us, who can be against us? He that spared not his own Son, but delivered him up for us all, how shall he not with him also freely give us all things? Who shall lay anything to the charge of God's elect? It is God that justifieth.

Who is he that condemneth? It is Christ that died, yea rather, that is risen again, who is even at the right hand of God, who also maketh intercession for us. Who shall separate us from the love of Christ? shall tribulation, or distress, or persecution, or famine, or nakedness, or peril, or sword? As it is written, For thy sake, we are killed all the day long; we are accounted as sheep for the slaughter.

Nay, in all these things, we are more than conquerors through him who loved us. For I am persuaded that neither death, nor life, nor angels, nor principalities, nor powers, nor things present, nor things to come, Nor height, nor depth, nor any other creature, shall be able to separate us from the love of God, which is in Christ Jesus our Lord." Romans 8: 28-39.

"If God be for us, who can be against us?"

You must learn to trust Him to choose your spouse when God chooses you. If you choose your partner, be aware that there will come a time when they will despise you and God. Your relationship with the Lord will become a contention between you and your partner. They may even give you an ultimatum to choose them or God. However, if God chooses you, your eternal spirit will remain connected. Initially, your dedication to God may seem crazy to your partner, but don't worry; your love for God will not go in vain. It's a choice between eternity and time.

Your partner may be in your life for a while, but God and His love are eternal. It is not meant to be if God chooses you and your partner leaves you. But if they stay with you through thick and thin, it is ordained by God for you to remain together, just as Jesus and the Father are one.

It is important to distinguish who is genuinely with you for who you are and not just for what you have or can do for them. If someone is meant to be in your life, they will love God as much as you do, or even more. However, you cannot force someone to love you or God. It is their choice to make without any external influence. Trying to manipulate someone into loving you is equivalent to practicing witchcraft.

Your love for God and your journey to know Him is a lifelong process. Therefore, your partner must also be committed to following God's will for their life. Being chosen by God comes at a cost, but it is impossible to quantify that cost. The Bible offers us a valuable lesson: the more significant the task you are called upon to fulfill, the greater the sacrifice you must offer. It may demand every fiber of your being, but God becomes your sole focus in return. If you put your trust in Him and give your all, He will undoubtedly reward you with His abundant blessings. Remember, your ultimate goal should always be to please Him, and He will make sure that you lack nothing.

Do not be impressed by people who hold ministry titles or appear prosperous without sacrifice. Their blessings may not have come from God, so stay in your lane. It is important to remember that God does not pay us upfront for our efforts. Some things require patience and time because "A faith that has not been tested is a faith that cannot be trusted."

In moments of uncertainty and discomfort, it can be challenging to trust that removing certain people and things from your life is for the better. However, placing faith in God and exercising patience can provide a sense of solace that the changes have a purpose. When God takes away something, it is not without intention. Instead, it is done with the plan of replacing it with something better suited for your life's journey.

Though this may entail moments of sadness and tears, it is essential to recognize that these experiences can be moments of growth and maturity in your spiritual journey. "Weeping endures for a night, but joy comes in the morning." It is also worth noting that sometimes, the people we interact with may not have pure intentions or believe in us, and as a result, God may see the need to remove them from our lives. By trusting in God's plan, we can find peace amid uncertainty and trust that everything happens for a reason and God will never leave us alone.

When God chooses you, He will call you to Himself. Some people may not understand this and may even consider you crazy for leaving those you love behind. However, we can look at Abraham's example of faith and remember that God required him to leave his family, property, land, and culture. Abraham chose to take Lot, his nephew, with him, and look how that turned out. In the beginning, you may face opposition from people you know, but after you have suffered for a while, God will send faithful people into your life who will bless you. This is not to prove anything to those who didn't believe in you but to those who do and will believe. Your best days are in front of you, unlike your enemy; his best days are behind him. Satan misses the good old days when he had free reign; this was, of course, before Jesus arrived on the earth and exposed him.

We must acknowledge that God has the right to do whatever He wants with anything He has created, including choosing you. In other words, God is the Boss. So I want to thank you, Heavenly Father, for choosing me.

I Knew

Chapter 2

In the book of Jeremiah, the Lord speaks to him the following:

Now the word of the LORD came to me, saying,

"Before I formed you in the womb, I knew you,

and before you were born, I consecrated you;

I appointed you a prophet to the nations."

Then I said, "Ah, Lord GOD! Behold, I do not know how to speak, for I am only a youth." But the LORD said to me,

"Do not say, 'I am only a youth'; for to all to whom I send you, you shall go, and whatever I command you, you shall speak.

Do not be afraid of them, for I am with you to deliver you, declares the LORD."

Then the LORD put out his hand and touched my mouth. And the LORD said to me, "Behold, I have put my words in your mouth. See, I have set you this day over nations and over kingdoms, to pluck up and to break down, to destroy and to overthrow, to build and to plant."

And the word of the LORD came to me, saying, "Jeremiah, what do you see?" And I said, "I see an almond branch." Then the LORD said to me, "You have seen well, for I am watching over my word to perform it." Jeremiah 1-5:12

Therefore, I already knew you before your mother and father had even met. I knew everything you would go through and all the mistakes you would make, even before you made them. Yet, I still love and want you. I knew you then, and I know you now. You don't have to pretend with me because I know the real you, the person nobody else knows. You were born with a purpose and are meant to fulfill that purpose. You are not a mistake!

Millions of sperm cells were released from your father to find an egg to fertilize. Do you know that God knew the day you would be reading this and wants you to know that, out of all the countless seeds that came from your father into your mother, "Millions of those seeds didn't make it, but you are the one who did?"

God knew you even before you were born. Your spirit existed within God's Spirit before your creation, independent of physical characteristics such as form, sex, gender, race, or origin. Know that God spoke something into your spirit; thus, you were created as a spirit being.

Even before we were given physical bodies, God communicated messages to us in our disembodied state. As we journey through life's twists and turns, we may encounter moments that oppose the core of existence.

However, our destiny and purpose are already within us.

God is in eternity and is eternal, while we are in time trying to judge what is timeless. When God spoke to Jeremiah, calling him to be a prophet, he was young and had no experience. He viewed himself as not qualified or old enough, and maybe this was not in the family's plans or view for his future. Jeremiah's father was a priest, and usually, the son following the father's footsteps was something expected.

His culture taught Jeremiah about God, but he did not honestly know Him. One day, God spoke directly to him. However, Jeremiah felt too young and inadequate to speak on God's behalf. This is a feeling many of us can relate to when we compare ourselves to others who may seem more qualified or capable.

The truth is, God has a unique plan for each of us, and He wants us to use our gifts and abilities to fulfill His purpose. For Jeremiah, God had something different in mind than his father, who was considered a holy man of God. God knew that compromises were made by the priests (including Jeremiah's father) in His name to please the ungodly and corrupt king. But how could Jeremiah know this?

God saw potential in a new generation and sought a young individual to impart fresh revelations and knowledge. This individual would be capable of receiving new ideas without any preconceived notions or religious rigidity. God tells Jeremiah that He knew him before he was in his mother's womb. He knew him when he was the spirit and had no flesh or body before he was a sex or gender. There are things that God spoke to our spirit from eternity before we were confirmed in time. However, at times, our spirit struggles to agree with the Creator due to the influence of external and internal factors. These factors include what we see and hear daily.

The power of agreement is everything to become what God has envisioned for us. We must align with God to get what He has purposed for our lives and His divine purpose. God tells him before time that he is a prophet called into time to speak to nations. So, do not tell me about your age or insecurities…I AM God. Remember when God called Moses to the mountain and talked to him about going to Egypt to tell Pharaoh to let His people go? Moses told God he was slow to speak, "Who made the mouth and tongue?" God said. Moses had no clue what was in him. Moses was dealing with his inabilities and insecurities. God gets the glory if we remain meek and humble but powerful and effective.

You have to decide whose word you're going to believe and follow. Not doing what God tells us to do is a betrayal of ourselves and God. Judas betrayed himself first before he betrayed Jesus because Jesus had chosen him for good, telling him his purpose. He listened and followed the other voice and went for the money instead, becoming famously known for being a betrayer. We have plenty of examples of people God has called with imperfections, and God has blessed them, so they start to believe that they are great themselves, forgetting when they had no confidence or experience; now, they are without integrity and the original purpose God had for them…ultimately, they become a god to themselves.

"Do not say you are too young," says God; you must go to everyone I send you and say whatever I command you. Do not be afraid of them because I AM with you and will protect you." God already knows his creation and how cruel and evil people can be when they are told something against what they want to do, so they destroy messengers because they can't reach God to attempt to kill Him.

In Jeremiah's time, there were false prophets who pretended to do the work of God but were actually doing the devil's work in disguise. These individuals would tell the king and people in authority what they wanted to hear, attaching God's name to their words. They skillfully mastered the art of pleasing people by telling them what they wanted to hear rather than warning them about the destructive future that awaited them as per God's message. This highlights the importance of being cautious and discerning when it comes to those who claim to be doing God's work.

* * *

Our world operates in cycles and patterns, including different seasons. No one can receive only positive messages from God. We need a balanced message that feeds our souls, just like a balanced meal provides our bodies with good health. This is crucial for our spiritual well-being.

God cares for us; it is reasonable to assume that warnings of impending destruction would be given in advance to give us a chance to change course and avoid calamity. During the time of Jeremiah, false prophets were misleading the kings and priests by telling them that God was pleased with them while they were committing wrongdoings. Jeremiah's assignment was to bring attention to these false prophets and to encourage people to recognize their mistakes and correct their ways. This highlights distinguishing between truth and falsehood to live a righteous and just life.

Feeling a solid and persistent urge towards something could be a sign that God has called you. Some individuals, when they disregard this call, turn to harmful relationships, substances, and other destructive behaviors. You might be surprised that many people engage in inappropriate actions but still talk about God, yet do not follow His will. This internal conflict can lead to mental torment. These individuals may struggle to fit in, even though their true mission is to do God's will; they are constantly misunderstood. Sadly, their demise is seeking acceptance from others.

If you have been living in a way unaligned with God's will, it's never too late to make a change. God loves you, is with you, and does not seek to harm you. He knew you would struggle and lose your way, but He welcomes you back into His embrace. Remember, God is with you wherever you are, but He will not impose Himself upon you. You must say yes to His will and open your heart to Him more than you have for the wrong relationships.

The world constantly imposes expectations on you, telling you who you should be and what you should do. However, God, who created you, is eternal, and His plans for you are not limited by time. The Eternal God knew you even before you were born, before your parents met and had an attraction toward each other. God has a purpose for you. The world may see you as an object, but God sees you as His daughter with inherent worth and value.

This applies to both men and women, as false narratives have been spoken over both genders. Women, in particular, have been subject to derogatory labeling and mistreatment. However, God sees beyond physical appearance, sex, and gender roles. He sees you as a unique individual with a nurturing heart, and His plans for you extend far beyond any betrayal or disappointment you may have faced in life.

* * *

You, as a woman, were targeted and attacked as a little girl, and that little girl is still in you, needing love, protection, understanding, and answers for why you were abused and mistreated even by your mother. You were left and entrusted with someone who did things to you that you can't even utter. God knew and knows you. He knew what you would go through. When these bad things happened to you, you thought you were alone, but you were not.

You have spiritual witnesses who knows what was done to you. You were never alone. I can't express enough how important it is for you to see the bigger picture. When you take into account everything terrible that happened to you, and you survived it; you are the victor, not the victim. In my book, "God, the Woman, and Her Enemy," I talk about how everything in this world came from hidden things from another world. There were and still are evil things hidden in Lucifer's heart. He's being exposed for judgment. These things have to be in time, making whatever it is temporary. Trouble can't last but for so long.

Do you know every rape, molesting, murder, lie, betrayal, and the list goes on? Every evil you can and can't even imagine has an origin. Lucifer's heart is the origin. These things must happen to be recorded and used to judge him and his followers on the day of judgment. You have the Internet bullies and beyond making fun of the invisible God and the "pie in the sky" thing, but it won't be funny when they leave this world, and they will. These people are not as powerful as we think. Wouldn't they have conquered death, their greatest threat and enemy, if they were? They act like they are gods, so where is their eternal power?

God said to Jeremiah, "I have put My words in your mouth. See, today, I have appointed you over nations and kingdoms to uproot and tear down, to destroy and overthrow, to build and to plant." The masses want a false prophet and voice to tell them what they want to hear and glorify their flesh and ego. They will hate a prophet who gives instructions and rebukes them for correction.

They would instead make people think they are unique and in good graces with God, but when you look around, why are our conditions in our communities, cities, states, and nations in such disarray? Why is the crime rate climbing rather than diminishing? Why the murders? Why do hate and the degradation of a people come through music messages that promote rebellion and wickedness as though it is something to admire and glorify? Satan is copying God's skills and turning it for evil by using his false prophets to speak a word. How long do we as a people and nation think we're going to last?

God asked Jeremiah, "What do you see?" What do our pastors see? What do our prophets see? This is important to God because if it weren't, He would not have asked a young man who had not yet been infiltrated by society that question. He asked him before a false narrative could influence him. Do you know what our leaders see? They see money and opportunity. The true prophets and pastors will see what God sees. The world and the church are in trouble, and our pastors are posting vacations, cars, houses, clothes, shoes, fashions, parties, and vanities of this world and think they are doing God's will and His people a service. They are blinded to the fact that they see what Satan sees. The same devil who said to Jesus if he will bow down and worship him, he will give him the kingdoms of this world and all the glory that comes with it, is the same devil who is giving most of these money hungry pastors their lifestyles, because they DID BOW to the devil! On the day of judgment, God will have their knee prints along with their finger prints for stealing.

Our pastors and bishops are looking to be accepted by the world's standards and are imposing these ungodly principles onto God's people right in church through their preaching and teachings. On top of that, they are doing an ungodly pyramid scheme by asking you to sow a seed into it; the seed is the money. These leaders have people who are thirsty for God, chasing after the gods of this world because they trust their pastor.

They have the people praying for vain things to come into their lives in Jesus' name. God has true prophets in this world, but most will not receive them because they are not conformed to this world. They are rejected just as Jesus and the prophets of old were rejected. We have been conditioned to think that blessings are things we can buy when, in fact, it is having a relationship with the God of the things.

We have become worshippers of vanity; we do it in the name of Jesus and God. For this reason among others, God is turned His face toward women in these last days as prophets…true prophets to speak His word and not sell him out for vanity."In the last days, your sons and daughters will prophesy," says the Lord God. These ignorant preachers, pastors, and orators will say God said, "prophesy," He didn't say to preach. Think about the culture, and the times when this was spoken. When the prophet Joel prophesied this word, women were considered second and third class. Women didn't have any rights. The other thing was you had to be a man and at least 40 years of age to be considered to be endorsed and accepted as a prophet, meaning by the authorities of men, by way of certain tribes. If you check biblical history, you will see several prophetesses have already been recorded, image all of thoses who were not recorded.

God used a prophet to proclaim this End Time Prophecy because God knew He would act as the women and young people's Emancipator. So, if God tells us what we are called to do, we rebel against God if we don't. The older prophets have been corrupted because their predecessors had groomed them, and in return, they have become groomers to the young who want to be prophets. They are easy targets because they want fame and fortune. The older leaders give them the attention they are thirsty for because they know what they want; it just has to be brought out of them. The young aspiring prophet/preacher believes God has favored them to bless them with this opportunity.

It is concerning that some individuals who call themselves apostles and bishops are in their early 20s and claim that God has called them. They are willing to sell their souls for money and have been deceived into thinking that the mark of a true calling from God is in material possessions. As a result, they relentlessly pursue financial success to validate their self-proclaimed titles. However, the true mark of an apostle is having a personal relationship with Christ, being tried, and leaving worldly possessions, making God first, suffering, and being persecuted for Christ's sake, with blessings as mentioned in the Bible. Not greedy, carnal, fleshly desires and calling it persecution. I am not against blessings, but I am against "The love of money is the root of all evil." We have sold out our own people for a dollar, in and out of the church. I was guilty of it, but I repented, meaning everything the devil gave me on pretense, I let it go. I have nothing that belongs to him. This is why my messages to him and his followers are lethal and diabolical.

* * *

Likewise, the true mark of a prophet is giving up everything to follow God and do His will. If someone cannot walk away from everything to let God become their everything to fulfill God's will, then they have not been genuinely called by God. Satan may have called them, and as a result, they will be blessed with temporary worldly things that will lead them to lose their soul and be full of pride. Pride will be their marker, and fulfilling their carnal desires will be their curse and downfall, which will eventually ruin their ministry. To the wannabe apostles and bishops, Paul said it like this, "I'll let nothing separate me from the love of God." This is a true fact, if God let you suffer for years with no blessings, will you still preach the gospel? Who are you following that have you so messed up that you see God as your personal Genie? First things first, know who your father is.

This is a reminder to stay grounded and wise when claiming to be called by God. It is important to remember that Jesus said to "Follow me" and that we are like sheep among wolves. Therefore, it is crucial to be wise as a serpent but harmless as a dove. When spreading God's message, it is best not to take any extra belongings, such as a coat, prepared message, or wallet; in other words, don't take vanity with you and hype. Instead, trust that God will speak through you and provide for your needs (your labor is worthy of its pay). This is how Jesus taught and prepared his followers for ministry, not filling their heads with worldly possessions. Near the end of his ministry,

Jesus talked to them about how they would be blessed. God wanted to be able to trust them, but Judas failed the class.

It is also advised not to go from church to church, exploiting your gifts. Instead, focus on blessing one house with your anointing and spirit, leaving peace in that place if they receive you. Ultimately, let revival break out in one place and allow the people to gather at that appointed place, letting God work through you without making propaganda out of God's message. Is this real enough for you?

I don't believe having material possessions is inherently wrong, as I have owned and enjoyed them. However, it's essential to ensure your things don't consume you. I have faced the difficult decision to walk away from my possessions to answer my calling. As a builder, making money was my top priority until God challenged me to trust in Him as my source of provision. As I followed His guidance, everything I had acquired through my efforts, including relationships, left my life. I've learned to trust God, and now I have a freedom that cannot be explained. When I speak, everyone who is of God, including the devil, who came from God, knows that my words come from God. I speak the words God has put in my mouth with the understanding that He is my Boss. God knew me before I was formed in my mother's womb and knew the day would come when I would speak His word and not be on Satan's payroll.

* * *

I know I don't have anything that belongs to the devil. I used to serve him in my ignorance, and now I can say I know Satan, and he knows me, and what he knows best is God knew me first and knows me, and it is Him only that I serve. I will never bow down to the devil again but cast him and his offspring out. I have seen many church leaders who are gifted and skilled in delivering the Word but do not know the Word, which is Jesus. They sell Jesus just like Judas sold him. So, what tree will they hang from if they don't repent?

When God called Abram, later known as Abraham, he was challenged to leave behind his home, land, and family to answer God's call. During his journey to where God was leading him, he suffered losses and deaths of people who believed in him and were following him. He had to move several times because circumstances were not in his favor.

He also faced a severe famine where he lost everything he had. Abram was an idolater then, and everything he considered a blessing came from other gods. He did not realize that what he thought was a blessing from God was a gift given to him and his family for generations by idol gods (the Devil). After he had nothing left but his promise from God, God made the king of Egypt bless him with something called "A trespass offering." From then on, everything Abram possessed came from The Most High God of the Universe.

* * *

Ultimately, God would bless him, change his name from Abram to Abraham, and give him the son of promise. God knew his name was Abraham before He called him, but sometimes, it takes time to shed the idolatry and things of the world. God will make no mistake knowing what is His and what belongs to the devil. The true miracle of Abraham is something given by God that money can't buy.

The true mark of God's church was purchased and birthed by the blood of the Lamb, which is the power money can't buy. The apostles had power from heaven to do things that money couldn't do, undeniable miracles. The Pharisees had money, the temple, and prestige, but the true church, run by the apostles, had angels ascending and descending upon them to do what money couldn't; for this reason, the religious leaders wanted to get rid of them. Just like today, "There is nothing new under the sun." These leaders today don't want a true prophet because they know the church is their hustle; they don't want the real Jesus in there because he would disperse their offerings to the people who are in need. Jesus would overthrow the tables used at most of these events, as he did at Passover when he rebuked those money grubbers, and he would say, "My Father's House is a house of prayer. You have turned it into a den of thieves and a house of merchandise." Who do you think Jesus would be talking about?

* * *

That one incident or the eternal spirit of Lucifer who comes as an angel of light but is a wolf dressed in sheep's clothing, a serpent, seeking to deceive and destroy God's people. Where are The Houses of Prayer? We don't have enough time or access to come together for prayer in our churches. Our nation is in trouble, and we need to be unified in prayer and worship. We have built multimillion-dollar churches and facilities, but they are open only on Sundays and Bible Class nights. What about the rest of the week? When investors build hospitals, they intend for them to be open 24/7 because they know that crises can happen at any time. But when we need the church, it's closed more than it's open. The church was not built to meet the needs of God's people. Even the Pharisees didn't close the doors to the temple. And yet, we as pastors have the nerve to preach to the people about how we are living in terrible times… Hypocrites, all of us! Destruction is coming, and if we wait until it hits to gather for prayer, it will be too late.

You have no clue as to how many people believed in these leaders and did everything to attend some of these conferences and did not see God; they saw gods, lovers of money and vanity. These people needed God. Not all meetings are bad, but the money-grabbing ones should be ashamed of themselves, leaving the people broke and disgusted. Before they can recover the losses of the one conference, Satan is already pushing the next one. This is the same commercialized spirit of retail. Before one holiday is gone, they are already putting merchandise on the shelf for the next holiday, you can't get a break from the world. The church has adopted the same spirit and principles from the principalities fallen from heaven, the gods of this world.

What has happened is Lucifer has come in and taken over the church. Whether it is arrogance or ignorance, branding has become routine. Pastors now have built their brands like Walmart, Apple, Amazon, Google, and Disney, for example. These pastors and prophets learn from one another how to develop their own brands. The problem with this is that they used God and His people to build it and did it in the name of Jesus. Most of them come from nothing. They were not born rich or inherited wealth; they built it from God's people, and no matter how much they get, it's never enough; this is how you can tell that it is lust. Nowadays, companies prioritize protecting their brand over speaking about controversial topics or condemning immoral behavior.

They cannot afford to entertain anything that would be a threat to their brand despite preaching and teaching about Jesus. However, they do not follow in Jesus' footsteps to deliver people from the bondage and torments of the devil. Satan can't cast out Satan. They have surrendered to the devil on the mountain, and he is granting them the kingdoms of this world. They must be careful not to offend the god who gave them the idea for their brand. They use the sheep…God's sheep. What? You didn't know that God knew they were sheep and that sheep are innocent. This is why we have true prophets on record in the Bible, like Jeremiah chapter 23 and Ezekiel chapter 34, please read these chapters when you can make time. Allow the Holy Spirit to talk to you. How often do pastors preach and teach from these books, chapters, and verses of the Bible?

I want to make sure you understand that some preachers have been instructed by officials who serve Satan to protect their brand at any cost. These officials can recognize these preachers' gifts, talents, and anointing and use them to entertain and impress people. However, once they sell out, they can no longer cast out devils, heal broken hearts, set captives free, or preach restoration. Instead, they are constantly reminded of the high cost of maintaining their brand's relevance. For this reason, they are often sidetracked and have to cut off the Spirit of God to ask for money.

Many pastors and preachers have adopted the concept of sowing a seed into the Word because it is profitable. However, it becomes difficult for any preacher, regardless of gender, to preach the unadulterated word of God when they are spiritually committing adultery. The term 'brand' is a code word for god, and the church is helping these leaders glorify their worldly gods, which is idolatry. This is the very thing that God punished Israel for in the wilderness. These leaders have a tie and responsibility to the gods of this world. It raises the question of how one can give back to Satan all that he has. People believe God has given these blessings. When you hear someone talking about their brand, they are talking about and worshiping their false god. You thought you were helping to build the kingdom of God because this is what they told you, but instead, you were helping them to build their kingdom and brands. WOE!

The Lord God has commanded us, "Have no other gods before Me." So, no matter how much these pastors/ prophets may intend or want to help you, they can't because Satan will always be in their ear, reminding them of all the stuff he has given them and when they had nothing and how he has blessed them. Sadly, most think they hear from the True and Living God. This is why they keep saying, "Jesus!" They are trying and hoping they are ok in His presence, but they are deceived.

There are moments when people's hearts are in the right place; God may allow them to lose their status and reputation to save their souls. Sometimes, this happens through sickness and even death, but it is all part of God's plan. Although it may not be evident to the public, God is rebuking the Devil and giving people a chance to repent. Those who repent are forgiven and can still access the kingdom of heaven. This is when it gets tough for some people, but it is true if a person can repent, they too can be saved.

It's not up to anyone to deny God's forgiveness to anyone else. Some leaders who have repented and been forgiven by God have had to depart from this world before their time, but this is a necessary sacrifice to save their souls. While Satan may accuse the saints, when the accusations are true, God intervenes and forgives those who truly repent, regardless of the severity of their transgressions.

What is sad is that the women whom God has genuinely called suffer rejection from most clergy and get endorsed by the leaders who are pushing their brands. They believe this is a God send, only to find out they had been polluted with a spirit of the world. The woman of God has these men as their example of ministry. They don't know these men have been at the wrong tree eating the fruit Eve ate. Eve has been redeemed, but now these men need redemption but are too proud to admit it, like the Pharisees, who were full of pride. They use the woman for their desire, showcase her beauty, and then make her a brand (god). Don't sell!

As a woman, you have been through too much and have suffered; you need to be faithful to your calling without compromise. I am speaking to those whom God has indeed called to preach. Don't mingle with polluted blood. The blood of Jesus Christ is what has cleansed you.

Beware, for we are in the last days, and the devil is desperately seeking to devour you.

The worldview of you as a woman is, that you can't be a woman of God. They are looking for faults to disqualify you. It's funny how you can't preach. Still, you can be a prostitute, an exotic dancer, a whore, an adulteress, a magnet for lust, fulfill fantasies of desire, a water girl, bed warmer, mistress, police officer, a judge, a lawyer, in the military, a pilot, a nurse, a doctor, scientist, CEO, vice president, president, porn star, church clerk, cook, maid, fundraiser, chicken and fish fryer, but just not a preacher or pastor. Says who? Who is allowing and endorsing women for all these professions, but preaching and pastoring are off limits? It is incredible how many men and women support these beliefs. What made a woman believe she could master the pole as an exotic dancer and be gifted enough to tempt individuals to give them mortgage money, rent, and car payments because they got caught up in the fantasy that she sold?

On the other hand, what made a woman believe she was called to be a pastor? Do both of these have a calling? Did they both hear a voice or voices telling them they could do it? Both of them take skills and endurance. Both of them serve people, but neither one could do what they do if they did not believe and pursue it. One is selling fantasies and lust, while the other is giving truths of realities and love. One is a giver, and the other is a taker.

What is dangerous about the two is if the woman of God forfeits her calling as a preacher/pastor, she could become a taker and sell fantasies to the people; she will take people's money in the name of Jesus. If she is not grounded in the truth, convicted of her faith and calling, she will use her other gift to seduce you right in the church or church conference and you won't know what happened until it happened. You'll go home talking to yourself like someone who was on crack because it is a spiritual drug and it is illegal.

This is the reason we have so many male pastors/ preachers getting money like they are pimps. We all have to be sure that we are not on the mountain meeting with the devil, bowing down to get the kings of this world handed over by him, and then feeling like we have done some great thing. How many churches will be built that are open only two days a week? We say we are in the last days, but churches aren't available for prayer but open for business. Tithes, offerings, building funds, and fundraisers, but we can't pray during the week.

The world is in a spiritual pandemic, and hardly any churches are open. Imagine during the pandemic crisis, most hospitals were closed with a sign saying Sundays at 10 am and Wednesdays at 7 pm. Are we blind or just in denial? What do we think God is saying about this? How does Jesus feel about the church if it is His church? How can the church serve the community with these hours?

Why do churches have so many pastors, elders, and leaders if we are open just two days a week? What are they doing all week long?

God had me challenge people to give Him seven minutes of prayer starting at 7 am, whatever your time zone. Seven minutes of dedicated time to God, no cell phones, no devices, no multitasking, no interactions whatsoever with anyone or anything…Just seven minutes. Seven represents perfect, full, and complete. Start your day with seven, God's perfect number. Seven days of creation (1000 years equals a day), seven days of the week, seven spirits of God, seven churches, seven candle sticks, seven colors of the rainbow, seven years of plenty, seven years of famine, seven trumpets, seven last words of Christ, seventh day sabbath, seven days holy week, Passover seven days, seven days of unleavened bread, enslaved people released in the seventh year. Wouldn't it be powerful to know that around the world, believers are praying together on one accord as they did in the upper room on Pentecost? As the Body of Christ, we must find a way to unify.

The world loves its own; I don't know why believers are trying so hard to fit in with the world and be accepted. You will never fit in as long as Christ and His kingdom are in you. Don't lose yourself trying to be something you were not ordained. The ungodly are not accepting you; no matter what you do, they will drag you down in the mud and make a mockery of you; they are waiting for the opportune time to expose you and bring you down. The Devil is not your friend; no matter how much pleasure you get from him and his demons, it's a trap.

He is the accuser of the saints daily; let them be accusations; don't give him facts. Don't you know that the day will come when we, as the saints of God, the followers of Christ, will judge Satan and his followers? Don't find yourself on the wrong side to be judged when you are supposed to judge the wicked. This is why we don't judge now; time is for building the case, and eternity is for judging and condemning evil in The Supreme Court of God, where the charges will stick.

I cannot emphasize this enough: RIP Rest in Peace is not for the Believer. This deception comes straight from the Deceiver; he wants you to believe you will not be accountable after this life. This is not true. Christ is the Resurrection. "We are appointed once to die, and after death is the judgment." No justice, no peace. How can we believe there is no eternal accountability when we are accountable for our actions here on earth? If we have a court in time, we must know there is a court in eternity. No one gets away with evil. Even the judges will be judged on how they ruled cases in time, their lifetime, or their career. You gave time to these people when you knew they were innocent. We are not talking about the cases where you were not sure of them being guilty or innocent, but there

are clear-cut cases where you railroaded the innocent…
Woe unto you! These judges literally had people's lives in
their hands. If they were not just in their rulings or took
bribes, they would have to face the people whose lives
they had ruined. The great deception is the Devil wants
you to believe you will not be accountable. All of this evil
is because of the love of money.

The "Prosperity Gospel" has become the church's
"Fool's Gold"; the false prophets have painted rocks gold
(pictures of success and blessings) and made as many
people who believed they were messengers from God to
give to (sow a seed) them for the gold. They deceived the
people into giving their money for a golden life, only to
find out later that they gave their money believing they
would get the same gold as the messengers had.

The preachers showed them real gold (a successful
lifestyle), but the gold they sold to you were painted rocks,
and they are the ones who painted the stones when they
prophesied lies to you, and by doing so, they would get
you to sow. They manipulate people into believing you
would get the same result by giving to them. The gold
paint is wearing off; you have worthless painted stones
and feel foolish. You are left with doubt, anger, and
betrayal and wonder where God is.

We know and understand the ministry needs financial
support, but everyone cannot be rich, at least not in this

world. If you support a church or ministry, then support them and give, but don't give all you have unless you are sure God is telling you to. Otherwise, it's like playing a lottery, hoping you will hit big. The Bible is loaded with principles of giving and sowing to work, and God will always honor His word; what I am saying is don't be taken in by these greedy false prophets playing on your emotions, causing you to be an emotional giver, God has nothing to do with that. We need to build the kingdom just like we build our cities. But understand, it is work, not magic; God works miracles, and I have witnessed miracles.

Many preachers used the story in the Bible of the widow and her son, who was in a famine, and how the prophet asked the widow for something to eat. She told him she only had enough for her and her son to eat, and they would eat the last food she had, and then they would die. The prophet tells her to bake the bread, give it to him first, and then feed her and her son. She believed him to be a man of God (meaning he was sent to help her and her son, not harm them) and fed him first. As a man of God, she understood he could not be selfish enough to eat her last food and leave her and her son to die.

The man of God stayed until the famine was over. Every time they needed to eat, God provided flour and oil so she could make bread to feed all of them as long as the man of God was there. God honors obedience, sacrifice, and faith. The woman and her son survived along with the man of God until the famine was over. She then was able to grow crops from her own land and prosper. Do you see how the prophet stayed with her and her son until the famine ended and assured them they would be ok? God knew the famine would be over before it was over.

God sent the prophet to the widow at the beginning of the famine to take care of her and her son; he was the answer to her prayers. He was not sent to take her last but to demonstrate the Godly principle of sowing and reaping. She sowed into him so he could sow it back into her. He did not take her money and run. Neither did he go to the next desperate widow to take her last and run home, then count how much he accumulated from his preaching, calling it blessings.

How many conferences have you gone to, and the preacher asked you to believe God and sacrifice in giving all you have in the offering and watch how God will have a blessing waiting for you when you get back home? You give but are afraid, but believe the prophet. You get on the plane to head back home with so much expectation; now that the conference is over, you're feeling nervous because you gave money all week, money that you didn't have. Every day and night, each speaker was so annoyed and so good when they asked for the money you gave. You have covered your transportation, hotel, and food, but this conference cost way more than expected because of the extra giving. With all you have given, God has something great waiting for you back home.

You arrive home only to find out God is not there with any gifts for you. You are hit with tremulous problems, and money is at the top of the list. You're trying to be optimistic and believe in a miracle because, at this point, a miracle is what you need. All hell is breaking loose; the preachers call it a test of your faith. In the meantime, someone is telling you about the next conference. You haven't even settled back home yet, and they are offering discounts for next year. You have to be asking yourself, is this God? You don't like how you feel but are too ashamed to tell anyone.

You keep talking about how good the conference was, but you're disappointed and disgusted. You're not trying to be critical, but maybe these conferences are for groupies rather than believers. What happened to the church Jesus died for? Where can you find the kind of miracles that money cannot buy? Why can't we shift the focus towards people truly seeking answers instead of those just chasing goosebumps? You may have felt good while attending the conference, but now you feel like you've been taken for a ride. You're struggling to get your finances back on track after overspending at the event, almost like when you were younger and didn't know any better and would overspend during Christmas.

The people who give to false prophets should know they are not from God because they only offer empty promises. Have you ever received a gift in the mail from someone you've been financially supporting for years? And now, when you're going through a tough time, did this prophet receive a message from God that you need help? No, because they are a false prophet. You are only on their mailing list as a giver, and while you receive letters with encouraging words, you never get a check. If they can send you letters asking for money, they can also send you a letter with a check made out to you as a token of their appreciation for all the support you've given them. False prophets charge money for everything, even prayer. Why are you not getting paid? After all, you gave your last penny to them, thinking they were messengers of God. Don't worry; God will judge these false prophets and leaders. You will be there on the day of judgment as a witness to how much God loved and knew you.

God has countless ways to bless you as He owns the entire world and can do anything He wants. To receive His blessings, pray, read, and study His word, and ask the Holy Spirit to teach, lead, and guide you. Don't be afraid of His answers, as He is our comforter. The Holy Spirit is powerful and honest and will only reveal the truth to you. You can trust Him because He is God's Spirit Witness. It is essential to find what God asks of you and do it. Remember when Jesus said there was no man greater than John the Baptist, who had walked away from all his material possessions? John had none of the material things we often seek, thinking they are blessings. Therefore, do not judge your life solely on material things because you may miss out on the most significant part of God. God is Spirit, and His blessings are eternal. John lived a fulfilling life by doing what he was meant to do.

It is a fact that prosperity cannot be achieved without going through tests and trials. It is important to understand that no matter how much you give, not everyone is meant to be rich. It's important to stay in your lane and be content with the level God has called you to. People should not be upset with God as if He has deceived them.

Jesus warned the church, saying, *"Not everyone who says to me, 'Lord, Lord,' will enter the kingdom of heaven, but only the one who does the will of my Father who is in heaven. Many will say to me on that day, 'Lord, Lord, did we not prophesy in your name and in your name drive out demons and in your name perform many miracles?' Then I will tell them plainly, 'I never knew you. Away from me, you evildoers!' Matthew 7:21-23 NIV.*

However, as we mature, we may make our own plans instead of surrendering to our Creator. We start to do our will rather than the will of God. We think we know our own heart, but we do not; only God can know the heart. There are things in our hearts we have no clue that they are there. This is why some people can do things that others find unbelievable.

"And he who searches our hearts knows the mind of the Spirit because the Spirit intercedes for God's people in accordance with the will of God. And we know that in all things, God works for the good of those who love him, who have been called according to his purpose. For those God foreknew, he also predestined to be conformed to the image of his Son, that he might be the firstborn among many brothers and sisters.

And those he predestined, he also called; those he called, he also justified; those he justified, he also glorified. What, then, shall we say in response to these things? If God is for us, who can be against us? He who did not spare his own Son but gave him up for us all—how will he not also, along with him, graciously give us all things? Romans 8:27-32 NIV.

Isaiah chapter 53 in the Bible reveals that God did not spare His own Son, Jesus, who is referred to as "The suffering servant." As believers, we may face difficult times and be tempted to think that we have done something wrong or that God has abandoned us. However, it is important to remember that this couldn't be further from the truth.

1 Who has believed our message and to whom has the arm of the Lord been revealed?
2He grew up before him like a tender shoot and like a root out of dry ground.
He had no beauty or majesty to attract us to him, nothing

in his appearance that we should desire him.

3 He was despised and rejected by mankind, a man of suffering and familiar with pain.

Like one from whom people hide their faces, he was despised, and we held him in low esteem.

4 Surely he took up our pain and bore our suffering, yet we considered him punished by God,

stricken by him and afflicted. 5 But he was pierced for our transgressions, he was crushed for our iniquities; the punishment that brought us peace was on him, and by his wounds, we are healed.

6 We all, like sheep, have gone astray, each of us has turned to our own way; and the Lord has laid on him the iniquity of us all.

7 He was oppressed and afflicted, yet he did not open his mouth; he was led like a lamb to the slaughter, and as a sheep, before its shearers are silent, so he did not open his mouth.

8 By oppression and judgment, he was taken away. Yet, who of his generation protested? For he was cut off from the land of the living; for the transgression of my people, he was punished.

9 He was assigned a grave with the wicked, and with the rich in his death, though he had done no violence, nor was any deceit in his mouth.

10 Yet it was the Lord's will to crush him and cause him to suffer, and though the Lord makes his life an offering for sin, he will see his offspring and prolong his days, and the

will of the Lord will prosper in his hand.
11 After he has suffered, he will see the light of life and be
satisfied; by his knowledge, my righteous servant will
justify many, and he will bear their iniquities.
12 Therefore I will give him a portion among the great, and
he will divide the spoils with the strong,
because he poured out his life unto death, and was
numbered with the transgressors. He bore the sin of many
and made intercession for the transgressors.

It is a fundamental truth that the Lord Jesus can understand any form of human suffering. The Lord endured trials and rejection, and, above all, he humbled himself before his creation, even as they inflicted harm upon him. The Lord showed us the ultimate level of selflessness through his actions, which serve as a testament to the enduring power of humility and compassion in difficult situations. Jesus is our example of how to overcome our fleshly desires. Jesus can feel any pain we go through; he understands. This is crucial because many great leaders have fallen from grace and power due to their inability to pass this test. To have power and authority over the devil, we must not possess any of the devil's property, including the pleasure of the flesh that occupies our hearts and lives illegally. It is impossible to cast out a devil Sunday morning if we were with him getting pleasure on Saturday night. Due to the sensitive nature of the subject matter, many religious leaders may refrain from addressing the issue of demonic possession, let alone attempting to exorcise a demon.

The omniscience of God is such that He possesses a superior understanding of His creation, surpassing that of their own. Consequently, there is nothing we experience in life that is beyond the knowledge of God. He knows, and He knew. God, the creator of this universe, created each one of us with a unique purpose. If He had not loved us, we would not have been born and given a chance to fulfill our purpose. This purpose could be anything, ranging from serving humanity to spreading love and kindness, as long as it is aligned with the will of God. So, it's our responsibility to seek the one who made us find that purpose and work towards it, as it will give us a sense of fulfillment and bring us closer to God's plan for us.

The wilderness is a place where hidden things are revealed. When God chooses you, you must go through the wilderness before receiving anything God has promised you. The wilderness is between you and your destiny. This is the proving ground. Although it may seem like a cruel and lengthy journey, the wilderness is a necessary step in our spiritual journey. We may feel forgotten or abandoned by God during this time, but in reality, we are called to the wilderness because God loves us. God wants us to confront our enemies head-on. This is where and when we can get to know God for ourselves and to know His voice. So, we will not be easily moved or influenced when someone quotes scripture but cannot live it.

In our life, ministry, or blessed place, the enemy may try to use everything against us. However, he will try to do it in the wilderness. If we pass our tests in the wilderness, we will have authority over the serpent when we come out. If we defeat the devil in his familiar and powerful house, he won't be able to defeat us in our own house, whether it's our home, church, or business. If we forget what we have learned in the wilderness, we won't stand a chance in life. We must be careful and watchful. Many of our leaders fall because we get caught up in prosperity and forget the lessons of lack and how we depended on God for everything. Having the bare necessities was a test, but we would fast and pray, then wait on God to get us through. We've shed tears when we thought we wouldn't make it. While we are going through the most challenging times, it is in these times that God is anointing us, pouring more of His spirit into us. We should not covet someone else's anointing; the devil will not respect an anointing stolen or borrowed. Whatever is in us that's not like God will come out in the wilderness. Remember, the children of Israel were in the wilderness for forty years.

"Remember how the LORD your God led you all the way in the wilderness these forty years to humble and test you in order to know what was in your heart, whether or not you would keep his commands. He humbled you, causing you to hunger and then feeding you with manna,

which neither you nor your ancestors had known, to teach you that man does not live on bread alone but on every word that comes from the mouth of the LORD."
Deuteronomy 8:2-3 NIV.

They were tested on every side, and most of the time, they failed the test. They would choose gods they couldn't see over the invisible God, who is The God I AM, who brought them out of Egypt and slavery. They continued to choose false gods that gave them immediate gratifications that were only temporary, and they had to go around the wilderness again like someone doing laps around a hot track at practice. The wilderness is our place of practice… it's rehearsal. We must get it right in rehearsal (time) before we are granted access to the kingdom (eternity). Rehearsals are strenuous when you don't know your part, but when you get your part tight and right, you feel good and confident and are ready for showtime. God wants us to be prepared for showtime.

The devil does not miss any rehearsals. He is at rehearsal, watching every move and sound we make. He knows if we complain against God rather than be thankful, we will be required to stay in the wilderness a little while longer. Thus, he gets more time to play with us and calls us to fail. He knows if you got it or are faking it, and God allows you to get through it, or it will destroy you on that stage. You may die in a place of disgrace and shame and never attempt to walk with God again. Moses did not understand his destiny, and timing is everything. Nothing happens before it's time, no matter how hard we try. God knew Moses before Moses had a name. God used the circumstances of Moses's escape to give him a name and an education. The Pharaoh's daughter gave Moses his name. Pharoah was trying to kill the Hebrews, and God put a Hebrew right in the house of the enemy.

When Moses killed the Egyptian, he was driven through the wilderness and to the land of Midian. He spent forty years in the wilderness, learning and practicing being a shepherd. Then, after four decades of tending to sheep, God spoke to him and instructed him to go to Egypt to demand that Pharaoh let His people go. Moses spent the next forty years leading the same people in the wilderness, where he wrote the Torah. Little did Moses know that God was preparing him for greatness. He probably thought it was a life sentence for his sin. While tending the sheep, God was humbling and training him.

Moses, a prince of Egypt, was humbled to the position of a shepherd, which was considered a job for the undereducated. Although he was born a Hebrew-Israelite of the Tribe of Levi, he was raised as an Egyptian Prince and enjoyed all the splendor, education, and glory it had to offer for forty years. Later, he would go into exile and live in Midian as a shepherd for another forty years before delivering God's people from Egypt and leading them as God's prophet for another forty years. Moses died at the age of one hundred and twenty years. Interestingly, Jesus accomplished in forty days what it took Moses and the children of Israel forty years to achieve.

When we think God has forgotten us or is taking too long to bring us out, this is when we are tempted to go back to our old lives. Settling for a life searching for good times and feeling good, sometimes no matter the cost. It's the place where we are most comfortable in our sins. The familiar place doesn't have to be perfect, just legally ungodly. We can become addicted to pleasures outside of the wilderness and be deceived into believing it is better without God than with God on His terms. This is certain: God will not cheat on our scores. If we pass the tests in the wilderness, we will be granted authority over the enemy in all that we do. Moses said, 'I'd rather suffer the afflictions with the people of God than to enjoy the pleasures of sin for a season."

The devil continues to use the same old tricks, firstly because they work and secondly because he doesn't have any new ones. Faith that has not been tested is a faith that cannot be trusted. To please God, one must have faith. The wilderness serves as an environment that can evoke unexplored strengths and latent talents. In traversing the wilderness, the individual is confronted with challenges and adversities that can test and refine their character while bringing forth a transformative experience that would not have been possible within a comfortable and predictable environment.

It's the pressure that puts our faith to the test because God is not going to pacify us every minute, and for this reason, sometimes we think we are getting away with some things, but we are not. It's the carbon that's under intense pressure, about 725,000 pounds per square inch that bonds the carbon atoms to each other in a unique arrangement: one carbon atom to four other carbon atoms. That's a lot of pressure. This is what makes a diamond hard. See, 1 plus 4, this is where grace comes in: 5 is the number of grace. We are not able to see in our fleshly earthen vessels that we are made from the similar pressure God created us to make diamonds. You are stronger than you think! You have to see you in the realm of the spirit, not the flesh. Believe this: the enemy knows your value. Given all that you have gone through and the pressures you have endured without being crushed, you are a diamond. You are made of many layers of value when you allow God to take you through life. Three undeniable components that make you priceless with God are pressure, heat, and time. The devil knows you're a diamond and how valuable you are, but all you see is carbon right now. Just give it some time to know your worth.

It can be challenging for human beings to accurately gauge their abilities and powers to endure until they face specific challenges or circumstances. This lack of self-awareness can make it difficult to predict how we will react in certain situations or what we can accomplish. Some people can bring the best out of you while, on the other hand, someone else can get the worst out of you. Who we connect with in life is essential. It is never too late to make a change in your life.

Remember that each individual's circumstances are unique, and it is necessary to surround yourself with people who bring out the best in you. The power of influence can't be denied. One out of three angels followed Lucifer over what God had for them and was kicked out of heaven, losing their eternal place and relationship with God. The greatest deception is that they thought they were getting away with their hypocrisy and thought God didn't know…but He always knew. He knows our beginning and end, our first breath and our last. God is supreme, all-knowing, and knows the end from the beginning—the Omniscient God.

God was the only one who saw iniquity in the heart of Lucifer. No one could have imagined how lethal iniquity was and is. Iniquity is the root sin and the producer of all sins, the fruits that threaten life. Every murder, rape, lie, molestation, adultery, fornication, jealousy, betrayal, and hate crime, just to name a few, are fruits from its tree; it is because of iniquity. God knew you would be abandoned, God knew he would leave you for another lover, God knew she would walk out of your life, God knew they were living a double life, God knew he was on the down low, God knew your abuser, God knew you would leave home at an early age, God knew Satan would want to be your stepdad, God knew your molester, God knew you would end up divorced, God knew he or she was the wrong one for you, God knew your mother would believe her boyfriend over you, God knew when he came into her life he would touch you in the wrong way at an early age, the devil sent him, God knew you would end up on drugs and become an addict, God knew you would get sick, But God also knew He would die for you and everything you would ever go through…He's got you! God knew you would get this word, God knew they lied to you, and He is here telling you that you still have the victory. You can get through this. God knew you would be the victor, not the victim! You are saved, converted, and safe!

He knew that losing your loved ones would hurt, but God took care of death, and those who believe in Him will never die. If they are in Christ, they are not resting but living. In eternity, you don't get tired; you don't have flesh or a mortal body for that; you will be immortal. Don't feel sorry for those who have preceded you in death because they are having the time of their lives. Be sure that you don't mourn forever over them; remember the good times you shared with them in time because, in eternity, there will be no end to the love and good.

For all of the evil we experience in this world, it's only

temporary. This is God's doing, and it had to be. It ends in time and will be judged in eternity after this life. God is building a case against Satan and all of the evildoers. They get to spend eternity with themselves in the absence of sound and good people. This will be one of the principal torments for them. Evil only gets off with pleasure when they make the good suffer. They won't have any more good people to do evil to. Evil only feels good when they can abuse the good God has created. Well, not anymore!

Jesus did not have to suffer the way he did. He could have had a quick death, but God wants us to know that He is not a coward. He suffered because the devil has made you suffer, but He made sure that your suffering could not last forever. Pain to be delivered, God had to go through pain to give birth to us. Born again is our saving grace. God's love for us…it's an everlasting love. No one gets away with evil. God will judge every case, so forgive your enemies; this doesn't mean to have to put up with them or even see them. Forgive that you don't become bitter and lose your power or forfeit your calling and purpose in God.

Continue your work and serve your God. DO NOT make a god out of your pain, but turn your pain into power! Remember that justice will be served. Satan's best days are behind him; believers in Christ's best days are in front of them. Don't believe the devil's hype. He knows he has a short while, so he deceives people to get wild, expressing through them how he wishes good could last forever, but it can't and won't for him. He uses the weak to express his perversions through. He's using every generation to party and do his kinky stuff. Look throughout history with the rich and powerful; they don't know what to do, so they use their demonic imaginations to do lustful stuff. The poor do not know what to do with poverty, so they overly indulge in things to escape the pains and realities of the dire state they are in with daily reminders.

The angels were deceived by Lucifer, who transformed into Satan, and they wished they could do it all over again. If you are a follower of Satan, you will have days when you wish you had another chance to make it right. So, I admonish you to think about what the devil got you doing…I did. I repented and cried because my eyes came open, and I didn't want the Devil to be the mastermind behind my evil doings. The evil is tied somehow to your desires, and he gets you by tempting you with something you may like but gets you into trouble; then, he hides when you get caught, leaving you to hold the bag and take the charge or penalty. Do you know how many countless people there are incarcerated because of this evil tactic? Don't cover for that devil because he's certainly not going to cover for you. I am compelled to warn the people who are supposed to represent God, like preachers, pastors, bishops, prophets, and gospel/Christian artists, can not serve two masters! Don't allow the devil to make a fool out of you.

What he is doing to you, he did to the angels. The angels thought they were getting away with being a hypocrite, too, when they were in heaven because God didn't say or do anything about it for a long time. God is no fool; it's His love, and He's merciful. He hopes for our sake that we will come to our senses and turn away from evil. The angels cannot turn; it's too late for them, but not you and I. Expose that devil! God only sends warnings because He loves us. God is not evil, neither does He get joy from seeing anyone's demise…not even Satan's.

The uninfected angels may not have understood when God put the angels out of heaven, maybe not knowing they were infected with iniquity; this separation caused a war. It would help us as humanity to know why we are here on this planet in the first place. Lucifer and the fallen, rebellious angels were put out of heaven before iniquity was birthed in eternity. They were cast down to this planet, the only planet we know of that has gravity, and gravity has a law that limits their access. They are here, and we are here being quarantined. They are confined to this world until judgment. We are born here and do not remember having a physical body in the heavens. We are Beings that can manifest anything, whether good or evil, based upon what we choose to listen to or obey. We have a will and are created free moral agents; we get to choose good or evil. We have been given the liberty to act on our will or submit to God's will or the adversary's plans. We inherently will choose to do our Father's will, whether that is God or Satan.

Don't let any man deceive you. We decide to do what is pleasing to our Father. If you belong to God, you will eventually get it, but if not, you will not be denied your right to be with your father, the devil. People don't understand this kingdom order, that your heart belongs to your father, whoever he is, because you are his seed…his offspring. If it's God, well, He died for you; if it's Satan, well, he has yet to die. Let's see if he is willing to die for you…not that it will do any good.

"The Lamb was slain before the foundations of the world." God knew the devil would come after humanity, especially the women. God knew that they would eat from the tree and sin. God knew he would send his Son to save the world. God knew that Lucifer-Satan-The Devil- False Prophet and Serpent would not be able to refrain from such an easy opportunity to rule a world. Lucifer wants to be God and is willing to do whatever it takes to get this position of power…even if it's the world versus the universe; he's so desperate to be like God. To be God is his fantasy, and the naive is helping him with his fantasy. Our hearts are where ideals are planted and, if acted on, will manifest whoever places them there. Are we evil or good? Righteous or unrighteous? Godly or ungodly? Saint or sinner? Giving life or taking life? Building the kingdom or tearing the kingdom down? Loving and kind or mean and hateful? We cannot serve two masters!

After listening to the serpent and obeying, the Devil won this world by default. If we choose the fallen angel to serve in time, we have made him our father. If we reject him and seek the Lord for reconciliation and restoration, we are born again, and God is our Father. We have to choose. One out of three angels chose Lucifer, and he is their god. Our purpose in life is to choose who we want as our eternal god. What life do we want to possess, good or evil, life or death, love or lust, faithfulness or promiscuity? We have to choose. God will not force Himself on anyone, but He will let us know He is interested and knew us before our parents ever met. God knew the day we would be born and the day we would expire…He knew. If we choose the world, Lucifer, and lust in time, then we would have eventually chosen evil in eternity if we were born there first.

The purpose of time is to build a case against evil and judge it, condemn it, throw it in the trash, and burn it. We don't keep garbage in our homes, and neither does God. We make it complicated but are dedicated to the god we want to serve. This is why people hate God because they serve another god. Everyone has the right to be with their father, and God will not keep Satan's children away from him…He is the Just Judge. If you hate God in time, you will eventually hate Him in eternity. Look at the manifold wisdom of God to create a place called time to allow the creation the freedom and liberties to choose between good and evil, and it has no bearing on the universe and eternity. Whatever we do here stays here. "Flesh and blood cannot inherit the kingdom of God." This world is designed to hold us down, and the fallen angels cannot rise above the first heaven. The law of gravity does not bind the rest of the heavens (universe).

We are so arrogant that we question whether life is anywhere beside the earth. We are the most fragile form of life because we've been confined to a temporal state of being. Our needs, like food, water, air, and oxygen, are not supplied on the other planets to our knowledge. Death releases us from that state of being, and our eternal part (soul) is set free and is not bound by the law of gravity when we belong to God. We don't want to believe in hell, but we throw away trash every day. We take the good part (in the packaging) and throw away the containers or packages. The package our goods are in did its job if we can get the goods from inside the package undamaged.

When we choose God, we put our lives in His hands and allow Him to get what's good inside us and throw away the package. Our souls are inside, and our bodies are the package that gets thrown away. On the other hand, when we choose evil, we are damaged inside and out. Therefore, the package and what's on the inside gets thrown away in the trash and is incinerated for energy…

usable power. This is what happens to our waste and with technology. Do we think we are the true innovators of such things?

God knew when He created the earth that the man was in the earth, the woman was in the man, and the children in the man and woman, "I knew your food was there, I knew your pets were there, I knew your seafood was there, I knew the birds were there, I knew the animal and mammals were there, I knew your medicine was there, I knew the house was in there, I knew the boats and ships were in there, I knew the planes were there, I knew the bridges were there, I knew the oil was there for gas, diesel, and the cars and trucks, I knew your job was in there, I knew the iPhone was in there, I knew, the atomic bombs were in there, I knew the technologies were there, I knew materials to build were there, I knew the gold and silver was there, I knew weapons of mass destruction was in there.

"I knew your shoes were there. I knew all means of transportation were in there. I knew that when you started to discover what I already knew, you would begin to worship the works of your own hands. I knew your dining ware was in there. I knew everything was there. Do you get the point? I knew! Who do you think put all of those things on the earth? 'God said, Let there be,' and it was. It took humanity thousands of years and generations to discover what I already knew. There are a lot more hidden things in the earth that God has not yet revealed. Revelation means 'the unveiling of the previously revealed.' This means it was there all along but was hidden. Why do men think they are more intelligent and wiser than Me?"They can outthink Me. So, I AM telling you that I knew you, and I know You! You cannot surprise Me with anything you think, say, or do because I knew, and I know."

"So listen, woman, I knew you were going to be born in this generation, and I knew they would fight against you like they did Jeremiah because of your age and gender. I knew that they would not win against you. I knew that one day, you would get this message and get yourself together so you can preach this gospel of the kingdom and bring glory to My Name. I knew you would finally get it and let nothing and no one turn you back to what you used to be…because you know what I already knew."

The Apostle John had a vision where he saw a countless number of people, so vast that there was no number to describe it. However, God knew you, and I would be a part of that number. It's unlikely that God would be angry at you for helping to achieve that number just because you are a woman. The truth is that Jesus will not return until we reach the number that John saw because he showed John the number. John did not mention the gender of the people he saw; what mattered was that they were in that number. So, what's important is that you contributed to the work of achieving that number. Don't let the devil make you doubt yourself. Remember that God is real and is solely focused on His will being done, not your gender.

It is a fact that those whom God has called to preach have been chosen by Him even before the foundations of the world. This divine calling is not only a testament to the deep-rooted faith that these individuals possess but also a testament to the omniscience of God, who knows the destiny of every person even before their birth. Therefore, it is essential for these men and women of God to heed this divine calling and to preach the gospel with all their might. Doing so will fulfill their obligation to God and spread the good news of salvation to all lost.

As such, it is important for us to recognize the divine nature of this calling and to support those who have been chosen to preach. Through our support and encouragement, we can help these individuals carry out their mission and reach out to those in need of salvation. You have been anointed to spread the Gospel; instead of fulfilling their true purpose, some have chosen to use their anointing for personal gain or other purposes. The prophet Isaiah had a vision of the anointing of the Holy Spirit. This anointing is meant to empower preachers to bring good news to the poor, bind up the brokenhearted, proclaim freedom for the captives, release prisoners from darkness, and preach about the year of restoration, getting back all the enemy has stolen from you.

It is a sacred gift that should not be misused or taken for granted. Jesus Christ left us an example of how to use this gift properly. We should know what our anointing is for, use it accordingly, and always remember that God knew us before we knew ourselves. Your predestination is that of God, who has foreknowledge of us even before we became aware of our existence. Despite this knowledge, many of us find ourselves plagued by worries over how others perceive us. However, it is essential to recognize that these concerns are often the enemy's work, which seeks to disrupt one's relationship with God.

To resist these attempts, remaining centered on your faith, calling, and destiny is crucial. God has a unique plan for each person, and by staying committed to your spiritual path, you can align yourself with this purpose. Through this alignment, you can find a sense of direction and purpose, even in the face of adversity. Moreover, it is essential to recognize that God has a timing for everything. Your journey may include moments of hardship and struggle, but these experiences can serve as opportunities for growth and self-discovery. By embracing these challenges, you can move closer to your true destiny and fulfill God's plan for your life. In essence, by remaining steadfast in your relationship with God, faith, and purpose, you can overcome any obstacle and stay aligned with your divine calling. God knew you would be an overcomer. Tell your story, and to God be the glory.

You have been called, anointed, and ordained by the Lord God Himself to carry out His divine mission. He has given you His words to preach, prophesy, lay hands, cast out demons, and heal the sick. God knew that you were the one to accomplish this great purpose, so go forth with the assurance that God will be with you every step of the way. PREACH!

If we engage in activities like praising God, worshiping Him, singing hymns, preaching, laying hands, and organizing revivals without conquering sin, we are not doing anything new. We are doing the same thing that caused Lucifer and the angels to be cast out of heaven. They thought they were deceiving God by pretending to worship and serve Him while having iniquity in their hearts. Therefore, if you are okay with sin, you are deceiving yourself and others.

Lucifer had convinced some angels that God was unaware of their actions. According to him, as long as they continued praising and worshipping Him, it didn't matter what they did. Consequently, they continued to transgress against God, living a double life. However, God, in His mercy and love for them, allowed them to keep doing this for a while, hoping they would come to their senses and repent. If only they had asked God for help and expressed their desire to be holy and pure, God would have helped them. But instead, they thought they were wiser than God and continued with their selfish ways. We must learn from those who used to reside in heaven and how they lost their place. Iniquity is not our friend! "Depart from Me; you are workers of iniquity."

So, when God concluded that they were not going to repent, not going to change, God cast them out of his sight, and they came to this world. So, those same fallen angels and Lucifer are doing to humanity what they did to the angels in heaven; "there is nothing new under the sun." "Be hot or cold; if you are lukewarm, I will spit you out of My mouth." So, who is speaking through you talented, gifted, and anointed lukewarm folks if God is not? How many of you like your coffee hot or cold, and your tea, hot or cold, not lukewarm? Do anything hot or cold; at least with God, you would have a chance to be saved. If you play both sides like Lucifer and the angels did, then when you need help, you will have nowhere to go. What do you do when God and Satan don't want you?

Why don't you open up a nightclub, strip club, or boutique, write songs on the other side, perform R&B, rap, or hip-hop, or be a motivational speaker and leave Jesus' and God's name out of your mouth? Do anything that does not require a lifestyle modeling holiness and righteousness of the kingdom of God. Why do you have to be in the Christian and gospel industry being filthy contaminated? Have respect for God, have some respect for yourselves and your families, and your marriages. Making a mistake is one thing; we all make mistakes. But if you can continue in sin and do praise, worship, and preach as if you have not done anything, that is not a mistake; that is a purpose; it is nothing short of wickedness; this is a warning to repent. The Lord is saying before I come upon you swiftly and cut you off.

Women, I know you know a lot of secrets and have maybe just as many; you are a lethal weapon. God knows everything about you, me, them, and everything in between, but He wants you and still is calling you in these last days to preach the gospel; understand this: He doesn't need any more fake preachers and false prophets to add to those already in operation. He wants to put his words into somebody's mouth, who will choose to live holy since the men can't keep it in their pants, just like the Pharisees couldn't. God is calling you, but make no mistakes about it; He wants you to keep your panties on and use your mouth to preach the gospel, not to put it on anybody's flesh. You know that man is not your husband, then who's husband is he, and who sent him to you? Why you? Why are you in love when he's not? Be careful and watchful!

You are a chosen woman to preach the gospel. If you remain faithful, you will be exalted because you will have God's glory and anointing with you to preach the gospel. However, always listen to the right voice…the Voice of God; if you cannot live the life, refrain from being a pastor or prophet and preaching about Jesus Christ and the scriptures. It's better to leave it alone." 'God knows my heart" is Lucifer's greatest deception of an excuse ever spun. Yes, God knows your heart, and He knew iniquity was in Lucifer's heart, and look at what it got him. Do you understand what it means to be the top preacher and gospel singer and not be required to live a holy and righteous life?

Imagine winning a top gospel award and God didn't honor you or the award. Because if you're not living a life in alignment with what you're singing about, then God did not give you that award….the devil did. It's the same thing Jesus turned down on his 40-day fast when he was on the mountain with the devil. The devil showed him the kingdoms of the world and said, "I will give them to you if you bow down and worship me." Jesus rejected him and his offer. If you're not living the life, it means you bowed down, and he will give you your desire. You got your awards and top chart song from Lucifer, so the devil blessed you, not God. You thought it was God, but it was the devil in disguise who blessed you. Those who continue to live this life of deception will share in Lucifer's rewards from God.

Have you ever thought,…why can't I live right or be faithful to my spouse? Because Lucifer gave you some of the songs he wrote before he was cast down out of heaven. We all must know by now Lucifer was the very best singer-songwriter, arranger, and producer in the universe. This is why you can't live a life of holiness; neither could Satan.

That's why you can sing about it but can't live it. That's why you can preach it but can't live it: you bowed down to the wrong god and listened to the wrong voice. Ultimately, you may become a false god, revered by idol worshipers who offer temporary worship and accolades.

However, when all is said and done, we will stand before God and give an account of how we have used the gifts He has given us. God gives gifts without repentance, which means He knew how we would use them before He gave them to us and still hasn't changed His mind about it. Trying to impress people is a temporary high and a lie. In contrast, we will all awaken to the truth when we face God in eternity, where truth is uninterrupted. Please understand that everything Satan blesses you with is stolen. Things like glory, honor, life, joy, peace, unity, praise, worship, gold, every precious thing of value, and the ultimate our souls and Adam's dominion and authority. The man and woman were not created to be Satan's slaves or servants but his master. The devil is bribing you with your own stuff.

Don't let the devil make a fool out of you. I am only writing this because I allowed him to make a fool out of me at one point in my life. But no longer! Hear me when I say that! Adam, in turn, lost everything to the devil through disobedience to God; this is why obedience to God is so vitally important…don't you understand… is it redemptive? Do you know what makes the devil such a

great liar and deceiver? It's because he knows the truth…
the real truth! That's why we must know the truth, too. I'm
referring to actual facts: God has never lied because He is
the truth. There is no falsehood in Him, and a lie cannot
survive in His presence. Although Satan is a liar, he has to
tell the truth when he is in the presence of God. For
instance, when God asked Satan, "Where have you been?"
he had to answer truthfully."

*"Now, there was a day when the sons of God (angels)
came to present themselves before the LORD, and Satan
(adversary, accuser) also came among them. The LORD
said to Satan, "From where have you come?" Then Satan
answered the LORD, "From roaming around on the earth
and from walking around on it." The LORD asked Satan,
"Have you considered and reflected on My servant Job? For
there is none like him on the earth, a blameless and upright
man, one who fears God [with reverence] and abstains
from and turns away from evil [because he honors God]."
Job 1:6-8 AMP*

*"Be sober [well balanced and self-disciplined], be alert
and cautious at all times. That enemy of yours, the devil,
prowls around like a roaring lion [fiercely hungry], seeking
someone to devour. But resist him, be firm in your faith
[against his attack—rooted, established, immovable],
knowing that the same experiences of suffering are being
experienced by your brothers and sisters throughout the
world. [You do not suffer alone.]"*   *1 Peter 5:8-9 AMP*

It is unfortunate that some individuals preach about Jesus and write songs praising and worshiping God but do not live according to these beliefs. This behavior suggests that they do not truly love or fear God, nor do they honor Him. These observations are based on factual evidence. Unfortunately, some people may not want to share these things with you because they hope to benefit from your fortune. As a result, you may have been surrounded by "Yes" people assigned by the devil, who are inclined to agree with you, resulting in no accountability. When someone exposes another person's misdeeds after the money runs out, it is not an act of justice, righteousness, or responsibility. Instead, it is driven by hate, revenge, or extortion. It's important to consider how you would feel if you were in their shoes and faced the Judgment Seat of Christ or the White Throne Judgment alongside the person who paid you to expose them.

Don't be overly concerned about what people think of you; what matters is what God knew about you before you were born and what He knows about you, period. If you feel out of line with God, make up your mind to get back in alignment with Him; remember, He loves you and knows you better than anybody, including yourself. Just come back home to your Heavenly Father and stop allowing the devil to play the role of your stepfather. You know Satan always wanted to be a father and mother…he-she is dangerous!

Repentance is a powerful tool that we, as human beings, can use against the devil. It's a little-known secret that out of all of Lucifer's gifts, repentance was not one of them. When we repent of our sins, we strip the enemy of his power over us. But when we keep his secrets, he gains control over our lives and becomes our lord. Assess your life; look around at where you are, the things in your life, and who is in your life. Is Jesus Lord of your life or someone else? Do you see God as your Father, or is Satan your Father and or stepdad? Do you know who your birth father is? You're trying to obey both fathers; they are not equal but are opposites. Whoever you follow with zero resistance is who you belong to. When you obey the devil, he invites other demons into the room. You will seek to please the one you love. The tree is known by its fruit…

No matter how much you have achieved, be it awards, money, houses, cars, or deals, you can never find true satisfaction through them. It is because the desire for more is rooted in lust, which is like a deep black hole with no end. The devil will make you do anything to find satisfaction, but ultimately, it will only lead to emptiness. Don't you know that call you received asking you to do crazy stuff was Lust…lust made the call. On the other hand, love is satisfying within itself and can work with a little and turn it into more than enough. Love produces life, while lust abuses it and destroys it.

God knows exactly why you are rich and miserable,

and you should, too. The religious leaders were so popular and wealthy, having so many followers and influence over the people. On the other hand, the disciples, who used to be ordinary people, were witnessing how many people were following Jesus and them. This was astonishing to them knowing they were the successors of the ministry. Jesus warns them not to become prideful like the Pharisees because he knew the disciples would be apostles and people would hail them as great and even gods. He warns them of the pride that can come with success, even in the church to have—so many followers. John the Baptist had so many people following him and believed his message. It was God in John. Can you imagine John here today? Where is John? Why are we not hearing the message of repentance? Do you know Jesus said there was no man born of a woman greater or more successful than John? John had no material belongings except what he wore. How can this be? Do not judge your success by another individual's. True success is when you fully understand why you are here and what God wants you to do, and then do it. John did his job and left…this is true success. Look how we are continuously talking about what he did and his contribution to the Christian faith.

"In the meantime, after so many thousands of the people had gathered that they were stepping on one another, Jesus began speaking first of all to His disciples, "Be continually on your guard against the leaven of the Pharisees [that is, their pervasive, corrupting influence and

*teaching], which is hypocrisy [producing self-righteousness]. But there is nothing [so carefully] concealed that it will not be revealed, nor so hidden that it will not be made known. For that reason, whatever you have said in the dark will be heard in the light, and what you have whispered behind closed doors will be proclaimed on the housetops. "I say to you, My friends, do not be afraid of those who kill the body and after that have nothing more that they can do. But I will point out to you whom you should fear: fear the One who, after He has killed, has authority and power to hurl [you]into hell; yes, I say to you, [stand in great awe of God and] fear Him!
Luke 12:1-5 AMP*

Social media has become one of the most excellent tools for revealing all things done in secret. This is what Jesus prophesied for the end times. Although it can be messy, you know the devil has to do his thing…the evil.

I'm alluding to the paradoxical nature of wealth and happiness. I emphasize that being rich does not guarantee a life of contentment, and there may be underlying reasons why an individual with substantial wealth may still feel dissatisfied. Wealth alone cannot provide fulfillment, and other factors contribute to an individual's happiness.

Mortality is a unifying factor that transcends social status or wealth. Death is an inevitable event that touches all human lives, regardless of their perceived fortunes. This serves as a reminder that even those deemed exceptional or privileged are vulnerable to the same fate as everyone else. Without God, all the little gods will have no value when they leave this world.

Imagine being the Creator who created all beings, and the beings you created sing about you and talk good things about you, but do not know you. They're saying and doing all of the things they think you want to hear or do but won't take the time to get to know you. How about most all beings see God as an opportunity? Even the ones He gave His life for have hidden agendas. God has given a great deal of love but has not received much love in return. Despite this, God has so much integrity that He will not use His powers to force anyone to love Him. He continues to show kindness to both the just and the unjust.

Consider this: what if Lucifer and the fallen angels had loved God for who He is instead of trying to seize a kingdom that was already theirs by inheritance? It's a common human flaw to desire more than we can handle, even when we've been given the best gift of all - yet, somehow, that still isn't enough. We go to great lengths to sing, preach, and attend church, all while offering God things we think He wants from us. But in reality, these offerings are no different from those of Lucifer and the angels - they were given without love for God, only for His gifts. If we continue to sing and preach with a hidden agenda, we are worse than Lucifer himself. Lucifer was not made in the image of God, yet we were, and yet we still fall prey to this same destructive pattern of behavior. What hurts most of all…God already knew we would choose things He had created over Him who created them.

Although we were created in the image of God, we tend to break records of rebellion originally set by the fallen angels from heaven. However, we often prioritize worldly things over our creator. Many of us tend to misunderstand God, the ultimate embodiment of love. We often fail to recognize that He has a heart full of emotions and feelings. Instead, we treat Him like a mere problem-solver, turning to Him only when we want our complaints and issues resolved. It's painful to think that despite this, God still showers us with unconditional love. It's high time we break this pattern and choose to put God first in our lives, above everything else. Surrender to God all your past regrets, bad decisions, toxic relationships, vengeful thoughts, pain, and sorrow. Entrust you and your children to Him and have faith that God will transform everything for your benefit. No matter what it looks like, it's not over yet. Remember that your life is not your own; it belongs to God, so offer it to Him. He has always known every decision you would make, and it has led you to this point. God knew…He always knew.

Have you ever thought about apologizing to God? We all have strayed from the path He has set for us, indulging in worldly pleasures and disrespecting His creation. But it's not too late to seek forgiveness. Let us ask for His mercy and repent for our sins, promising to serve Him from this day forward. Remember, God knew we would make mistakes, but it's up to us to take responsibility for our actions. Join me in saying this prayer: "Lord, I am sorry for all the pain and disappointment I have caused You. Please forgive me for my sins, past, present, and future. I repent and promise to serve You for the rest of my life. In Jesus' name, Amen."

God knew, God knows, and God always knew what the end would be because… He's God The Omniscient!

A Voice

Chapter 3

In the time of Herod, king of Judea, there was a priest named Zechariah and his wife, Elizabeth. They were both righteous in the sight of God but were childless, as Elizabeth could not conceive. One day, while Zechariah was serving as a priest in the temple, an angel of the Lord appeared to him, standing at the right side of the altar of incense. When Zechariah saw him, he was startled and was gripped with fear. But the angel told him, "Do not be afraid, Zechariah; your prayer has been heard. Your wife Elizabeth will bear you a son; you are to call him John. He will be a joy and delight to you, and many will rejoice because of his birth, for he will be great in the sight of the Lord.

He will never take wine or other fermented drinks and will be filled with the Holy Spirit before he is born. He will bring back many of the people of Israel to the Lord their God. And he will go on before the Lord, in the spirit and power of Elijah, to turn the hearts of the parents to their children and the disobedient to the wisdom of the righteous—to prepare a people prepared for the Lord." Zechariah asked the angel, "How can I be sure of this? I am an old man, and my wife is well along in years." The angel said to him, "I am Gabriel. I stand in the presence of God, and I have been sent to speak to you and to tell you this good news. And now you will be silent and not able to speak until the day this happens because you did not believe my words, which will come true at their appointed time."

Zechariah doubted the angel's words; consequently, he became unable to speak (lost his voice) until the day the prophecy was fulfilled. Elizabeth became pregnant and was in seclusion for five months of her pregnancy. She gave birth to John, who would later prepare the way for the Lord.

John's birth was considered a miracle as he was born to Elizabeth and her husband past their childbearing age. Elizabeth had been barren all her life, and John was believed to be conceived by the Holy Ghost. John clearly understood his purpose in life, which was to be committed to the work and ministry of God. He was tasked with preparing the way for the Lord by being a voice for God and speaking His truths without any political games or selfish gain. John's parents were Levites, devout followers of the law of Moses and the Levitical Priesthood.

John was raised as a preacher's kid and was a descendant of Aaron, Moses's brother, who was a priest. Religion protocols were a significant part of his life, and he knew the rituals and traditions involved. Being the son of a priest, John was brought up to follow in his father's footsteps. The priests in those times lived luxurious lives and were highly educated. They were expected to know the law of Moses and the prophets thoroughly, as they acted as the intermediaries between God and the people, providing counsel and guidance.

They offered up blood sacrifices for the sins of the people, especially during Holy Week and Passover. This was a massive deal during this time for the Israelite (Jewish) people. They would bring their lambs or sheep for their offering of the sacrifice for the atonement of their sins. Every year, John would see this act of forgiveness of sins and played an essential role in this orientation. John knows and understands the importance of repentance and forgiveness of sins. As elderly parents to John, they would pass away while John was an aspiring young man. The temple of God and priesthood is his inheritance. He had no life outside of the temple and Jerusalem.

One day, John leaves his life of the priesthood behind. No lavish clothes, priestly robes or shoes, no money, family or friends…nothing. John leaves his inheritance behind and follows a voice calling him to preach in the wilderness. This goes against everything he's learned about serving The Most High God and his people. Who is John without his priesthood and temple? John obeys the voice calling to the wilderness, an undesirable place. They were taught about the children of Israel and their forty years of experience in the wilderness before getting to the promised land. The wilderness can be seen as a place of punishment, neediness, and a very undesirable place. This is the place where you leave the noise of people, many voices of humanity. John goes because one voice is above all the others. I can imagine how many people would say, "John, why would you leave? Where will you go? What will you do for work…how will you live? The Voice of God drowned out all of these audible voices.

John is called to a unique assignment - to baptize people in the Jordan River and preach the message of repentance because the kingdom of God is at hand. He is devoted to obeying the voice in his spirit above men's voices. John is doing something new by dressing in animal skins to represent the blood sacrifice and covering placed on Adam and Eve after they sinned. He has given up everything to follow God's voice and is willing to obey God rather than men who are priests.

John has isolated himself from social activities, such as eating and drinking with people, to focus on the voice that guides him to fulfill his calling. He now consumes a diet of locusts, wild honey, and water and has sworn off any food or drink prepared by human hands. He has renounced all worldly pleasures and embraced a sacrificial way of living, all because of the voice he trusts completely. John's preaching differs from traditional preaching, and his message is simple: "Repent." Despite not being able to prove his divine calling, many people believe in his message and have been baptized. However, his growing influence has also drawn the attention of other leaders, particularly the priests and Pharisees.

"And in those days cometh John the Baptist, preaching in the wilderness of Judaea, saying, Repent ye; for the kingdom of heaven is at hand. For this is he that was spoken of through Isaiah the prophet, saying, The voice of one crying in the wilderness, Make ye ready the way of the Lord, Make his paths straight. Now John wore a garment of camel's hair and a leather belt around his waist, and his food was locusts and wild honey. Then Jerusalem and all Judea and all the region about the Jordan were going out to him, and they were baptized by him in the river Jordan, confessing their sins. But when he saw many of the Pharisees and Sadducees coming to his baptism, he said to them, "You brood of vipers! Who warned you to flee from the wrath to come?" Matthew 3: 1-7

"Bring forth, therefore, fruit worthy of repentance: and think not to say within yourselves, We have Abraham to our father: for I say unto you, that God is able of these stones to raise up children unto Abraham. And even now the axe lieth at the root of the trees: every tree therefore that bringeth not forth good fruit is hewn down, and cast into the fire. I indeed baptize you in water unto repentance: but he that cometh after me is mightier than I, whose shoes I am not worthy to bear: he shall baptize you in the

Holy Spirit and in fire:" Matthew 3: 8-11.

It is possible to imagine the expressions on the faces of the priests from the Holy Temple, who were referred to as holy men. John, who grew up in the temple and witnessed horrific and terrible acts committed in the name of God, called them out. John could cleanse himself of all the sins he was exposed to through repentance and sanctification. Sometimes, our most uncomfortable experiences prepare us for our mission. John was likely bothered by seeing some of the individuals he believed in and admired engage in ungodly acts of greed and infidelity. John's message was impartial, and he did not alter or manipulate its content. He preached repentance to everyone without any political bias in his delivery.

We must be careful about which voice or voices we listen to. If we obey the wrong voice, we can become a voice of destruction, rebellion, gossip, discouragement, and torment. We will not experience peace if we listen to the wrong voice. Both your voice and God's voice are powerful. If God has given you a voice, why would He tell you to be quiet? If He has called you to preach or pastor, why would He send other voices to tell you that you are out of order and not in sync with Him? The reality is that God's voice is supreme to all other voices. If God has called you, He will not stop talking to you or calling you until you convince Him that you do not want to do His will.

Do not let your obedience to man lead you to lose joy

and peace while disobeying God. Just like Eve, who listened to and obeyed the wrong voice, what voice is telling you not to preach? Will God punish you for doing His will? Will He reward you for obeying man over Him or flesh over spirit? When God said the woman's seed would crush the serpent seed's head, He meant that you should not remain silent. And truth be told, you are not going to be quiet anyway. So why not do what you were created to do?

Use your voice to bring God glory and save lives. When you preach and see people respond and get saved and delivered, whose voice do you believe they heard? Was it the enemy or the devil, or was it the voice of God that caused them to repent and cry out, wanting to give their life to the Lord? Remember that man can appoint you, but only God can anoint you. Did God anoint you to preach? If yes, why are you struggling with the voice of no reason for your calling? God is looking for a voice to represent His voice. Too many have deceived people by becoming the voice they need for a price. Do what God has told you to do, and be the voice that God can say, "My sheep know my voice, and a stranger they will not follow."

Are people following your voice, your calling, or your flesh? Are you serious about what God has ordained you to do? Then, be the voice of God with no condemnation. Satan wants you to be silent so he can have his way with you, your family, your children, and your marriage. This is why we are having so many divorces; the voice of God is not in the household. Other voices are running that marriage into the ground.

Die-Voice, Di-Voice-Divorce, killing the voice of God in the marriage will end up in death. When two individuals who once shared a common bond and mutual understanding find themselves in a state of disagreement, effective communication becomes elusive, leading to the death of the relationship. In such cases, searching for a more harmonious voice becomes paramount, as it offers solace to the individual left in a state of emotional turmoil with their partner. However, caution must be exercised when seeking counsel, as listening to a voice that only feeds our ego can lead us astray. In such circumstances, parting ways may seem inevitable.

When two individuals in a marriage fail to agree on something, it is essential to remember that the voice of reason should come from the God whom you consulted and leaned on when you first met and truly wanted the person. More often than not, a foreign voice or voices may come into play, making it difficult for the couple to reconcile their differences. This can lead to divorce, which is unfortunate. It is important to remember the vows made before God and witnesses. Each party must be willing to listen to the voice of reason, which can be challenging when both parties feel justified in their opinions. It is essential to remember that God is the truth and was present at the altar when the vows were made.

Marriage requires dedication, love, and commitment; we should strive to keep these values throughout our lives. However, today's world has so many options that it can be challenging to maintain a healthy and long-lasting marriage. Remember this: if you are satisfying your flesh (physical needs at any cost) or leaving the one you made your vows to for something or someone that looks better and or something lifting you up in pride, then you find yourself wanting to be accepted by those who love vanity. You are probably listening to the wrong voice or voices. Nonetheless, Lust can't replace Love.

There are too many voices in the marriage, and where is the voice of God? One voice says no, the other says yes… what voice is of God? It was not God's voice telling you to cheat or be unfaithful; he didn't say to that preacher / pastor to be unfaithful in the marriage. "Women be silent" is not what God is talking about being silent while being abused.

The pursuit of faithful, dedicated, and trustworthy leaders is of paramount importance to God. Their voices, not their gender or personal agenda, should be the guiding force, driven by genuine love for God and His people. Disrupted homes, families, and churches are often the result of having listened and acted upon the wrong voice. Therefore, careful discernment and obedience to the right voice are essential in maintaining a healthy and functional society.

Build a genuine relationship with God, make Jesus your Lord and Savior, and get to know his voice. Being a woman called to ministry has its unique challenges for sure, but be honest, have integrity and Christ-like character, and do your job to the best of your ability. "God is not the author of confusion." Let's be clear: this is not about promoting or endorsing rebellion, nor disrespect of authority, but the complete opposite; this is about submission and doing the will of God over our own.

Jesus demonstrated his submission to God in the Garden of Gethsemane, saying, "Not my will, but your will be done." Sometimes, our submission doesn't seem glorious in the beginning, but in due season, if we don't quit, our submission to the cross, crucifying our agendas and dying to our own will, we will resurrect and rise above all of our adversities, and to God be the glory. So… hold on!

Standing up for your right to speak and be a voice for God is important. In these troubled times, we need all the help we can get in the Body of Christ. Who will the children listen to if the righteous lose or give up their voice? According to God, our seed has the power to dominate, and we must not let that power go to waste. When God spoke to the serpent about the war between his seed and the woman's seed, he referred to a spiritual conflict that would manifest physically. Men have always known that they carry the physical seeds that lead to a baby, but they didn't realize that they also carry spiritual seeds until the prophets explained it.

On the other hand, women don't produce physical seeds, but they can still nurture and grow spiritual seeds by speaking God's word. We have the ability and authority to release physical and spiritual seeds that can become the destroyers of our enemies. This is how people become born again, by hearing God's spoken word (seed) and believing in it (spiritual conception). So, let us use our voices to preach God's word and release our spiritual seed into the world. "The seed requires soil, and the people are the soil where we are tasked to plant God's word. If we continue to spread God's word, it will bear fruit, resulting in some being saved thirty-fold, some sixty-fold, and some a hundred-fold.

You cannot defeat the works of the devil by staying silent. When God created Adam, Eve was already inside him, and Adam became a living soul capable of speaking; in other words, he became a speaking spirit. This can only mean that Eve also became a speaking spirit. This is why the enemy talked to her, and she talked back. So, the original woman was created to speak and have a voice. The Garden of Eden is where the enemy tried to take away your voice by causing you to obey the wrong one so you would become a destructive one. However, your power lies in answering your calling from God and preaching the gospel of the kingdom. They may try to tell you that you can't preach, but they use you for everything else. You can be on committees, fundraise, pay tithes and offerings, fry chicken and fish, sell dinners, organize events, comfort those who are mourning, visit the sick, arrange funerals and homegoings, sing, praise worship, handle budgets, type and manage sermons, and much more. But the one thing you cannot do for God is to be a voice. That's ridiculous! God is not like that. So, get out there and use the voice God gave you!"

If you don't allow God to use you, then you set yourself up to be used by the same enemy that deceived Eve in the first place. Redemption is about restoration. Have we been redeemed from the curse or not? If the woman is not set free, then the man is still in bondage, too. Why is he preaching? If the bishop or pastor told you that you cannot preach because you are a woman, did you not know that Gentiles (non-Israelites/ Jews) were not allowed to touch God's word, never to preach? We have been reconciled to God and restored to our original place with God, but "cursed is the ground for our sakes." Not cursed is the woman. If you believe you are under a curse, then be silent or be the voice for the devil and his kingdom, but if you are redeemed of the Lord, You better say so! Open your mouth and preach this gospel of the kingdom, daughters of the Most High God. If God has called you to preach… you better preach! He's listening for His voice through you!

Many leaders often refer to the letter written by the Apostle Paul to Timothy to support their stance on women preachers and teachers. However, it's essential to understand the cultural context in which Paul wrote the letter. At the time, Timothy was the youngest ordained pastor, believed to be around 21 years old when Paul installed him as a pastor. According to the Law of Moses and the prevailing culture, men were not appointed as priests and leaders until the age of 40, which was considered a reasonable age of maturity. For instance, one must be at least 35 to be elected President of the United States of America. Also, to be a priest, you must be approved by the Pharisees. Paul, a Pharisee, made this exception; he understood how to set order.

Apostle Paul wrote this letter; " *These things command and teach. Let no man despise thy youth; but be thou an example to them that believe in word, manner of life, love, faith, and purity. Till I come, give heed to reading, to exhortation, to teaching. Neglect, not the gift that is in thee, which was given thee by prophecy, with the laying on of the hands of the presbytery.*" **1 Timothy 4:12**

Please note that Paul, originally known as Saul and before his conversion, was a Pharisee, a devoted leader committed to following the Law of Moses. Those trying to set order to the house (church) were not allowed edifices during this time, so they had worship services in their homes. Imagine Timothy, being so young, and using this house for church services when his grandmother and mother are used to running the house. Why would they think Timothy would not need their help running the church? "The mother is saying, "Timothy is my son, and the grandmother is saying, "The pastor is my grandson, this alone could make it challenging to see him as their pastor and spiritual leader. It can be pretty embarrassing when someone interrupts or corrects a teacher while they are teaching.

It is reasonable to consider the letters written to Timothy as a general guideline for the church. However, it is essential to note that these letters were written explicitly to Timothy as a new and young pastor. They were addressing a particular situation involving his family and congregants.

What if saints complained about how Pastor Timothy's mother and grandmother seemed to think they had the parental rights to tell Timothy how to do things? Timothy's father was absent for the most part, so they may have considered him a mama's boy. His father was a Gentile Greek pagan worshipper who did not believe in the Israelite God or Jesus Christ of Nazareth. The Pharisees prohibited women from worshipping in the temple, while the Gentiles were indifferent. This illustrates the diverse challenges that Paul faced when writing letters to Timothy.

Women were now allowed to attend services with the

men and, of course, not speak according to the Law of Moses. To put this into perspective, let's go over a few things women weren't allowed to do as a Jew.

- Women couldn't sit under a Rabbi's teaching
- Women couldn't speak to men in public
- Women weren't allowed to worship with men
- Women weren't counted as people (Joseph was called to register for the census now; Mary went along, but she wasn't counted). Feeding the 5,000, they counted the men, not the women and children.
- Women were divorced for any reason at all (Jesus addressed this in Matthew 19:3-9)
- Women couldn't testify in court
- Women had no legal rights
- Women were not allowed to touch the priest

The apostle Paul faced similar challenges as he tried integrating women into the community. This was perceived as a departure from the traditional customs of Jewish temples and synagogues, where women were not allowed to participate in public worship. The church was in a class of its own and still is. When women were accepted into the church to worship with men, it was a definite slap in the face to the Pharisees. Nevertheless, the church was a new movement and was facing a lot of scrutiny and persecution. The newly established churches required pastors, and Timothy, who his devout Jewish mother and grandmother raised, was a believer. Although some people might have had concerns and objections regarding his young age and ability to lead, the church made an exception for Timothy's age for the sake of the church and ministry.

Also, the Law of Moses said that a man could not go in public if his beard was shaven or cut off; as a man, you were considered disgraced to have a clean-shaven face. In the Law of Moses, it was considered shameful for men to shave their heads. The law compared a man's appearance to natural elements, such as the male lion's mane, considered a symbol of masculinity. The reason for this was the concern that a man with a shaven beard and long hair could be mistaken for a woman, leading to confusion.

When Apostle Paul wrote his letters and established the church, he didn't start by preaching to the Jews. Circumstances prohibited him from preaching to his own people; as a result, he preached to the Gentiles, and many of them were saved and filled with the Holy Spirit. Therefore, Rome was one of the Gentile cities where he was called to preach. The Romans were the opposite of what Paul was accustomed to religiously and culturally. As part of Roman and Greek culture and government, men were required to shave and be clean-cut as a sign of wealth, education, and civilization. The Roman military made it a law for short haircuts and a shaved face. This was their way of life about 200 years before Christ. Paul faced the challenge of teaching the church of Rome about

Grace through Jesus Christ and the Kingdom without imposing the Law of Moses upon them.

The Jews, on the other hand, saw Gentile people (non-Jews) as ungodly, heathenistic, and rebellious to the Laws of God. Imagine the challenges Paul had as a Jew but also a Roman citizen, bringing together two distinct groups of people. As an apostle, he worked towards bringing together the Jews and Gentiles through the power of the Holy Spirit. He ensured that the differences in their respective customs, beliefs, and traditions did not create obstacles for their established leaders. During the early days of Christianity, the Galatians church witnessed some challenges regarding including women in worship alongside men.

This was the view of their society during this era, and I remember Paul saying, "I am a Pharisee of the Pharisees." He explained to the religious leaders why he was defending his position with the church. He reminded them of his knowledge and adherence to the Mosaic Law. However, he had now realized the importance of grace and mercy. He had been accepted into the church through Jesus Christ's grace and did not intend to disregard the law. He wanted the leaders to understand that he was aware of the law but was now saved through grace. Now an apostle, Paul is trying to establish order in the newly planted church. So, to keep down confusion and not appear opposed to the law of Moses (which he wasn't), he was now a product of grace, and this was his message. The observers would accuse Paul of breaking the laws of Moses by allowing women to worship with men and participate in the order of services. Apostle Paul was given revelations like no one else in the New Testament.

We must understand that Paul was addressing the church or churches by sending letters when he could not attend service in person either because of ministerial duties elsewhere or being detained in jail or prison. Some were converts who were Jews, and others were Gentiles. Jews were under the Law of Moses, whereas many Gentiles knew very little, if anything, about these ordinances that were so sacred to the Israelite people. The Jews lived and died by these laws, and it's what was used to govern them as a people. Paul, in turn, would be used to reach other people who may have otherwise been left out of the gospel.

"For there is no distinction between Jew and Greek: for the same Lord is Lord of all, and is rich unto all that call upon him: for, Whosoever shall call upon the name of the Lord shall be saved. How then shall they call on him in whom they have not believed? and how shall they believe in him whom they have not heard? and how shall they hear without a preacher? and how shall they preach, except they be sent? even as it is written, How beautiful are the feet of them that bring glad tidings of good things! But they did not all hearken to the glad tidings. For

Isaiah saith, Lord, who hath believed our report? So belief cometh of hearing, and hearing by the word of Christ. But I say, Did they not hear? Yea, verily, Their sound went out into all the earth, And their words unto the ends of the world.

But I say, Did Israel not know? First, Moses saith, I will provoke you to jealousy with that which is no nation, With a nation void of understanding, will I anger you? **Romans 10: 12-19**

Paul's challenge is bringing two different cultures and people together under one God without all of the laws and traditions of religion.

Paul's ministry was under enormous pressure, as he was on the run from the Sanhedrin (the Religious Leaders of Jerusalem) as a fugitive. Many of Paul's writings were inspired by God while he was in confinement. Little did he know that his letters would become a part of the best-selling book of all time. Paul is credited for writing almost three-quarters of the New Testament. His teachings and revelations have undoubtedly inspired countless Christians in the Body of Christ. As Paul grew in grace and maturity, his writings and teachings reflected his growth, just as it would in any of us who are called by God to feed his sheep and gain experience.

If God has called you to preach, it means that people in this world are assigned to you. You may be the only voice of God they will hear.

Jesus said, "My sheep know my voice and a stranger they will not follow,"

Jesus is the living word of God; the word has a voice. When you speak God's word, he has given you the authority to be a voice submitted to his voice for his people to hear from God. *Jesus said," You are clean through the word I have spoken to you." John 15:3*

Here are a few examples of how important a voice is to God: "Why would God silence you and not allow you to have a voice in His house, where His people can hear you? After all, He is your Father, and your voice is important to Him."

- **With my voice, I cry out to the LORD; with my voice, I plead for mercy to the LORD. (Psalms 142:1)**

- **I will cry unto God with my voice, Even unto God with my voice; and he will give ear unto me. (Psalms 77:1)**

- **Lord, hear my voice: Let thine ears be attentive To the voice of my supplications. (Psalms 130:2)**

- **Thou heardest my voice; hide not thine ear at my breathing, at my cry. (Lamentations 3:56)**

* * *

- I love the Lord because he heareth My voice and my supplications. (Psalms 116:1)

- Abraham obeyed my voice and kept my charge, my commandments, my statutes, and my laws." (Genesis 26:5)

- Hear my voice, O God, in my complaint; preserve my life from dread of the enemy. (Psalms 64:1)

- If I summoned him and he answered me, I would not believe that he was listening to my voice. (Job 9:16)

- Give Ear to My Voice O LORD, I call upon you; hasten to me! Give ear to my voice when I call to you!   (Psalms 141:1)

- "In my distress, I called upon the LORD; to my God, I called. He heard my voice from his temple, and my cry came to his ears.   (2 Samuel 22:7)

- Hear my voice according to your steadfast love; O LORD, according to your justice give me life. (Psalms 119:149)

- O LORD, in the morning you hear my voice; in the morning I prepare a sacrifice for you and watch. (Psalms 5:3)

* * *

- **Behold, a voice from heaven said, "This is my beloved Son, with whom I am well pleased." (Matthew 3:17)**

- **Jesus answered them, I have told you so, yet you do not believe Me [you do not trust Me and rely on Me]. The very works that I do by the power of My Father and in My Father's name bear witness concerning Me [they are My credentials and evidence in support of Me]. But you do not believe and trust and rely on Me because you do not belong to My fold [you are no sheep of Mine]. The sheep that are My own hear and are listening to My voice, and I know them, and they follow Me." John 10:25-27**

Jesus talked about His sheep without specifying their gender. He emphasized the importance of knowing His voice, which can only come from having a close relationship with Him. Similar to recognizing your spouse's voice in a conversation, you should be able to distinguish God's voice from others when He speaks to you about your salvation, life, or any other matter. You should know His heart and character so no one can easily deceive you. It doesn't matter how many scriptures you have memorized or quoted if you cannot recognize God's voice speaking through them. Therefore, knowing your God and His voice is crucial to avoid being misled by imposters.

"This is about relationships, whereas the law was about religion. The law can be compared to dating God and learning about His ways of thinking and moving. Grace, on the other hand, is like being married to God. In marriage, there are joint responsibilities that outsiders cannot deny or govern. Many things that work while dating won't work in marriage because marriage requires a different level of commitment. It's not helpful for the best friend to keep reminding your spouse of how you knew them before. The Law is like a best friend, but grace is like a wife. If you keep competing with or finding fault with the wife, you will eventually lose the relationship with your best friend. "You are saved by grace. Your voice is restored through your relationship with Christ.

The law says I knew God first, but grace is saying everything he was building was for me all along. So don't be jealous of me because he is the one who said, "The first will be last, and the last will be first." I have been made first, and you still want me to be last. To be silent and not have a voice. Religion introduced me to God (the Law); Grace through Jesus Christ is my marriage to God, and this bride has become One with Him and has a voice. I will preach and teach the gospel of the one I love and who loves me.

In Eden, God told the serpent he would crawl on his

belly, not the woman. God put us at war, and the woman cannot win this fight with a closed mouth. She must preach and teach how the enemy has tried to take her voice, mind, and family. No one can tell her story and testimony the way she can; I'm trying to convey this message so she will wake up before the anti-Christ comes on the scene. He is going to use her and her voice to commit evil. He's attempting to keep his enemy (the woman) close to him because he knows the prophecy is she will produce what will crush his offspring. Woman, you are powerful! Your voice is powerful through God. Scream his word! Your pain will not allow you to be quiet.

The Bible tells a story about Jesus being tempted by the devil in the wilderness. The devil tried to persuade Jesus to use his power for selfish reasons instead of fulfilling God's plan by using the scriptures. Similarly, God has blessed us with a purpose - to serve His people humbly and not to boast in pride or consider ourselves superior to others. We should not hide our talents but use them to fulfill our God-given mission.

In the absence of God, sometimes we are inclined to listen to the voice that tells us what we want to hear rather than what God is saying to us. Jesus demonstrated in the Garden of Gethsemane that he did not like the idea of submitting himself to his enemies, being judged, condemned, and put to death. However, this was the purpose of his coming to this world. So, he humbled himself to his Father and said, "Not my will, but your will be done." Even when it hurts and sometimes makes us appear weak and helpless, we are strong enough to deny our flesh and feelings for the bigger picture. We have been anointed and given power and authority to save, not destroy.

"For God so loved the world that he gave his only son that whoever believes in him would not perish but have everlasting life. God did not send his Son into the world to condemn the world; but that the world through him might be saved" John 3:16-17.

After Jesus finished praying, his enemies arrived to arrest him. Shockingly, one of his hand-picked disciples, Judas, was leading the pack. Judas betrayed his Lord and sold him for money. Ensuring that you are in ministry for the right reasons is important. If God has called you, do not let money sway you. Make sure you are serving God and not the love of money. Money will come, as God knows our needs before we ask. But do not allow the enemy to reduce you to a dollar. As a daughter of Christ, you already have to fight for your rights. Do not sell your anointing and soul like Judas did for selfish gain. Be authentic and fearless in your delivery. Remember, "If God is for you, who can be against you?"

Some challenges come with following God's calling. Sometimes, people may not feel ready or willing to engage with the challenges that come with their calling, but it is important to trust God's voice and have faith that he will see you through. When we understand God's voice created the universe and everything in it. We should be encouraged to use our anointed voice as a sign from God rather than waiting for more signs. God has given us a voice to make a difference in the world. "So, don't wait any longer and go into the world to preach as God has commanded."

The woman was created to listen and to speak. Her enemy deceives her by pretending to be a friend. He knew how powerful of an influencer she was created to be even before she knew. With a voice, the enemy deceived her and, in turn, used her voice to cause her husband to disobey the voice of God. The sin is contributed by allowing an outside voice to dominate the sanctioned relationship. The marriage consists of 3 voices: the husband, the wife, and God, who put them together, like the preacher at the wedding officiating the wedding ceremony.

When God addressed the transgression in the garden, he only asked to hear from 2 voices, the husband and the wife. He didn't ask the enemy to speak because he was in violation for even speaking into this marital relationship in the first place. Marriage is an institution founded and ordained by God and is only honored by God (the Officiator). He is the only voice over the other two voices, making the marriage vows a covenant. The husband and wife become one flesh, as Jesus and the Father are one. This is a covenant relationship. It was doomed when they allowed another voice besides God to come into their relationship. The same goes for today. We have so many divorces (di-voice, dead voices, opposing voices) because of too many voices that have no life-giving power to the marriage.

The story is about a woman who was created to listen and speak. Unfortunately, her enemy deceived her by pretending to be her friend. The enemy knew how powerful of an influencer she was created to be even before she realized it. The enemy used her voice to cause her husband to disobey the voice of God, which resulted in sin. The sin occurred because an outside voice dominated over the sanctioned relationship. A marriage consists of three voices: the husband, the wife, and God. It is a covenant relationship, and only God can officiate it. When the enemy spoke to the woman, he violated this covenant. When God addressed the transgression in the garden, he only asked to hear from the husband and wife's voices, not the enemy's. This violation doomed their relationship. Similarly, many modern-day divorces occur because too many opposing voices dominate the marriage. No matter how close you may be with others, supernaturally and divinely, you can only be one with your covenant, the one you're married to.

* * *

"And Pharisees came to Him and put Him to the test by asking, Is it lawful and right to dismiss and repudiate and divorce one's wife for any and every cause? He replied, Have you never read that He Who made them from the beginning made them male and female, And said, For this reason, a man shall leave his father and mother and shall be united firmly (joined inseparably) to his wife, and the two shall become one flesh? [Gen. 1:27; 2:24.] So they are no longer two, but one flesh. Therefore, God has joined together, let not man put asunder (separate)." Matthew 19:3-6

It is a divine thing for a man and a woman to enter into a marriage covenant and operate as one through submission to the Spirit of God. Have you ever wondered how three can become one in the spiritual realm? This concept may sound familiar because it's the same way the Triune God works. The Triune God is three persons in one: the Father, Son, and Holy Spirit. Similarly, the triune man comes together as one in body, soul, and spirit, just like the type and shadow of Abraham, Isaac, and Jacob.

If Abraham had not heard and obeyed the voice of God at the age of 75, he and Sarah would never have given birth to Isaac, their miracle son. Without Isaac, there would have been no Jacob; without Jacob, there would be no 12 sons who became the 12 tribes that ultimately formed the Nation of Israel, the Jewish people. All because Abraham heard and obeyed the right voice. The nation was conceived from a seed of obedience to God's voice. The Bible says that Abraham's obedience was counted as righteousness to him, even though he was an idolater when God originally called him. It doesn't mean that Abraham did everything right, but his obedience to the voice of God moved God to justify him as right. Obedience to God is greater than any and every sacrifice we can give him.

It is crucial to understand that regardless of our present condition, we must always endeavor to honor God by obeying His instructions. We are responsible for heeding God's calling and obeying His instructions. Everything begins and ends with His Word, so it is crucial to prioritize listening to His voice above everything else.

The question of whether a woman can preach is a common one in religious circles. If a woman has been called, anointed, and ordained by God to preach, and she ignores that calling because of the voice telling her not to preach, then she would be disobeying God, just as Eve did in Eden when she listened and obeyed the voice of God's enemy. It's important to remember that disobedience to God is a sin, and we have been given the power to do His work through the sacrifice of Jesus on Calvary's Cross and the sending of the Holy Spirit.

How will they call on him whom they have not believed? And how are they to believe in him of whom they have never heard? And how are they to hear without someone preaching? And how are they to preach unless they are sent? As it is written, "How beautiful are the feet of those who preach the good news!" But they have not all obeyed the gospel. For Isaiah says, "Lord, who has believed what he has heard from us?" So faith comes from hearing and hearing through the word of Christ. But I ask, have they not heard? Indeed, they have, for "Their voice has gone out to all the earth, and their words to the ends of the world." Roman 10: 14-18

As believers of Christ, you are children of God and belong to the kingdom of heaven. DO NOT allow anyone to call you "GOAT." This is idolatry at its best. We'll know who the greatest is when we are standing before the throne of God and the holy ones of heaven. The phrase "Greatest Of All Time" is a temporal assertion that denotes a momentary status. According to biblical texts, when Lucifer was expelled from heaven, he was bound by the constraints of time, which means he is serving his sentence in this world, which can be viewed as a prison…he's here on death row.

When you understand we were created to worship, if we don't worship God, we will find something to worship. As human beings, our ultimate purpose is to worship. We'll be held accountable for this when we stand before the throne of God and the holy ones of heaven. It's a humbling thought, but it's important to recognize that if we don't worship the Creator, we'll inevitably end up worshiping something else - whether it's money, power, or even ourselves. Let's strive to be mindful of our worship and devote ourselves to the right cause. By doing so, we'll be fulfilling our true purpose and living a life of meaning and fulfillment.

Know who you are and who your Father is. You're either sheep or goats, but you can't be both…and the wolves are a whole other story…

The demons asked Jesus, "Have you come to torment us before our time?" No matter how much we beautify this world, the Devil knows nothing can compare to where he used to live, which is in heaven.

Jesus said, "When the Son of Man comes in his glory, and all the angels with him, then he will sit on his glorious throne. Before him will be gathered all the nations, and he will separate people one from another as a shepherd separates the sheep from the goats. And he will place the sheep on his right, but the goats on the left.

Then the King will say to those on his right, 'Come, you who my Father blesses, inherit the kingdom prepared for you from the foundation of the world.

Then he will say to those on his left, Depart from me, you cursed, into the eternal fire prepared for the devil and his angels.

And these will go away into eternal punishment, but the righteous into eternal life."

When he has brought out all his own, he goes before them, and the sheep follow him, for they know his voice. A stranger they will not follow, but they will flee from him, for they do not know the voice of strangers.

And I have other sheep that are not of this fold. I must bring them also, and they will listen to my voice.

My sheep hear my voice, and I know them, and they follow me.

John the Baptist was once asked about his identity and the message he was preaching. He responded, *"I am a voice crying out in the wilderness, calling for repentance, for the kingdom of God is at hand."*

In those days, John the Baptist came preaching in the wilderness of Judea, "Repent, for the kingdom of heaven is at hand." For this is he who was spoken of by the prophet Isaiah when he said,

"The voice of one crying in the wilderness: Prepare the way of the Lord; make his paths straight.'" Matthew 3:1-3.

Do not let ignorance, hatred, or any other reason stop you from doing the work God has chosen and anointed you to do. Whether you are male or female, be the voice of God and do His work.

It is essential to note that people cannot come to God unless they hear His voice. Irrespective of the gender of the preacher or the content of the message, individuals who do not belong to The Lord will not be drawn to Him.

Therefore, it is imperative to recognize that non-believers will not be swayed by any voice or message despite one's best efforts.

Sometimes, people come into your life because they have heard about the blessings God promised you. This was the case with Abram. His nephew, Lot, left his home to follow Abram to a faraway land because he had heard God's voice and believed that Abram was the one who had received a promise from God. On their journey, Abram lost livestock and servants to sickness and famine, and despite getting older, he still had not been blessed with a son. However, God blessed Abram in Egypt and restored everything he had lost. Abram also blessed Lot with some of what God had given him. Later, Abram discovered that Lot had recruited his people and raised livestock separately from him. Some people will follow you with their own agenda, and if God takes too long to bless you, they may use you to start their own thing. Lot told Abram he was leaving to make a living in a different place, and Abram let him go.

Lot took his family to Sodom and Gomorrah, where he lost everything, including his wife and two of his four daughters. His wife turned into a pillar of salt for turning back against God's word, and two of his daughters married men from Sodom. When destruction came, the two daughters were consumed, while the other two daughters ran to the mountains with their dad. Lot was too proud to find his uncle Abram for restoration, and he ended up making children with his two younger daughters, and they became cursed people known as mountain dwellers. Lot tried to claim Abram's blessing that he had heard from God's voice, but God had spoken those things to Abram, not to Lot. Some people can partake in your blessing, but they cannot run with your blessing because your anointing is just that…your anointing.

There are many examples in the Bible of people who were unsure about a message and asked God for confirmations or signs. Abraham is an example of someone who waited 25 years for a word from God to come to pass. He thought it was taking too long for him to have a son, and his wife got the idea of using a surrogate for them to have a child. But later, they discovered that doing it their way brought pain and frustration. They decided to wait and ultimately learned to trust God to do what He said He would do. When God told Abram (Abraham) that He was going to bless him with a son, it took 25 years for that word to come to pass. In the twenty-fourth year, God showed up to bless Abram and his wife Sarai and changed their names to Abraham and Sarah. God then told them they would have a son from both of their bodies, and they were ancient. He said, "By this time next year, you will have a son, and his name will be Isaac., meaning laughter." At the same time, God went to destroy the city that Lot was in. Abraham tried to intercede for Lot, but God was done.

* * *

Get this lesson as well; you take everyone with you because they will compete or be jealous of you, and you are changing within while you are being obedient to God and following Him. God changed their names before He gave them their much-awaited blessing. Sometimes, some things take time, and the times and seasons are in God's authority alone.

After Abraham had waited all those years for a son, God would ask him for the long-awaited Isaac to offer him up as a sacrifice. Abraham hears a voice telling him to go up to Mount Mariah and give God a sacrifice. This means the promise God made to Abraham was riding on this son of his. But what if he offers up the life of his son?

The prophet Elijah killed some false prophets on Mount Carmel who served Jezebel. When Jezebel heard that the prophet Elijah had slain her prophets, she became furious and sent messengers to threaten Elijah. She said she would do to him what he had done to her prophets by the same time the next day. Fearing for his life, Elijah fled and ended up in an isolated place where he fell into a deep depression. Jezebel's message had weakened him and taken away his confidence and courage. God spoke to Elijah and asked him why he was sitting under a tree. Elijah explained that he had killed the prophets who had sold out for money and become Jezebel's prophets. Elijah had been a prophet of the Lord for many years and had trained these prophets. However, they had gone astray, becoming prophets for Baal (money).

* * *

We find that the prophet Elijah was distressed and anxious about the threat that Queen Jezebel posed to his life. However, instead of addressing Elijah's concerns about Jezebel, God gave him instructions for his next mission. Although Elijah was upset and wanted God to intervene against Jezebel, the Lord had a different plan in mind for him. He commanded Elijah to prepare himself for a journey. We have to be careful of which voice we listen to and believe. As powerful as the prophet Elijah was, we see how listening to the voice of God's enemy can paralyze us with fear, disabling us from doing our job and causing us to be stagnant and lose focus.

"There, he went into a cave and spent the night. LORD And the word of the LORD came to him: "What are you doing here, Elijah?" He replied, "I have been very zealous for the LORD God Almighty. The Israelites have rejected your covenant, torn down your altars, and put your prophets to death with the sword. I am the only one left, and now they are trying to kill me too." The LORD said, "Go out and stand on the mountain in the presence of the LORD, for the LORD is about to pass by."

Then a great and powerful wind tore the mountains apart and shattered the rocks before the LORD, but the LORD was not in the wind. After the wind, there was an earthquake, but the LORD was not in the earthquake. After the earthquake came a fire, but the LORD was not in the fire. And after the fire came a small, still voice. When

Elijah heard it, he pulled his cloak over his face and went out and stood at the mouth of the cave. Then a voice said to him, "What are you doing here, Elijah?" He replied, "I have been very zealous for the LORD God Almighty. The Israelites have rejected your covenant, torn down your altars, and put your prophets to death with the sword. I am the only one left, and now they are trying to kill me too." The LORD said to him, "Go back the way you came and go to the Desert of Damascus. When you get there, anoint Hazael king over Aram. Also, anoint Jehu, son of Nimshi, king over Israel, and anoint Elisha, son of Shaphat, from Abel Meholah, to succeed you as a prophet. Jehu will put to death any who escape the sword of Hazael, and Elisha will put to death any who escape the sword of Jehu. Yet I reserve seven thousand in Israel—all whose knees have not bowed down to Baal and whose mouths have not kissed him."   *1 Kings 19:9-18 NIV.*

We often worry excessively about potential problems or people who may use us for their benefit, and it's normal to feel lonely. However, we should not worry because God is always there for His purpose and will. If you are in God's will and He is still talking to you about an assignment He wants you to do for Him, then nothing can happen to you until God is done with you or until your assignment is complete. You are not going anywhere yet, but your enemy lives on borrowed time. "Regardless of the situation, it's crucial to recognize and heed the voice of your God. Make sure to listen attentively and follow through with obedience."

Elijah understood the importance of recognizing God's voice and waiting for Him. It is crucial to discern when God speaks to us through His written word, spoken word, audible voice, or our inner thoughts. Sometimes, God may send messengers, preachers, prophets, or even angels; our responsibility is to be sharp and skilled in recognizing His voice.

The Bible warns that Satan can come as an angel of light, so we must not be too anxious or desperate for a word, as the enemy might deceive us by sending a counterfeit word or an impostor messenger. It is not uncommon for specific individuals to claim that they have received a message from the Lord and that it should be passed on to someone else, even if they have not received such a message. As a result, we must maintain a balance that allows us to understand when we need to be humble and acknowledge that the message may indeed be from God. However, we must learn to wait patiently for God's message. The waiting period is the most challenging aspect of receiving a genuine message from the Lord. Waiting for a message to be fulfilled can be complex, especially when seeking immediate deliverance.

Sometimes, the fulfillment of a word spoken by God may happen immediately, while at other times, it may take years or even generations. That's why knowing and discerning God's voice when He speaks is important. If a word doesn't happen immediately, we shouldn't conclude that a false prophet said that word. Instead, we should always inquire of God concerning any word supposedly coming from Him. And if we need confirmation, we can ask the Lord for a sign. There's nothing wrong with that. However, we must be careful. After we get our sign, no matter how complex or lengthy the wait is, we owe God respect and should pray for patience to wait on Him. Know Him and His voice; then you can be *A Voice* that echoes truth and light, where we will find life eternal.

The Voice

Chapter 4

I had become addicted to cocaine and heroin, weed and alcohol I was living. The life of lust wasn't dedicated to anything but pleasure. It started as fun, but I felt disgraced and ashamed. I didn't want to live like that anymore, but at the same time, I didn't want to die either. I'm smoking cocaine and getting high for three days and three nights, not eating, just drinking, getting high, and having sex. My chest is hurting. I'm in pain, and I want to stop, but something is telling me to keep hitting the pipe to keep sniffing, and I'm in tears because I have no power over these voices that are within me.

I tried to lie down and get some sleep, and I heard a voice speaking in my ear. It said get up, for today is the day of salvation. It scared me so badly because I didn't know the meaning of the words, and I didn't understand. My heart was racing, feeling like it was going to burst. I was panicking and wondering what it was. I tried to lay back down but hadn't slept in over three days, and I was trying to sleep but had no peace.

I felt a tap on my shoulder like a finger poking me, and

I could feel the wind from the breath in my ear as if it was a human being saying, get up and go to church, for today is the day of salvation, and at that point, I jumped up because of fear I looked around. There was nobody there except the woman that I was with. I ran to the bathroom and threw water on my face. I looked in the mirror, and it was like I wasn't looking at myself.

I didn't like what I saw; something had taken me over like I could see into my soul. This is not me. I don't like this person not beginning to cry and ask to help me. I took a shower, got dressed, turned on the television, just trying to find peace, and heard a song by a group called The Winans singing, "Straighten my life out again." I began to cry; I missed my innocence. I started to miss the days when I went to church and was clean of the dirt I'd subjected myself to.

I grew up in the Pentecostal Church (PAW) and (PCAF); both denominations were very strict, taught, and preached holiness… baptizing in Jesus's name and the filling of the Holy Ghost. I left the church at the age of 18.

I had not been in church in over ten years; now, I felt nervous about returning. I didn't know what to expect, and it had been so long. I was a teen when I left, but up til then, church was all I knew. I'm thinking, why am I feeling nervous?

Amazingly, after my encounter with the Winans, I

didn't touch the drugs anymore while I was getting dressed. I didn't realize something had started to break me free. I went out the door, and as I was driving, I thought I was going to my home church where I grew up.

This church used to be my home away from home, but now I feel like a stranger. But it's where I'm headed. They have not seen me in over ten years, and I don't know what to expect. To my surprise, a voice said to me, go to your mother's church, what?! I didn't want to go there. You see, my mother was a pastor. She started pastoring right before I left our home church. Although she was starting her ministry, she told me to stay at our home church.

Our pastor at the time of our home church made it known openly, even in his sermons, that a woman is not called to be a pastor; I was a little confused because there were maybe a few women pastors I knew of. Perhaps it's my mother who has heard the wrong voice? Maybe she is rebellious in pursuing this calling of preaching and pastoring. She was good at missionary work, praying, church dinners, and fundraising. Perhaps she should stick to that and stay in her rightful place.

I loved my pastor like a father; he was good to me and treated me like a son. He taught me about serving God, being faithful, having faith, and believing in God. I learned church order and protocols here; this was my family. Our pastor was a working man. He had oil trucks and dump trucks; he was always working. He was a man's man; he was the most outstanding example to me as a man, second only to my father. He allowed me to work for him, and I started driving his oil and dump trucks when I was only 16 years old.

When I was about 10, maybe 11 years old, I wanted to play organ and piano. Our church went through a transition where we had no musicians. Our pastor put me on the organ on a Sunday morning service. I did not know music. I didn't even know any notes. I was so embarrassed to be up there. This would go on for several weeks. One Sunday morning, the Holy Spirit fell on me, and I could feel His presence. My eyes were closed, and I was doing what my pastor told me to do; he said, "Play!" I was hitting keys…making noise.

Suddenly, the sound changed; I could not believe what I heard. I thought it was Chris; he was the one I looked up to as an organist; he could play that Hammond and was so anointed. I thought he left his church that Sunday to help us out because I was pitiful; I knew nothing about music except I liked it. When I opened my eyes, I looked for Chris, but he wasn't there. My hands and feet were moving, and I was playing…It was me playing…this was a miracle….my miracle!

From that day forward, I started to have an understanding of music that I could not explain. I would see chords in my head, and I would practice, and the pastor sent me to take piano lessons. I became the lead musician of our church. I applied myself and was there with everything happening at the church service. I practiced and practiced.

Within a few years, I was being exposed to other churches and ministries because of music. I was helping a friend, Tony, the choir director at the time, with this church, and I liked it there. I started to feel at home, and I was spiritually growing. I started to go to this church more frequently. I began having dreams about two places; on one side, things were hard, and on the other, things were easy.

I heard a voice tell me to go to the church where you are growing up. Seeming out of nowhere, I was forbidden to go to this church; I was told by my mom and pastor to stay away from that church…to be obedient; they said the church was a cult (I didn't have a clue as to what a cult was) I was devastated. I found myself sneaking over there whenever I could. Attending church was so much pressure, but I liked it there.

Sometime after this period, my mother asked our pastor if she could help her former pastor. He had asked her for her help. This is the church and pastor where she first received the Holy Spirit. She was going to have prayer services at noon there. Our church was on the east side of

Baltimore, but we lived on the west side, and the former church and pastor were on the west side. I would hear our pastor's messages changing and his tone. He appeared to be more frustrated, and it was coming through his messages. Was he frustrated about what? I didn't know. His messages started to reflect how we need to know what voice is speaking to us. He truly believed my mother was hearing the wrong voice. I feel like they are not attending to the voice talking to me.

Eventually, my mother would leave to help the other church while I was feeling like a cheater in a relationship; I was between two churches. I had a secret, and it didn't feel good. I am 17 at the time. As time passed, my mother informed our pastor that her former pastor was going to another state and wanted her to take care of the church. Eventually, she became the pastor of this church. The former pastor went south and gave her charge.

This did not sit well with our pastor. As hard as he tried to be diplomatic about the situation, it was getting unbearable. I started to feel like my mother was being slandered, and it was bothering me. Our pastor wanted her to return to our home church and leave that church alone. My mother refused, and my world turned; things could never return to what they used to be. During almost every service, I heard how people think they hear from God, but it is another voice. "God did not call that sister to pastor," he exclaimed in his sermon. I was starting to feel like I couldn't wait until I was old enough to leave on my own.

A guy showed up at our church but was outside asking the usher to give me a message that he wanted to see me. I went outside on break, and this guy did not look like a church. I had never seen him before, and he invited me to join his band; he said he needed a bass player. It was a secular band, and I had never played in a secular band before, even though we dibble-dabbled with all the top 40 songs. But playing in a band was like blasphemy from where we come from. I told him I wasn't interested, and then he said the magic words, "Your cousin Richard is in my band." I loved my cousin; he was an incredible musician and played several instruments. I learned so much from him. I'm wondering when my cousin left church. He played for the church up the street. "Hey man, if you change your mind, here's my number; my name is Jimmy," he said. I returned to the church service with the number in my pocket and thought about my cousin.

In the meantime, I was continually hearing messages relating to what my mother had done. It seemed like a crime. She had a good name in the church, but now I was starting to feel ashamed of what she's done. I don't know what to do. I love my mother, but that's it; she's my mother, and I loved my pastor as my pastor. Why is my mother trying to be a pastor? Bishop is going on about not being called to pastor and how some people are rebellious and disobedient to leadership.

* * *

I could not help but feel a certain kind of way, knowing the stones were directed at my mother. My mother was a faithful member and known as a prayer warrior; she has never given the pastor any trouble…he used to use her as an example. The bishop/pastor could call on her for some sincere praying when it was called for. When I left the church, I didn't believe in women pastors; I didn't believe that a woman could be called to the office of pastor and preaching, not in that regard. A woman may be a missionary or prayer person, not a pastor or preacher.

"While all of this was happening, I had a secret plan in my mind. When I grew old enough, I decided to leave the church. I have learned that people who walk out on you have been considering going for a long time before they do. One Sunday, I decided not to attend church. Instead, I dressed in my Sunday best and went downtown to the Hippodrome Theatre, a movie theater in those days. I had to wait until the theater opened as we could not attend movies while growing up.

Well, I'm old enough to go, and I am going and didn't tell anyone at the time. They opened from 11:00 am until 11:00 pm, and I stayed there all day and ate popcorn, candy, and hotdogs while waiting for Jesus to get me for this sin. It sounds a little ridiculous to many of you, but this was serious in the Pentecostal church back in the day. Back then, it was just one big room where they played the premiere movie in rotation while playing older movies. I stayed until they put me out. I had a ball; it was my birthday treat and fell on a Sunday. When my mother asked where I had been because the pastor had been calling asking for me, my pastor probably thought I had gone to my mother's church since she started her ministry. Then, I told her I went to the movies, liked them, and had a blast.

Sometimes, we can make our children so thirsty that they are willing to drink from any fountain, while other times, we can give them so much to drink that they are never satisfied with what they drink. Thus, we must find a balance between having no access at all or too much access too fast.

This was the day I told my mother I wasn't returning to church. She was shocked and asked, "What do you mean you're not going back?" She was shocked and asked, "What do you mean you're not going back?" I told her I was done with church. She said, "Well, now you can come with me to my church." I said, "To your church, Mother, no disrespect, but you are not a pastor; God did not call you to preach." She asked, "What do you mean by that?" "I'm just saying, all of these bishops and pastors I have played for and backed up on the organ while they preached, I know I can't go with you." I didn't mean to hurt her feelings, but I had issues. I had no clue that I was a bigot, sexist, and discriminatory man. I had been misleading, and I misunderstood.

This would be the fallout between my mother and I. Eventually, my mother would get my father involved (he did not attend church during this time). He called me downstairs and asked, "What is this your mother is telling me about you not wanting to go to church anymore?" I said, "Yes, sir, that is true." He said, "If you are going to stay in this house, you will go to her church, And you are going to quit that band that you're in and go to work with me, do you understand? "Yes, sir," I said. I would not disrespect my parents, so I went upstairs and immediately packed my clothes. I didn't pack anything they had given me or gifted to me.

I had worked since I was 10 in my father's business, so I had my things. After about 2 hours, I came downstairs with my bags to leave, and my mother asked, "Where are you going?" I don't know, but I am not going to your church and not quitting the band, so I'm leaving." This is how I left the church and my home at 18 years old.

I had some real issues and was too ignorant to know it. I was the one who told my mom God did not call her to pastor. But I eventually helped her behind the scenes with sound systems, instruments, and construction, and I even taught my brother how to play enough to get by in the church services. He's incredible today, of course. But I would not attend church services. So, I had never heard her preach or teach; I just prayed. I knew she could pray!

So, knowing my background, when the voice said, "Go to your mother's church," I was freaking out but was desperate, so I went, and I obeyed the voice. When I got there, it was a brother from the old neighborhood who used to do dope and stay high all the time. We used to call him Quinten, and he was standing at the door when I walked in. It was like a sign to me because he was so clean-cut. He was wearing a nice suit, which was unusual for me since I had never seen him dressed like that before. He was an usher at my mother's church. I was surprised and asked him what he was doing there. He laughed and told me that he had been attending the church for over three years and had been clean for the same period.

He said this was his church and asked me why I was there. I was hesitant to answer, but he offered to help me. He asked me where I wanted to sit, and I replied that it didn't matter. He then directed me to the front. As I walked in, my mother was already preaching her sermon. I heard the Bible slam with the sound of the podium mic, and she said, "God just changed my message. He said today is the day of salvation for somebody in here." As I walked to my seat, I thought, "This is the third time I have heard this phrase in one morning.

I was sitting there, feeling ashamed because I had been high for days, and she was preaching about Jesus in a way that I had never heard before. Even though I grew up attending church, she spoke about his love and sacrifice, and how he died for our sins resonated with me. It hit home, and I realized I didn't know Jesus like I thought. While she was preaching, I grappled with the secret I had been hiding from my family. But the pastor's words gave me a sense of comfort and hope. When it was time for the altar call for prayer, I felt compelled to go forward, but I was afraid.

I wanted to go, but the voices were saying, everybody is looking at you, man; you know you're high; you don't want to go up there like that to embarrass yourself and your family. Get yourself together and come back later. I want to say this: you can never get yourself together. Jesus did not die for you to get yourself together. If we could get together, Jesus would not need to come and die for our sins.

You come as you are, please hear me, prodigal sons and daughters, people hearing the gospel being preached, listen for God's voice; he loves you, He can use anyone, forget the foolery, this is real, you can't get yourself together. Go as you are you, but you will not stay as you are ("to as many as believed, He gave them the power to become the sons of God"). I was ashamed, and the voices said, "Don't go up there, don't do it, don't you do it, get yourself together." It's like they were panicking inside of me.

* * *

I sat there, and the brother next to me tapped me; he said, "Hey brother, do you wanna go up to get prayer?" I said no, I was good, knowing that I needed to go up there; I was saying to myself, "I don't know this man," but in a way, I was glad for the invitation; I was just afraid. I realized the same voices that were speaking to me not to get prayer were the same voices telling me to be hard, to get drunk, to be unfaithful in my relationships, and the more the pastor was speaking at the altar, and praying for people, the more I started to believe God.

This voice had to be God's spirit speaking through her because it was talking to my heart, soul, and inner being. I was being convicted, and the shame was leaving, and I was beginning to feel that it was going to be ok. It was like I was paralyzed; I couldn't stand up and go, although I wanted to.

I don't even know what that fear was. I was so afraid to move, and I said to myself, "Lord, I need your help; if that brother asks me to go up for prayer again, Lord, I will go." That brother was already in the prayer line waiting to be prayed for, and he just started moving, getting out of the line, and walking. I thought he was going to someone or somewhere else, trying not to be suspicious for looking at what this brother was doing. He walked across and came through the church pews, excusing himself all the way, and found his way to me and said," Brother, are you sure that you don't wanna go up to get prayer with me? Let's go up together," and I said yes, I knew that was my sign.

See, it's okay to ask God for a sign. It's OK to ask God for help because He knows those demonic spirits have taken hold of you. These demon spirits need a body to express themselves and work through. That's why Jesus said when the spirit is cast out of a person, they'll wander in dry places and can't find rest. They cannot find peace, so they will return to their old places with their old ways. They will return to the same person whom they used to manipulate and control, get high, be unfaithful in marriage, and be a fornicator, liar, cheat, or thief. Regardless of your title or position, the devil doesn't care; we must come to terms with these things. He's out to get all of us and any of us who let our guards down. We must pray for one another.

These are demonic spirits I had in me to do the things I did; this is not normal. This is a demonic presence when you can't be faithful in your marriage and make excuses for it because of your position or title while preaching the gospel of Jesus Christ and the kingdom. These are demonic spirits of lust when we can't keep it in our pants, so we operate off of our gifts and talents rather than the calling, the anointing, and the purpose in the will of a holy and righteous God.

* * *

We have examples of men and women walking away from everything to please God because they didn't want pleasure over His will or lust over love. If fulfilling your lust with a man or woman or money is more important than what God has told you to do and say, He cannot trust you any more than He could Lucifer—Satan—the Devil.

By faith Moses, when he was come to years, refused to be called the son of Pharaoh's daughter; Choosing rather to suffer affliction with the people of God than to enjoy the pleasures of sin for a season; Esteeming the reproach of Christ greater riches than the treasures in Egypt: for he had respect unto the recompense of the reward.

By faith, he forsook Egypt, not fearing the wrath of the king, for he endured, as seeing him who is invisible. Hebrews 11:24-27

If God cannot trust us in this world, how can He trust you in the next world? That's why Lucifer betrayed him because Lucifer was trying to fulfill his lust and desire that was outside of the will of God for the betterment of the kingdom of God. Judas was a bishop; he was over the money. Money pleased him like a woman would a man, so he betrayed Jesus for the lust of the eye, the lust of the flesh, and the pride of life, something that was outside of the will of God. He had to have it! Forget these titles of Bishop, Pastor, and Prophet…it doesn't matter…death is the great equalizer.

* * *

You can't take the money with you, and neither can you take the feeling from lust with you…it's an illusion if you can't control your lust and your flesh. You are an enemy of God, and sometimes God allows the enemy to attack your flesh and kill you in the natural that your soul may be saved if you repent. Some say they didn't make it to heaven with everything they did. We don't know that because their punishment could have been to destroy their flesh, their earthly body, the earthly blessings and riches that they had, and got cut short so that they could be put on a bed of affliction to give them time to repent, to seek God's mercy and Grace.

I was in my seat now, thinking about all of the stuff I did in the name of pleasure, having fun selfishly. We don't even realize we are helping Satan build his kingdom. I needed to repent of the sins I had committed against God and guess whoever the people or persons that committed the sins against God were with you. Hearing the voice of God was doing something to my spirit and mind, somehow making me aware of things I never paid attention to.

I went up there with Brother Haskell and was in the prayer line, and now I was trying to negotiate with God in my heart. I said, Lord, if you give me two, maybe three months to straighten out my mess in the street because I had drugs out in the street, I had people to answer to, I had money to collect, and I think I need to handle this business. What I didn't know was those demon voices were talking to me and didn't want to let me go. They had been with me for so long that I thought my inner voice was talking to me. They didn't want to move out of me because I had become a good place for them to live in.

Here I was trying to negotiate with God, and when it was my turn to get up there for prayer, I was going through like the pastor was a woman who is my mother. I remember I told her years ago when she started pastoring, saying, "God did not call you to be a pastor. I said, how can you think you are supposed to be a pastor?" I did not know that I was a bigot; I did not know that I was sexist. I did not know that I was prejudiced, and I was not. I thought I was just being honest about the place of a woman, the fact that God cannot use a woman and would not use a woman to Pastor, and now here I am standing there ashamed and don't want my mother to know that I do drugs that I'm a drug addict.

I stayed away from her whenever I was high, and I'm standing here now, in my worst state since doing drugs. I hadn't slept in three days and was high as a kite, and I was trying to cover it, and she looked into my eyes, and I saw it wasn't her. There was something different about her; the spirit of God was on her, and she tapped me in my chest and heart and said," God just said you can't fix it. He got to fix it, and I began to cry; I couldn't hold back the tears. I thought, pull yourself together, but that didn't work.

I knew that God was talking to me through this woman, through my mother, and she said, "Lift your hands and call on Jesus!" She said, "Because today is the day of salvation and the day that you hear God's voice hard, not your heart," I began to cry because I felt something breaking me loose on the inside. I began to call on Jesus harder and louder. I lifted my hands and surrendered, and I kept calling his name, and I kept calling.

Then I heard a voice say within me, "How can you crave a hamburger if you never tasted one?" The voice said, "The devil introduced you to the taste of cocaine and drugs, like a mother introduces her baby to their first table food, just as a mother introduces the baby to a brand new taste of something good for them; he said, the devil did that to you and said, "I'm going to take this taste out of your mouth." I'm listening simultaneously as I'm still calling on the name of Jesus. While this was going on, all of a sudden, I smelled cocaine as if it was being cooked on a stove; then, I could taste it like I had eaten raw cocaine. I could taste it like I had swallowed a gram, which was bitter in my mouth and stomach. I felt like I had to vomit, and I felt myself beginning to choke while I was still calling the name of Jesus.

I could hear voices outside me saying, "Don't stop,

keep calling on the name of Jesus, don't stop." I could feel myself gagging and getting sick to my stomach, and I was tempted to stop, but the voices on the left and the right, which were the altar workers, were saying, "Don't stop… don't stop, keep calling Jesus, don't stop…don't stop and I pushed my way through. I kept calling on the name of the Lord Jesus, and all of a sudden, it felt like somebody took their hand with the whole arm and supernaturally reached into my mouth, down my esophagus into my stomach, and pulled everything up out of me that didn't belong in me. I could feel it when it lifted out of me, and I began to praise God. I could hear myself speaking a language I did not know, according to the witnesses, who said it for almost 2 hours. The two voices on the left and right were Sisters Beverly and Louise. I learned these were laborers for Christ; they were like midwives pushing that birth.; God has a sense of humor. The church was crowded when I went to the altar, and now the church is almost empty. I was the last one at the altar. God delivered me; I was born again; I felt brand new; everything seemed bright and new. I did not feel the weight I felt walking through those doors. I was made brand new.

The Pastor was there, my mother, and asked me, "How do you feel?" "Like new," I said. It scared me so much that I was ready to leave the church to kind of access what had transpired there. And I was trying to figure out what was going on, and my mother asked, "Do you have a Bible?" and I said, "No, ma'am, I do not, and they gave me a Bible, and I took it, and I went home. When I arrived home, I acted like I was running from something. I got inside my house, closed the door, and leaned my back up against the door. I was like, what had happened? I was pondering on what happened, and then I heard the voice say within me so clearly, "Clean up your house, get rid of the drugs, get rid of the scales, get rid of the bags, the vials, all the paraphernalia, get rid of your bar, your alcohol.

I began to obey the voice; it was soothing and peaceful. He delivered me, the One who said, "I'm going to taste out of your mouth." I began to clean up my house and put everything in contractor bags; I was a contractor, so I threw everything on the back of my dump truck. I flushed the drugs down the toilet. After that, I felt peace. I laid down, went to sleep, and had a peace that passed all understanding. This is not a cliché; this is a real experience.

I am a witness, and I woke up to another voice saying now get up and go back to that church and tell them your testimony. Tell them the goodness of the Lord and what I have done for you. I had not been in church in over ten years, and now I'm going twice in one day. I went, and when I walked through the door, they were already in service about to preach, and the pastor said, "We was wondering if he was coming to church tonight. What's so amazing is that I didn't know the church schedule or anything; all I had was a voice. "Do you have something to say?"

* * *

I was afraid but not like I was that morning, and I said," Yes, I do," because I knew the voice told me to tell the goodness of the Lord, and I began to tell my testimony. As I was speaking and telling my story, my mother, brother, and sisters looked like they had heard some rumors, but they couldn't believe it. My mother later told me that when I was telling my testimony, she wanted to go through the floor because she never knew that I was getting high, and when anybody even said anything about drugs, she defended me. She couldn't believe it, the selling and the using. That was on Easter morning when it happened so many years ago. I've never been high again, I've never been drunk again, I never did drugs again. I witnessed this thing, this salvation, this blood sacrifice that Christ did for us, and our sins are real. Jesus has all the power over that devil and his flunkies. I am convinced that demons are real because they were working through me.

The devil is real, he is evil and destructive by nature; we make light of it, but everything around us, from movies to shows to life, is letting us know; look at our superheroes and the Marvels and the magazines from the 50s and the 60s and through today; look at our life, everything is telling us that there is a war between good and evil and evil is always trying to take over the world, always trying to take over the government, always trying to take over something, that it may do it's evil. It's evil wanting to destroy the good. Why are we not getting this?

* * *

Evil is trying to destroy what is good. I witness Jesus saying," My sheep on my voice," it doesn't matter what you're saying; it doesn't matter what you're going through. Hear me: You better tune out the voices trying to destroy your life, destroy your family, destroy your marriage, destroy your career, destroy your legacy. You better rebuke those voices and call on the name of Jesus and submit to the voice of Christ that wants to save you, bless you, establish you, and give you success. If you can't be faithful in your marriage, don't make excuses because that voice tells you it's OK…no it's not! Don't be deceived… it's the wrong voice!

Please listen to me, leaders; I know by what authority I speak. I am no more significant than any other man except for my acknowledgment and understanding that I am a voice, crying out, don't let the enemy deceive you as he did at the tree to make you think that you can get it another way, that you are more significant than who you are, you are a voice, it doesn't matter how gifted you are, and talented that you are how smart educated wise that you are. It doesn't matter you are a voice. Hear me; none of us are more talented than Lucifer, at least not in our present state, which is in the flesh; this is why he uses the flesh so much because he misses having a body. He is using you, you think, because you're getting a feeling out of it that it's about you; no, it's about him calling you to oppose God. When God created Lucifer, he put vocals and trumpets down in Lucifer; he created Lucifer for praise, worship, entertainment, music for the production, glamour for beauty, and to be the host of the party. Don't you know Lucifer used to be the heaven host? This is why he knows how to throw a party—got people caught up in themselves. When people follow you because of your voice, not your beauty, not your money, they are following people for their beauty and don't even want to hear your voice. You have to understand which side of the spectrum you are on.

Don't be deceived; don't let the enemy fool you to make you think because you are a Pastor and Apostle, Bishop, Prophet, Evangelist or whatever your title may be, a politician or governor, president, a prince or king, CEO, whatever it is, you are a voice you are a government, a body of voices. You live by whatever voices you believe, the voices you continue to hear, and the voices you are listening to and obeying.

What voices do you believe in? Whatever you believe in is the world you will carry out; if you are listening and obeying the wrong voice in this world, it only means that you will hear and obey the dark voice in the world to come. It's the wrong voice telling you to be with that married man, to do drugs, to be with that man's wife, the wrong voice telling you to steal, kill and lie destroying someone's life. It's the wrong voice telling you to take all of them extra offerings, putting God's name to it, lying in the name of Jesus for money and profit. Using God to build your name and your brand, and you're still not satisfied, how much more do you need? The wrong voice is telling you to molest and rape, be careful of those evil voices making things sound sweet and ok, but it's not.

There are bishops and Pastors, apostles, and prophets having sex all over the world. Everywhere they have preached, there is some flesh you have left behind in those places. They have used the blessings that they say were given to them by God and used the same money from the offerings for their sex parties. Your DNA will testify against you, says The Lord. Repent before I come upon you suddenly! Do we understand that we have the potential to be God's enemy like Lucifer and the fallen Angels? That's why they got cast down from heaven because they listened to the wrong voice; pride was the voice that they heard and followed. Pride told them they could be greater than God, who is the one who created them. Pride told Lucifer you can exalt your throne above the throne of the Most High God.

People worship pastors and celebrities because we were created to worship and honor God. Born to praise but seeks praise, this is our weakness. People worship pastors because they can see them; it's something about them that connects with the premise of the fallen ones. It's easier or less challenging to follow a voice in a body because a voice in a body can be seen, while on the other hand, it takes faith to believe and follow the voice of an invisible God. Most do not know that Satan, the Devil, and Lucifer are the voices that talk to them, sing to them, and seduce them. This is why rap music is so huge; rap is the voice, the false narrative mixed with truth, that suggests everything for pleasure with the lie of no repercussions. The voice brought awareness, then turned around and destroyed family values in just one generation. Do know this and understand that A VOICE created everything we see!

These young people are listening, believing, and obeying the voice they hear in the music, and it's making them do some crazy things because of the voice. The voice tells them that they can have sex with anybody, do drugs, get money, houses, cars, jewelry, women, men, lust, and people can't get enough of it because the voice keeps telling them to go after the next thing. The next thing is simple: If you are a pastor, you are a voice; if you are a Bishop, you are a voice; Satan is trying to pervert you to make you obsolete so that you can forfeit your inheritance, which is in Christ it's not in the house, you have to know it's not in the car, it's not in the money because you can't keep these things, your true inheritance is in Christ, but we don't want to believe that there is accountability for everything we do. Whatever we can see naturally comes from something we can't see in the spiritual; the invisible world created the worlds we see…everything.

So, if we have a court system here in time, you know we have one in eternity. If we have a judge to deal with crimes and those who have broken the law, we must understand that God will judge us. If you have death row here, you have to know there's a death row there. If you can send somebody to prison to do life here, you can send somebody to do life there because this world cannot come up with anything that the eternal world has not come up with first. If you can come up with the question, the answer already exists. Don't be deceived; if you choose lust, the love of God is not in you at the time of fulfilling your lust. If you decide the pleasure of your own body, yourself, over the responsibilities, duties, and will of God for his people, then know you need to be born again. Then we are none of his. If you love the world, you are an enemy of God; Lucifer is the prince of this world, the ruler of this world; if you love this world, Pastor, you do not love God.

If you are fulfilling your lusts, whether with men or women or both, but dedicated to hindering women from pastoring and preaching and feeding God's sheep while you feed your lustful fantasies, you have to know Satan is your father; repent! I say that by the authority of God's word, the history of the leaders who have preceded us, like King Saul, who loved having power and the fulfillment of pleasure. He abused God's people, his God-given anointing, and misappropriated his power and authority. He was not concerned about doing the will of God. So, he got replaced, and God rejected him.

Lucifer wasn't worried about doing God's will; he wanted to do his own thing with God's stuff. Be sure you are not doing your own thing with God's stuff. God checked him; don't you see the parallels? He's got you believing because you are Pastors and Bishops and Prophets that you are something special. You are a voice, and you need someone who is not on Satan's payroll to tell you this. Because of your position of authority, you think you get a special pass; that is what the Religious Leaders believed in Jesus's day. Jesus said no man was born that's greater than John the Baptist because John the Baptist said I am a voice.

He was that voice for God and His will being done. He understood it doesn't matter what body I am in or the clothes, it doesn't matter what gender, it truly doesn't matter. After the cross of Calvery and the resurrection, it doesn't matter what your religion, race, or tribe is. Don't you see? Jesus did not die to give birth to another religion among thousands of others; He is "Alpha and Omega, The Beginning and The End, The First and The Last. He is in a category of His own…it is about the Kingdom and having a loving relationship with the King.

It's about the family of God, and don't nobody wants murderers, cheaters, adulterers, theft, and jealous-hearted people competing with the neighboring entity in heaven. Are we going to be looking over our shoulders? Wake up. If you could see the people you worship when it's time to leave this world, you may turn your worship back to where it belongs…to God.

* * *

It doesn't matter what tribe you are from or your bloodline. The Pharisees had more respect for John because he was from their tribe, Levi. John said I'm just a voice crying in the wilderness…repent. The wilderness is a wandering place. John went into the wilderness because he saw God's people as sheep wandering without shepherds. The people had no one they could trust to take care of them.

Do you think these people who have become rich from preaching have been given the blueprint to success? If so, you will find yourself worshiping personalities and chasing principalities! They are not superstars. They are Lucifer's lights. The devil wants you, your attention, and your worship. After all the suffering you've gone through from abuse, rejection, pain, loneliness, and sometimes even torment in your mind, don't you know you have survived all of that for a reason? Why would God silence you or tell you not to speak, preach, or pastor? If so, God's kingdom would be divided, and it's not; the church is because of men who have taken over God's house.

Don't let anyone silence you or steal your voice. *"My sheep know my voice, and a stranger they will not follow."* What voice is leading you? Cut it out…stop worshipping personalities and preachers. No, no, no, check out the voice; know who's talking to you. It's not ok to stay in sin.

The voice is saying to repent, for we all have sent

repent for the kingdom of God is that hand, if you are father Your voice if you are mother, your voice if you are son a daughter, you are a voice of brother Sister you are a voice Pastors you are a voice is pride and deception. There is no special pass. Please understand we're just voices representing The Voice.

Identify what kingdom you are from, and you will know your voice and the voice of the king you are serving. Light and darkness cannot occupy the same space; we cannot serve two masters, either God or Satan; choose this day whom you will listen to and follow.

Voices

Chapter 5

In the Bible, we read that after Jesus was baptized, he was led into the wilderness to be tempted by the devil. There are three tests: the lust of the eye, the lust of the flesh, and the pride of life. If the devil will destroy you and your ministry, it will be of these three; they are the foundation of destruction. This text inspires us to remember an important lesson about beginning ministry and fulfilling our calling in life.

It reminds us that passing the kingdom tests is crucial in gaining God's trust and being ready to face and overcome the devil's temptations. These tests are not administered by schools or universities but by the kingdom itself. We are encouraged to follow Jesus' example of facing and overcoming the devil's temptations and to be prepared to face adversity while being an example of ministry in the face of challenges.

"And Jesus, being full of the Holy Ghost, returned from Jordan and was led by the Spirit into the wilderness, Being forty days tempted by the devil. And in those days he did eat nothing: and when they were ended, he afterward

hungered. And the devil said unto him, If thou be the Son of God, command this stone that it be made bread. And Jesus answered him, saying, It is written, That man shall not live by bread alone, but by every word of God." Luke 4: 1-4.

Do you see how the devil came for Jesus in the sense of knowing he was hungry? Be careful who you allow to speak to when you're hungry and thirsty"? This applies to the spiritual as well. It's a powerful reminder that our physical needs can leave us vulnerable to temptation. The enemy may use our anointing against us, luring us into actions against our values and beliefs. It's essential to be aware that forces (voices) seek to lead you astray and cause you to engage in behaviors that could harm yourself and those around you. These negative influences may encourage you to indulge in activities that could negatively impact your relationships, professional life, and overall well-being. It's essential to stay vigilant and to prioritize the things that truly matter in your life, such as your values, beliefs, and the people you care about.

It is important to remember that our actions, talents, and abilities are accountable to God. The faith and trustworthiness we exhibit in our everyday interactions also indicate our character in spiritual matters. It is wise to ensure that we remain responsible and trustworthy in all our lives. In these last days, the fear of God is gone. Selfishness has taken over.

* * *

Jesus faced this same temptation, but he chose to deny himself and rely on the written word of God. Later, during his ministry, he encountered a group of over 5000 people (not including women and children) who were hungry and in need of nourishment. With only two fish and five loaves of bread, Jesus blessed the food and performed a miracle, feeding the multitude and demonstrating the power of God and his anointing.

It's worth noting that this same anointing and power that Jesus used to feed those in need was what he denied himself during his time in the wilderness. It's a powerful lesson for all of us - to be mindful of our vulnerabilities and to use our gifts and anointing in service of others rather than for our gain.

The next temptation, *The devil, led him up to a high place and showed him all the world's kingdoms in an instant. And he said to him, "I will give you all their authority and splendor (glory); it has been given to me, and I can give it to anyone I want to. If you worship me, it will all be yours." Jesus answered, "It is written: 'Worship the Lord your God and serve him only.'" Luke 5: 5-8*

In the biblical story of Jesus being tempted by the devil, we see that Jesus responded by quoting the written word of God. It is interesting to note that the devil himself acknowledged that he had the authority over the glories of the world, as Adam had lost his authority and possessions due to his disobedience to God. The devil presented the kingdoms of the world to Jesus and offered them to him on the condition that he betray God. This teaches us the importance of standing firm in our faith and not compromising our beliefs for worldly possessions.

If pastors have to lie, cheat, betray spouses, and compromise on the standards of holiness and righteousness for money, then Lucifer / the Devil, and Satan blessed them, not God, Jesus, or the Holy Spirit. When pastors have to resort to manipulation for money and fleecing the sheep, it's not God. If a pastor, prophet, or speaker asks for money to pray for you, this is not God; it's witchcraft. Never…ever pay anyone who asks for money before they pray for you…this is the temptation the devil offered to Jesus on the mountain, trying to get him to compromise for a prosperous and glorious ministry outside of God being the giver.

If Jesus had taken the bribe, he would never have been able to cast out devils and demons. This is why many pastors and leaders do not believe in casting out demons. Jesus said, "If Satan casts out Satan, then his kingdom will be divided and will come down." The devil continues to reward these kinds of preachers to deceive the people to continue to give money with the expectation of receiving the same blessing as the preacher who is asking for the money. The preacher demonstrates how many material things they are persuading you to give, and you will have the same thing. It's a pyramid scheme; you have no room at the top.

Biblically speaking, giving offerings is worship; don't let anyone fool you about this. In praise and worship service, we are providing to God and seeking communion with him…this is spiritual. Giving of our monetary is worshipping with our carnal things, honoring God with our substance. The same people who tell you that you have to pay tithes and offerings are the same people who have made it rain money in the strip clubs and paid for alcohol, drugs, and sex for pleasure. Some of them are still making it rain for sexual fantasies. We need to grow up and be honest. We should want to support the kingdom's work but, at the same time, avoid being exploited and deceived. We need to stop playing games.

When the pastor or prophet goes into the word or message, this is where God is feeding His sheep…giving to His people. This is the voice of God speaking to His people. When a speaker or pastor asks for money or monetary gifts after the message or after they have preached, and this is not the church's protocol, this is out of order, and I say that with the utmost authority. When people are crying and seeking answers from God, there should not be any surprises; we should be their protection from the enemy. The giving to God was another order of service, and that order of service and worship has passed.

Regarding the word and altar call, God only cares about people (souls) during this worship portion of the service; to involve money is a contamination and an insult to God and His people. This is an intimate time in the spirit.

Suppose you were being intimate with someone and stopped to ask for money while in the act; you are a prostitute. Suppose a preacher can stop the flow of the Holy Spirit while people are standing at the altar crying, repenting, and hungry for God, and that preacher ceases this moment to ask for money. In that case, they are not of the Holy Spirit of God; although it is a spirit talking to them, the god of this world took them to the mountain where they bowed. If you do not pass this test, it will follow you throughout your entire career, and you will think it's normal and you have God's favor, only to find out you are hearing and obeying the same voice Judas heard and obeyed.

The greatest gift you can bring God is your repentant heart. Why would God, who is a Spirit, want money from you while He is working on your broken heart and soul? God is a Spirit, and He's Holy and Righteous, and you are everything to Him when you are broken. You want God, and God wants you, but you are required to stop worship and the chance to get your healing because someone heard a voice say, ask for money right here at this moment. "Go to your seats, bring your offering, and sow a seed into this word. Who's voice was that to stop you from worshipping

God to give money? Look at God's history and character; you will forever know that God would never stop you from worshipping him to give money. You cannot recapture the moment; many of those souls are lost, and some will never go to church again, especially if they are new to this. The preacher is hearing voices. One minute, it is the spirit of God talking; the next, he hears the devil's voice and then his own. He may be preaching at the altar, but the devil is talking to him about getting more money, his bills, payroll, or taxes, or how much is in their savings, or just the greed of not letting this money moment pass.

This is where the human aspect comes in: what voice will he obey? Well, most people do not know what is taking place at that moment, but God does, and He can reveal this to His prophets. The devil will cut a deal with them, and his voice is so clear and convicting that most of them think that it really is God speaking to them. But the god of this world speaks to them; the love of money is the voice…they have to get that money because they are afraid of not having enough. They might miss an opportunity if they don't get the money at that moment. This is the spirit of greed and lust, which can never get enough. Listen to the voice telling you to get extra money for God's word. Who are we serving?

Have you ever heard of a true prophet in the Bible disrupting people who were praying and repenting to God to ask for money? Have you ever heard Jesus say, put money in my hands for you to get healed, or sow a seed into the word he spoke? The contradictions are ridiculously present. If the word of God is seed (and it is), how can you sow a seed into a seed? Seed needs soil; you sow seeds into soil; the people are the soil. The word is being preached to reach people's hearts (spiritually, the heart is the soil) to bring about changes and salvation. Salvation is the work of the heart, not the flesh.

Your ear serves as the entry point of nourishment for your spirit. It is through what you hear, whether it is good or evil, that you feed your spirit. Your eyes, on the other hand, function as your spiritual nose. When you see something, you are spiritually smelling it. After the smell, you decide whether or not you want to taste it. This is how the seed, which is the word of God, is planted in your heart - through your ears. Once you believe it, you mix it with faith, and it will eventually bear fruit.

Some people enter the church in one way, and when they leave, they are transformed, although not necessarily perfect. They are reborn and must be taught and nurtured in the teachings of God's word and the love of Jesus Christ so they can become like Him. This process takes time, but the change in them is evident. It is essential to provide them with spiritual nourishment, like a newborn needing milk. Jesus said, "If you love me, feed my sheep." He also said, "My sheep know my voice."

* * *

In this passage, Jesus commends John the Baptist for his selfless service to the gospel. John gave up all his worldly possessions and luxuries to preach the word of God in the wilderness, baptizing people for free. He survived on the bare necessities of life, such as locusts, honey, and water, and denied himself all forms of comfort and pleasure. Unlike some modern-day preachers who may resort to lying, stealing, cheating, or killing, John lived an entirely ascetic life. He did not dine out, handle money, accept food or clothing from people, or wear shoes made by humans. He preached repentance and baptized people until he was unable to continue.In contrast, Jesus socialized, ate, drank, and celebrated religious festivals but never manipulated His followers for money. So where did mainstream ministry get the idea to solicit money from their congregations for prayer or a prophetic word?

The third temptation; *And he brought him to Jerusalem, and set him on a pinnacle of the temple, and said unto him, If thou be the Son of God, cast thyself down from hence: For it is written, He shall give his angels charge over thee, to keep thee: And in their hands, they shall bear thee up, lest at any time thou dash thy foot against a stone. And Jesus answering said unto him, It is said, Thou shalt not tempt the Lord thy God. And when the devil had ended all the temptation, he departed from him for a season.*

Why Jerusalem? It was the headquarters of the Holy Temple. This is where you will find the holy of holies. The

Levitical priests, the Passover, and the places to go to pray and be forgiven of sins. This is where you offered up sacrifice to God. Jerusalem was called "The heart of God."

Jerusalem, an ancient city in the Middle East, was widely known as "The Holy Place City." Its priests considered extremely affluent and influential, held themselves in high regard and enjoyed a position of great privilege. They believed they were the chosen ones by God to have a unique position of authority. The city was considered a physical manifestation of God's blessings and favor, and the priests who lived there were seen as having the highest rank. People worldwide would make pilgrimages to Jerusalem to confess their sins, worship, and feel a closer connection to God.

The temptation of Jesus by the devil is a well-known incident in the Christian faith. The devil's suggestion to Jesus that He should sit on the pinnacle of the temple and force God's hand to prove His identity as the Son of God was a subtle attempt to incite pride in Jesus and encourage Him to act in a way that would elevate Himself above what is appropriate. This temptation is a classic example of the devil's strategy to lead people astray by tempting them to transgress against God. The devil's approach offers a false sense of glory and power, luring individuals with the promise of praise and worship, leading them to act in ways that are not in line with God's will.

* * *

This same tactic was used against Adam and Eve in the Garden of Eden and continues to be used today. It is a reminder that we must remain vigilant against the devil's schemes and resist the temptation to act in ways that are contrary to God's will. In conclusion, the temptation of Jesus by the devil serves as a cautionary tale of the dangers of pride and the importance of remaining steadfast in the face of temptation.

Death was considered the most significant enemy until Jesus finished his work at the cross, which included defeating sin and hell and showing up after his victory as the resurrection. Satan is uncertain about the outcome, but he knows one thing for sure -0The temptation of Jesus by the devil serves as a reminder of the perils of pride and rebellion against one's Creator. The Devil, known initially as Lucifer, was cast out of heaven due to his sinful nature and arrogance, which resulted in his transition to Satan the Devil. Through his experiences, he understands God has no tolerance for sin and pride. This is a cautionary record for individuals who believe themselves above their Creator, as the consequences can be dire.

Attention to all religious leaders, including apostles, prophets, evangelists, pastors, and teachers. It is essential to be cautious and vigilant of deception. In particular, bishops should know that there is no higher authority than God. We are the ambassadors of God, not merely the followers of human desires. Regardless of our actions, individuals in this world will always be influenced by the devil and will resist our efforts. We must choose our battles carefully and wisely, recognizing that not every conflict is worth our time and dedication. Moreover, it is essential to remember that God is the ultimate judge and will reward us accordingly.

If Jesus had chosen to perform for the devil, he would have been denied the anointing, power, and authority of demons, devils, sicknesses, and diseases. Because Jesus got his victory in a private place, he was able to authentically display the victory in public places now without shame because Satan knows our secrets. This is why most leaders and pastors dare not attempt to cast out demons in a service setting because the devil will call them out. "How dare you try to cast me out on Sunday morning when you were with me Saturday night," this is what Satan is saying because of what he knows about the person. So most modern leaders strive to have material things to shield themselves with, like Lucifer having a robe made of diamonds. When Adam and Eve sinned, they tried to cover themselves to hide their sins but covered themselves with figs rather than the blood. Designer clothes cannot cover sins.

Many leaders today conceal their wrongdoings through material possessions, making it difficult to distinguish the church from the secular world. Unfortunately, many people who are struggling financially are chasing after the very things that these preachers have purchased with their money. Believing that merely being associated with them will bring them the same blessings. However, this is not true. God has a unique and tailor-made plan for each individual, like their DNA or fingerprints. You must stay in God's word and pray to know His will for your life.

"What good will it be for someone to gain the whole world yet forfeit their soul? Or what can anyone give in exchange for their soul? For the Son of Man will come in his Father's glory with his angels, and then he will reward each person according to what they have done. Matthew 16: 26-27.

God knows every one of us, and everyone can't be rich. That is not how the world is designed. Each of us has a specific role and purpose in life. It is enough for all of us to meet our basic needs, but not necessarily to be wealthy. As someone who works as a builder and contractor, I understand what it means to be hired by someone to bring their dreams to life and be compensated for my work. Some people who hired me have more resources than I do, even though I am building their dreams. I do not have the means to replicate their dream for myself, as it is their dream, not mine. Most of us are meant to help others achieve their dreams, and, in turn, we can achieve our own. It is important to be content with our level of success and not envy others who may have more.

To maintain a sense of stability and avoid jealousy, I

endeavor to cultivate a mindset of dissatisfaction in myself. It is essential to recognize that the accumulation of material wealth is not the sole purpose of life and that we cannot honestly know the struggles and sacrifices individuals have faced on their path to success. While I appreciate life's finer things, my ultimate source of contentment is my faith in the Lord Jesus. As long as I have fulfilled my purpose here on earth and remained faithful to my calling, any possessions or wealth I may acquire hold little value. My primary objective is to serve the One who has placed me on this earth. Indeed, God has no problems with what He's blessed us with; He has a problem if the devil has blessed us, and we are saying God did it.

Trying to get Jesus to toy with death was his desperate attempt to see his power over death prematurely by committing a suicidal act that should cause God to intervene. Thus saying, do tempt God with the ultimate thinking if God loves me, He will save or stop this tragedy from happening. With everything in you, you must resist the devil; he cares nothing about you. Jesus demonstrates how the word can be misused and taken out of context. The devil was using scriptures to get Jesus to engage and hopefully think it was God telling him to fall. As believers and leaders, the worst thing we can do is allow the enemy to manipulate us into becoming gods of worship instead of worshiping God—misleading people and causing them to look at God like a genie who grants wishes.

* * *

We must know what voices are speaking to us in any situation. Know the voice of your heavenly Father like you would know the voice of your earthly father and mother.

Pastors preach about being blessed with material possessions and how God has supposedly blessed them. However, we should question who gave and blessed them with those things. Did they make a deal with the devil to obtain their wealth, or did they remain faithful to God to receive their blessings? It is crucial to resist evil and selfishness if your destiny and purpose are to sow good seeds in life. Sometimes, we become so self-absorbed that we fail to notice how our actions hurt others. Therefore, it's important to distinguish between doing the will of God and doing our own will. Pursuing the will of God may demand sacrifices from us. Lastly, we must remember that not everyone is going to like us.

It is crucial to remember that the enemy is always trying to find ways to enter your mind and heart. This enemy may present you with promising things intended to harm you. These destructive things and ideas may be disguised as alluring, charming, or attractive, making you feel good about them. Unfortunately, many people's lives have been ruined by things that seemed good on the surface but hid a hidden danger. Therefore, being aware of these dangers and protecting your heart and mind is necessary. Self-awareness and a clear sense of purpose are essential for personal growth and development. To stay aligned with one's purpose, it's advisable to surround oneself with individuals who share similar values and exude positivity. When evaluating advice or feedback from others, listening attentively to the message and understanding the underlying motives behind their words is crucial. This approach enables informed decision-making consistent with one's goals and values while remaining by God's divine will.

It's unnecessary to justify or excuse one's inherent talents or abilities to anyone other than God. Being accountable and dutiful with the gifts bestowed by the One True God who created you is vital. One's unique talents are an inseparable aspect of one's being, and it's perfectly acceptable to embrace and celebrate them without feeling the need to provide a rationale or apologize for them as long as they bring glory to God.

We are too caught up in using scripture to hold someone down, but God is looking for servants, sons, and daughters to live holy for Him. He's seeking a voice that will allow Him to speak through them. This world is made up of fleshly being terrestrial, and God is spirit, and everyone will not stand still to hear spirit as a voice. He's looking for someone who knows His voice and, in turn, allows Him to be the voice in you. Male or female… are you holy? When we start to understand everything we see was created by words (a voice), it is easier to accept why technology is moving so fast. Time is counting down, and the message must be released on the earth. Satan is in competition with God in spreading his message. We are governed by what we hear and see. As the gospel is being preached around the world, evil is being spread everywhere. The rap music industry has become the most influential and effective way for darkness. Look at how the world has changed in the past 50 years; it's because of the spreading of Satan's message and how a generation believed him over God. God's message is about giving and sustaining life, while Satan's message is about murder—taking life and destruction.

"And the earth was without form and void, and darkness was upon the face of the deep. And the Spirit of God moved upon the face of the waters. And God said, Let there be light: and there was light. And God saw the light, that it was good: and God divided the light from the darkness." **Genesis 1:2-4 KJV.**

The power of words and vision is demonstrated through divine examples. What one perceives, says, and believes profoundly impacts one's life. It is essential to be mindful of whose voice one hears. The prevalence of mental illnesses and confusion in today's society is a significant concern. During my tenure at a mental health hospital years ago, I frequently heard patients complain of the multitude of voices in their heads and request that they stop talking to them. The statement above alludes to the notion that disobedience to the devil will result in punishment in the form of physical or psychological distress. It is implied that the devil will inflict harm upon an individual who does not comply with his instructions. This can cause significant suffering and trauma, affecting one's mental and physical well-being. The severity of the punishment is subjective and may vary depending on the individual's interpretation of the devil's voice.

"And when he was come out of the ship, immediately there met him out of the tombs a man with an unclean spirit, who had his dwelling among the tombs. No man could bind him, no, not with chains: because that he had been often bound with fetters and chains, and the chains had been plucked asunder by him, and the fetters broken in pieces: neither could any man tame him. And always, night and day, he was in the mountains and in the tombs, crying and cutting himself with stones.

But when he saw Jesus afar off, he ran and worshipped him, and cried with a loud voice, and said, What have I to do with thee, Jesus, thou Son of the most high God? I adjure thee by God, that thou torment me not, for he said unto him, Come out of the man, thou unclean spirit. And he asked him, What is thy name? And he answered, saying, My name is Legion: for we are many. And he besought him much that he would not send them away out of the country. Now there was there nigh unto the mountains a great herd of swine feeding.

And all the devils besought him, saying, Send us into the swine, that we may enter into them. And forthwith, Jesus gave them leave. And the unclean spirits went out, and entered into the swine: and the herd ran violently down a steep place into the sea (they were about two thousand;) and were choked in the sea."   *Mark 5:2-13 KJV.*

It has been documented that Jesus was the first person to call out the spirits of those who were considered possessed. These spirits were known to be the vices of the individual's mind. The devil has always been able to reside in people and use them to carry out his desires without being seen as the perpetrator. This is in no way an excuse for evil behavior with no accountability. However, it is essential to acknowledge the reality that many people face daily, hearing so many unethical voices that only God can truly comprehend. It is imperative to shed light on this matter to aid in understanding and addressing the issue. Everything is not a demon, but we need to know when it is; we need to call a demon a demon and be the voice to call those spirits out.

Do we honestly believe that God will not use a woman's voice to call out and cast out demons? He will use whomever He's called and anointed for the job. I heard God through a woman's voice when demons were tormenting me. When you are genuinely in trouble and in need of God's help, you wouldn't care who and what it was as long as they have the power and authority to set you free.

* * *

The question of whether women can preach has long been a topic of debate. However, it is worth noting that women have been preaching for centuries, and their contributions have been instrumental in shaping religious communities worldwide. The notion that women cannot preach is rooted in patriarchal beliefs that have historically excluded women from leadership roles in many religious institutions. However, many who recognize women's immense value to the pulpit are increasingly challenging this view. It is important to note that the debate around women preaching is not only a religious issue but also a social one. The exclusion of women from leadership positions in many organizations has been a significant barrier to gender equality and has perpetuated harmful gender stereotypes. Furthermore, research has shown that diverse leadership teams, including those with gender diversity, are more effective and innovative than those that are not.

In conclusion, the question of whether women can preach cannot be answered with a simple yes or no. Women have been preaching for centuries, and their contributions have been invaluable to religious communities. The debate around this issue is important and speaks to more significant questions of gender equality and social justice.

The woman's voice is a beautiful and powerful creation of God, and its unique purpose is beyond human comprehension. No one has the right to question God in choosing her voice as a tool to achieve greater good. Her body, mind, and spirit belong to her God, her Creator. He has chosen her and her voice to use in these last days to crush the head of the serpent and his seed. God is not attacking the woman but the opposite. He has called and ordained the woman to be a voice in these last and evil days to destroy the works of the devil rather than working for him. Don't listen to the voices of these angry, lying prophets trying to silence the woman; these are the same men who have and continue to use her for pleasure. Her attack proves that God has called her to be a voice for his kingdom because if not, why is the devil so mad about her preaching the gospel? You're looking at gender; God is looking for a clean and holy vessel to work through, to allow His voice to be heard.

The following message concerns apostles, prophets, evangelists, teachers, pastors, and bishops. After delivering the message from God to the congregation and witnessing the people's response as they come forward to the altar, it is vital to acknowledge the voice of God that urges you to pray for them and cast out any unclean spirits that may be binding them. It is crucial to note that these individuals cannot deliver themselves, which is why they are present at the altar.

Therefore, hearing a voice suggesting you ask for a monetary contribution in exchange for their breakthrough is concerning. It is pertinent to question whose voice urges you to halt your prayers and appeal for money. Many of these people are in tears, sincerely seeking God's help. Can giving money at this time of spiritual and emotional need help them? Would Jesus himself pause his prayers to request money as a means of achieving one's breakthrough? God knows the ministry needs money; the tithes and offerings had already been collected, but asking at the altar and near the end of the service is the spirit of greed. I have been given the authority to say these things because they need to be told.

It is important to remember Jesus's warning, "If I had not spoken these things to you, you would be without sin, but now your sin remains if you continue to love money and not repent ("The love of money is the root to all evil"). "Woe to you, pastors and prophets who have led my sheep astray." The holy angels will usher you to the judgment seat of Christ, where you will be judged and condemned."

Why…because you listened and obeyed the wrong voice. The man is deceived in these last days; he's eating from the wrong tree and obeying the serpent's voice and is trying to get the woman to eat.

Jesus said, *Don't you believe that I am in the Father and that the Father is in me? The words I say to you I do not speak on my own authority. Rather, it is the Father, living in me, who is doing his work. Believe me when I say that I am in the Father and the Father is in me, or at least believe on the evidence of the works themselves. Very truly, I tell you, whoever believes in me will do the works I have been doing, and they will do even greater things than these because I am going to the Father.* **John 14: 10-12.**

Jesus said, "Not everyone that saith unto me, Lord, Lord, shall enter into the kingdom of heaven; but he that doeth the will of my Father which is in heaven. Many will say to me in that day (Day of Judgment), Lord, Lord, have we not prophesied in thy name? and in thy name have cast out devils? and in thy name done many wonderful works? And then will I profess unto them, I never knew you: depart from me, ye that work iniquity. Matthew 7:21-23 KJV.

Look at how the voices have changed in the past 60 years. See how the message went from uplifting others other than ourselves to everything about getting money, houses, cars, clothes, and jewelry. It went from praising and protecting the woman to openly abusing her and destroying who she is. This opened the door for the enemy to come in and take over on all sides, affecting the next generation's children. Love was replaced with lust.

The enemy came through a fight for rights in one area and went all the way to the left of many other issues that had nothing to do with the initial battle. Once we started celebrating victories prematurely, we lost focus; just like the children of Israel when they were delivered from Pharoah, they became distracted by their newly found freedoms and started worshipping the same gods who had put them into bondage; he did it in disguise.

Listen, people of God, there is a sound, a voice that belongs to God and is God where Heaven and Hell know it; angels and demons recognize it; even death knows this voice. This is why when Jesus was at Lazarus's funeral, he stood before him and shouted, "Lazarus, come forth!" Lazarus came to the mouth of the tomb with no assistance from human beings, although he was wrapped in grave clothes. Even death, hades, and the grave obeyed the voice of God and had to let Lazurus go! Lazarus heard the voice who created him, the voice who had spoken to him before he was in his mother's womb. This Creator's voice is the maker and giver of life. This voice was talking to Lazarus from the worlds on the other side of life that we call death. So you have got to know that the devil and demons recognize and tremble at the sound and presence of this voice. This is the same voice from creation that created everything with His (Word) voice.; we must remember this.

"The enemy will always try to imitate and duplicate what God has done and who God is. This imitation attack is known as false gods. One example is the power of voice in music, which has hurt our world in just one generation.

The next generation will witness the power of voice through AI, which has come to replace real intelligence. However, there is no intelligence greater and smarter than God. It's impressive to know that our intelligence was smart enough to create artificial intelligence, but we must use it wisely, being as wise as serpents yet harmless as doves. The question remains, what will we do with this intelligence aside from serving man and God?"

What voice do you recognize when someone preaches? Is it the voice or the gender that delivers God's message? Is it the messenger or the message that is important? Is it the clean vessel or the dirty vessels that have the connection to host God's word for themselves, regardless of how God wants a holy vessel? Is holiness even a concern anymore, or have we become a form of artificial intelligence preachers? We have no feelings, convictions, or fear of the One who created us. What happens to our fear and respect for God? As long as we preach, we don't worry anymore about the condition of our souls. Is God so desperate for male intelligence that He discriminates against female intelligence? Can a woman preach? Can A.I., of course, if its creator program it to. be programmed by its creator to preach from the Bible? Of course, a robot can. Therefore, if a robot can be programmed by its creator to do or say whatever the creator wants, it should be understood that God, as the creator of male and female, can give His creation the voice and means to preach the gospel. If man is more intelligent than God, of course not, God forbid.

* * *

This is why John the Baptist rebuked the Pharisees and the people. John said to the crowds coming out to be baptized by him, *"You brood of vipers! Who warned you to flee from the coming wrath? Produce fruit in keeping with repentance. And do not begin to say to yourselves, 'We have Abraham as our father.' For I tell you that out of these stones, God can raise up children for Abraham. The ax is already at the root of the trees, and every tree that does not produce good fruit will be cut down and thrown into the fire." God made man from the dust, and the dust thinks it is greater than God; just imagine if He made man out of rocks. Luke 3: 7-9*

As mere mortals, it is difficult to challenge God and believe we can succeed. Just ask Lucifer about it. Unfortunately, some preachers of this generation have been misled into thinking that they can live any way they want and still make it into heaven because they are followers and supporters of God. But like Lucifer, who believed that his good deeds were enough to guarantee his righteousness and peace with God, they, too, are mistaken. Even though he served, praised, and worshipped God, Lucifer's deception led to his downfall; iniquity was in his heart. Where do you think we get, "Depart from me, you workers of iniquity." Lucifer's name was changed to Satan, as he is now called, and his followers, who were once angels, were cast out of heaven and became demons, a species of derogatory. Pastor, prophets, and bishops, are you greater than Jesus? "He who knew no sin became sin and was smitten by God." Jesus did not commit any sin, but by his will and submission to God, he took on our sins. Therefore, becoming sin, God struck down the sins in his flesh, even when it was His own Son.

Are you so deceived into believing that you are so wonderfully satisfying to God that He will forfeit His own will and what He did to His Son for us? If we go into the presence of God with sin, it will be only because of our arrogance, rebellion, and disobedience to God. How disrespectful. Forget going to heaven, and rest in peace; there will be no peace without justice. After death is the judgment. Come on, pastors and gospel artists, is the money, sex, and power that you feel worth losing your souls? We know these warnings are in the Bible, but some need a reminder that God Is Not Dead! Hear the word of the Lord, "Stop ignoring My Voice!

It's important to remember that some people will always hate others and messengers from God, but their hate can only last while we're alive on this earth. Once we pass on, we leave all that behind. Those who have died before us are at peace and living well, while the wicked are constantly perishing. There's no point in hating on people who have already died - it's just a waste of time and energy. Instead, we should learn from those who have gone before us and those who are still here. No matter how rich or poor we are, we can't take our wealth with us when we die. The greatest torment for those who have done evil things for money is that they will NOT enjoy it forever because time is not your friend. However, we must all remember that the remainder of our actions is waiting for us when we look into the mirror, knowing that death has made an appointment with us and it cannot be canceled. Boom!

When you leave this world, you will be with Abraham, Isaac, or Jacob; it will not be Moses and the prophets that you will see; it will be the Lord Jesus, the Holy angels, and those who were sent to you in your lifetime and timeline warning you of the destruction to come if you Do Not Repent?!

How I express myself through written and verbal means does not indicate any political ambitions or an attempt to evade accountability. Furthermore, I do not seek to gather votes or followers. I request that individuals who do not share my adherence to the principles of Christ kindly refrain from seeking me out as a source of guidance.

Do you know Jesus was the first to break records in followers without social media, technology, posters, television, or other means besides "word of mouth?" When Jesus started his ministry, he said, "Follow me." This was the beginning of souls being snatched out of hell and the hands of the devil. When Satan started his counter ministry to destroy lives and souls, he said everywhere you look and turn, " Follow me and like me." He is the copycat of God, just the dark version of the real. Who's voice are you following? Who are you listening to regularly? Whoever it is, they are the architect of your life or death; either they are giving to you or taking away, telling you the truth or lying to you, feeding your egos by telling you what they've studied that the masses want to hear. Who are you listening to right at this moment? Because by reading this book, God is speaking to you. "Choose ye this day who you will serve? If God is God, choose Him, but if not, choose any other gods available to you who speak to your agenda, but by no means should you try to serve two masters, God and money.

I am compelled to tell any preacher, but to the woman, don't disappoint God as men have by being unfaithful in your marriages, preaching for money and prestige, and taking your panties down as some form of celebration for preaching a good word. Keep your dignity and integrity. Don't let anyone throw dirt on you so they can have dirt on you when all you are trying to do is answer your calling from God and do His will. BE HOLY!

Lucifer was replaced, and now it's happening again. God will replace those of us who choose idol gods over Him. "In the day of your troubles, call on the gods you served." How long will we cover iniquity? Iniquity is the sin of all sins because those who commit them know the word and do them anyway. Those who know God's word often overthink themselves. If we are supposed to be the lights of the world, why does the church feel the need to be like the world? Somebody's not the body of Christ. The Body is sick and needs healing, so judgment is coming to the church first. If we truly loved the Lord, why would we bring to Him as an offering or worship the very things and beings He kicked out of heaven? What is it? Do we think God is incapable of getting in touch with Satan without our assistance? How arrogant of us! I say, "We owe God an apology and repentance. Who told you that you were naked? Who told you that you are anointed? Who anointed you to use your anointing skillfully to sin against God? King Saul was anointed, but at the same time, God rejected him and allowed him to keep the anointing.

As anointed leaders - male or female - we have been entrusted with a divine responsibility. This responsibility involves managing the voices that guide us and inspiring others, always considering that God is the ultimate Voice! Did you know that a higher level is available to you if you pass the test on managing your anointing? That level is glory! However, God will never trust us with His glory if we prostitute our anointing. The anointing is not enough for all the troubles we presently have in this world; we need God's glory. Jesus even asked God for the God he once had when he was with God before the foundations of the world. It was the glory of God that got Lazarus out of the grave. It was the glory that resurrected Jesus from the grave.

* * *

"I urge leaders to understand that if we are tainted by greed and lust, we will never gain the trust of God's glory. I speak with the authority given to me, and the devil is aware of it, too. I have been ordained, anointed, and appointed to reveal the things that I speak of and have gone to hell and back to do so.

It is important to remember that before the preacher begins to speak, the time has been allocated to worship and honor God in all forms of giving, including monetary, praise, singing, music, and worship. Therefore, please refrain from bringing gifts or offerings to the stage/pulpit while the preacher is speaking. It is disrespectful to our God and considered idolatry and worship of self. Instead, wait until the preacher is finished preaching before making any offerings. These are ancient rituals to bring money to the altar while the preacher is preaching and they come with a spirit that loves money and self-glory. This used to include blood sacrifices from babies or children along with sexual perversions. The idol god worship would have monetary gifts given to the god they could see. We love to worship what we can see but lack the knowledge or understanding of idolatry. The Most High God does not want money mixed with His people who are at the altar crying for help and needing God to save them and deliver them from evil. For some, this may be the last time they attempt to find God, and a preacher blew because of their greed for money. Where are the (pastors) shepherds who will feed God's sheep? It's starting to make sense that when Jesus was born, the angels appeared to the shepherds who were in the fields at night caring for their sheep. The angels didn't even go to the temple to announce to the priests because it was obvious they were profane. They did not care about the sheep, they were in it for the money and lifestyle.

In the context of a kingdom, it is important to follow certain protocols. For instance, you should never approach the king while he is speaking, especially if you have something in your hands, without first seeking permission or speaking to him. Failure to follow this rule could have serious consequences, including loss of life. Similarly, if God is present and speaking through a preacher, it is important to show Him respect by not having any other gods before Him. Therefore, you should not have anything in your hands when approaching the altar if it is not offering time. Instead, it is appropriate to come to the altar with the gift of a repentant heart during preaching. This is a time to present yourself to God, not to make a monetary offering.

This type of offering was used in satanic worship in the offering up of idols (anything tangible with value/ substance) along with blood (usually a baby) and mostly some sexual or seductive type of offering. This is why a lot of preachers desire sex when they finish preaching; this is a demonic spirit of seduction and desire. We gave these spirits access when we moved towards the altar to give to idol gods; we summoned the gods of pleasure. The pleasure that a payday brings is eating, buying, speaking, and celebrating. All the things that come with the mood swings of a big payday.

When an exotic dancer/stripper dances for their audience, the sign of how well they are doing is acknowledged by how much money is given to the stage. People will bring monetary gifts(money) and throw them on the stage for her to go even deeper in her dancing of seduction. The more you give, the more she reveals and seduces…it's a spirit, not the Holy Spirit. She will finish her dance, then collect her offerings and count her money behind the scenes to see how well she did. The amount she received lets her know how seductive and enticing she was. Don't you know when she was dancing, voices were telling her what to do, how to do it, who to connect with, and who was the biggest giver?

We, as the church, must acknowledge that we have allowed the devil to infiltrate our churches. As a result, the church has lost its power. We must ask ourselves, what's the point of having the Holy Ghost if we are going to allow the devil to feel comfortable in God's House? In the Strip Club, Satan has us worshiping him through exotic dancers. I used to go there years ago and was ignorant of the devil's schemes. However, in the church, it's Lucifer who has us worshiping him through any means and all accounts. Both

Satan and Lucifer are the same devils, seeking worship from the world and the church. It's important to recognize that the devil is a thief.

So to the women God has called, Don't use your calling from God and prostitute your anointing or the gospel. God will have people to help you and give offerings to support your ministry. God has ordained it to be, "The laborer is worthy of her pay." This is the word and order from God, but do not seduce God's people by coming up with all of those satanic ways to get money, especially at the altar call. The altar call is when God wants to minister to His people, meaning the Shepherd is tending, healing, and comforting His sheep, not trying to get something else out of the sheep. We have been taught by leaders who were anointed but had been taken to the mountain by the devil and failed the tests of lusts and pride, who privately bowed down to the devil. In turn, they were taught by Lucifer how to pervert true worship to God. Lucifer knows the protocols of the kingdom; he used to live there and was in charge of worship. Then, who better to teach the church perverted worship? Did Jesus or his apostles ever preach and say," Come and put money in my hands because God has a word for you?" This implies that the person won't receive this personal word if they don't give the extra money. This is a seducing spirit.

We were so busy looking for Satan and the devil that we didn't realize we had given Lucifer (fallen angel of light) the High Seat in the temple, rendering our praise, worship, and preaching. Let me be clear: I am not saying all preachers have done this with the intent to deceive; what I am saying is it is wrong by any means. Many leaders have been taught how to raise offerings and even ask for money at the altar, but what I am saying is that the false prophet knows precisely what they are doing, and they are seducing you. I make no apologies to the devil and his agents. We have been seduced by listening to the wrong voices. As a people and church, we must admit to our wrongs and repent for our sins because we have lost our way. This is the only way we are going to have Revival. When Jesus said, ***"I AM the Way, The Truth, and The Life."***

Do you know what makes a great liar? When the liar knows all the facts, they know the truth and decide to lie. They can create their own narrative because without the other parties knowing the facts, they cannot successfully dispute the liar who knows the truth. The Devil created a narrative opposing God with the truth he knows about God, the kingdom, eternal life, and heaven. He knows that, as humans, we are constantly trying to figure things out. As children of God, it's important to remember that seeking acceptance from the world is a futile pursuit. The devil is incapable of love and loyalty, and his only allegiance is to himself. We must be vigilant against the many voices that tempt us daily, leading us away from God's will and our true purpose.

* * *

Let us pray, in the name of Jesus, for the strength to silence those voices and to remain honest about our struggles and fears. We must rebuke the evil forces seeking to destroy us and our families and fortify ourselves with God's shield around our hearts and minds. With so many voices vying for our attention, we must remember that there is only one voice we can trust, and that is the voice of God. Let us make intelligent decisions based on His guidance and seek salvation from the voices that seek to lead us astray. With gratitude, Lord Jesus, we thank you in advance for saving us from the perils of temptation and guiding us towards the light of your love. Amen.

We must strive to achieve absolute excellence by listening with discernment and wisdom to fulfill our sacred duty with utmost integrity and honor. In a world where numerous voices seek to undermine us, we cannot afford to be The Voices that people cannot trust. Instead, we should aim to be the voice that brings answers and solace by being the voice of the Resurrected Christ who only obeys the voice of God. May we, therefore, endeavor to spread the gospel of the kingdom, lifting the name of Jesus Christ, our Lord and King. May the peace of God be a gift to you and a blessing to all of our brothers and sisters who love God and are in Christ. No, this truth: while you are waiting on what God has promised you, there will be many other voices trying to get you to do things outside of what He has told you to do. Stay focused and be confident in knowing that you have paid the price to have your relationship with God and know His voice.

When you are a true prophet from God, He will give you some prophecies that will manifest immediately, and some will take years to come to pass. This happens with all true prophets. Some have taken hundreds of years, some thousands of years, because the generation it was spoken to doen't see it, it doesn't mean it didn't come from God. Such as Daniel, David, Jeremiah, Ezekiel, Isaiah, and even Jesus, to mention a few. There are times when God will give you prophecies of grandeur statue and may send warnings. People, most of the time, reject these prophecies because they don't line up with the flesh. Then, the prophet is rejected and called a false prophet. This voice becomes the amination through weak and carnal vessels to smear the name and reputation of the true prophet.

False prophets use immediate gratification prophecies to allure gullible and vulnerable people. They come to a town like a gypsy with a potion show, where they demonstrate the strength of their potion. They have a rehearsed show of a weak man drinking a powerful potion and then overpowering a strong man. With false prophets, they may tell you things they shouldn't know, like your name, address, or a lost family member, and pretend that they have a gift to share with you. In reality, they have a team that does their research and targets you. They look for reactions and prey on people for money. The more significant the reaction, the more they will ask for. However, it is worth noting that there are some gifted witches with authentic gifts, but they use them for dark purposes.

The purpose of this is for you and the spectators to believe that God has spoken through them. They are working on gaining your trust in a short period of time. The misfortune of this, in conclusion, if they had any doubt, they would look to their pastors who brought these false prophets into the church in the first place. The false prophet will surely give the pastor a great prophecy of monetary gain and praise them for being favored by God. False prophets are cunning individuals who manipulate people's beliefs for their own gain. They often use pastors as their endorsement to seem more credible. These false prophets have no fear of God and are only interested in sharing in the offerings collected from people's bank accounts. It's important that we do not allow these deceitful individuals to gain power over us and instead hold them accountable for their actions. Let us stand together against these wicked people and protect our faith from their harmful influence.

People often tend to seek out prophets who will tell them what they want to hear rather than what God has actually said. Unfortunately, many of these people end up losing their lives because they put their trust in false prophets who gave them false hope and led them to become prideful. They believed that they were too righteous and favored by God to repent. This false narrative has caused irreparable damage to the church and has led to infidelities. False prophets have led people astray and created a clique of transgressors who, despite being anointed, are equally rejected. These leaders are often fueled by listening and obeying the wrong voices, which tells them that they are blessed and highly favored by God. People continue to follow and give to these false prophets, which only encourages them to continue along their path. This is what happened to King Saul, who continued in his wicked ways for over 20 years despite being rejected by God. He was fueled by the belief that he was God's anointed, and he did not have a prophet like Samuel to tell him otherwise. It is essential to listen to the true voice of God and not be swayed by false prophets who offer false hope.

Saul even had supporters and assistance in trying to kill David to prevent the prophecy from coming to pass, with David being king. These people are so deceived, allowing a leader to think they have the power to stop God's plans. How can you ride on the fact that you are anointed but think you have the power and authority to stop another one's anointing? Didn't both of you get your anointing from God? The arrogant one will say to the others, the famous scripture, "Touch not My anointed, and do My prophets no harm." 1 Chronicles 16: 22, which is being used way out of context from what God was talking about;

this has to do with God's covenant for His people, not some greedy, selfish, and manipulative pastor. All the while, these false prophets have blood on their hands from the people of God and His true prophets, whom they have abused and killed. Sadly, they have been listening to the wrong voices for so long that they have deceived themselves into believing it's the voice of God telling them to do these transgressions. The devil is their father, no doubt, and he has made his voice sound like God. Lucifer is a liar and their Artificial Intelligence has studied God's voice and duplicated it. But he cannot fool God's very elect; this is why they are hated because know their Father's voice.

When you know that you know God gave you a word to speak, the enemy will definitely speak to you in many voices in hopes you will not do what God has told you to do. Don't be afraid of them or intimidated; they are flesh and bones with an expiration date stamped on them. Don't preach seeking the reactions of people or weigh God's word because you don't want to offend anyone. If you are going to preach, you must stay dedicated and faithful to God, remembering that He is the one who called you and anointed you. Do not sell out to the masses for open doors; those voices will talk you out of the will of God and His favor.

Do not let the lure of popularity or fame sway you from your divine purpose. Those panicking voices speaking within are not of God. God has never had a 911…He is the 911! Know and understand that His voice is steady and calm speaking to you unless He is driven to judgment and warning because of rebellion and disobedience. So, if you hear any voices that do not align with your godly values or divine message, recognize them as the enemy's attempt to derail you from your path. Stay strong, and trust in God's plan for you.

Every day, we are bombarded with countless voices. But which ones truly have our best interests at heart? To make the right decisions for ourselves and our loved ones, we must be able to discern between the voices that uplift us and those that tear us down. It's a difficult task, but it's essential for our well-being. So, take a moment to ask yourself, "Who am I listening to right now?" As you read these words, consider the voices that are shaping your thoughts and actions. Choose wisely, and remember that you have the power to silence the negative voices and amplify the positive ones.

Imagine Me

Chapter 6

How can someone explain the unexplainable? Some things God gives you are not for everybody... at least not at the time. How many accounts, even among people who claim to serve God and believe in Him, have a problem believing someone had an encounter with angels? Well, people are having encounters with demons every day! It is amazing how many times people have lost their faith because they had a divine experience and may have heard something prophetic or futuristic and are excited about it. Nothing seems to happen, especially the way they expected it, and they become discouraged and disappointed.

Mary is engaged to Joseph and there is excitement in the air about the wedding. They are planning to be married, most likely around harvest time. This is a time when prosperity is in the air and people are excited about the season. What a perfect time for the joining of two people to love one another for a lifetime. There is no greater celebration among the Israelite people than a wedding.

Joseph and Mary are residents of Nazareth. Joseph

speaks to the local Priest/Rabbi as their custom would be about the wedding and the arrangements and what family his betrothed is from.

Before Jesus went to the cross, salvation was based on the law, which meant that Gentile pastors and preachers were not allowed to handle God's word or preach from it. However, after Jesus' ascension, He sent the Holy Spirit to empower His followers and gave them the great commission to go into all the world and preach the gospel of the kingdom.

Before the dispensation of grace, the law was the only way to salvation, and it was given to Moses, not to a people outside of the seed of Abraham and the people He made a covenant with. However, when Jesus was on earth, He said that the message had to be preached to the Jews first since Israel was God's chosen people.

These twelve Jesus sent out, instructing them, "Go nowhere among the Gentiles and enter no town of the Samaritans but go rather to the lost sheep of the house of Israel. And proclaim as you go, saying, The kingdom of heaven is at hand.' Mathew 10:5-7.

So, Jesus was setting boundaries, outlining where this message should be preached. When Jesus was asked to do certain things, he would often respond and say, "It is not my time." It's important to know when it's your time so the timing doesn't confuse whether God will bless you.

Although there was a time when Gentiles could not preach the gospel or touch God's word, because of God's mercy and grace shown through Jesus Christ, now I have His Holy Spirit, and the gospel is being preached to me and my people. So, imagine me standing before looking for recognition and reward for standing in the way of anyone to preach the gospel. Paul said, "I can preach to others and myself be a castaway." This suggests that people know when they are fake and deceiving, preaching for the wrong reason. God will be their judge; I am not God.

Imagine me being free to preach around the world even as a gentile because of the work Jesus did at the cross. The concern is that any such bias would be akin to the actions of King Saul as described in the Bible. King Saul, the first king of Israel, was known for his attempts to stifle David's anointing and prevent his rise to power. The author suggests that any attempt to stifle the anointing of women in the church or ministry would be similar to King Saul's actions, actions of trying to stop or kill David and, therefore, completely unacceptable, especially being Gentile leaders.

However, it is not my place to impede anyone's anointing, as only God has the power to anoint. If someone claims to have been called and anointed by God to preach the gospel of the kingdom, then I must have the wisdom to respect their calling, as we can learn from the records left behind by the patriarchs. If I am unwilling to support them, then I must leave them be.

"Imagine me: using God's holy word to justify me but condemn others" seems to be a thought-provoking statement that highlights the issue of religious hypocrisy. It talks about a scenario where an individual is using the holy scriptures to justify their own actions and beliefs while at the same time condemning others who don't align with their ideology. This kind of behavior is not only unfair but also contradicts the very essence of religious teachings that promote love, tolerance, and acceptance. Imagine me being saved by grace but blocking anyone from the same grace.

The following excerpt invites the reader to reflect on the importance of upholding values such as equality and fairness in various spheres of life. Imagine Me contemplates the significance of applying biblical principles in everyday actions and interactions, particularly in instances where one's actions or beliefs might appear contradictory or hypocritical.

Imagine Me invites readers to imagine a scenario in which one uses religious texts to assert their freedom whilst simultaneously denying others the same freedom. The author highlights the importance of recognizing the value of all individuals through applying Christian principles and avoiding discrimination or inequality.

We as pastors and preachers should expound on the significance of acknowledging and valuing the contributions of women in diverse environments, including the establishment of families, churches, and enterprises, and the imperative to abstain from restricting their opportunities predicated on gender. By recognizing and celebrating the capabilities of women, we can create a more inclusive and equitable society that benefits us all. It is essential to appreciate the worth of women's contributions and to avoid gender-based discrimination that can undermine their potential and limit their opportunities for growth. Imagine a scenario where a woman of faith feels inadequate.

Imagine Me being the reason why someone who loves the Lord and wants to fulfill their calling cannot do so. If I were the one who blocked and sabotaged them, it would be a terrible thing. As Jesus said, "If you love me, you will keep my sayings," so preventing someone from following their calling would be a great injustice. Imagine thinking you're better than someone else in the name of Jesus. Imagine Me: I lied to Jesus using scripture and the law to have Jesus killed and thinking I was doing God a service. Imagine Me screaming, crucifying him, when Pontius Pilot was trying to find a way to let Jesus go free.

Image Me standing before God on that day to find out that when I abused them, I was abusing Jesus.

Imagine Me, the high priest who had Jesus arrested and brought before me and my counsel to judge Jesus and ask him to prove that he was the son of God.

Imagine Me living in a palace where Jesus had no home and looked down on him like a peasant.

Imagine Me is the sexist, racist, and biased bigot who preaches in God's name and thinks like the Pharisees that I am the apple of God's eye.

Imagine Me not thinking that one day I will give an account to God for the life that I lived.

Imagine Me hating people and being cruel to them and thinking I deserve God's love.

"For though we walk in the flesh, we do not war after the flesh: (For the weapons of our warfare are not carnal, but mighty through God to the pulling down of strongholds."

Casting down imaginations, and every high thing that exalteth itself against the knowledge of God, and bringing into captivity every thought to the obedience of Christ; And having in a readiness to revenge all disobedience, when your obedience is fulfilled.

Do ye look on things after the outward appearance? If any man trusts to himself that he is Christ's, let him of himself think this again, that, as he is Christ's, even so, are we Christ's. For though I should boast somewhat more of our authority, which the Lord hath given us for edification, and not for your destruction, I should not be ashamed: That I may not seem as if I would terrify you by letters. For his letters, say they, are weighty and powerful, but his bodily presence is weak, and his speech contemptible. Let such a one think this, that, such as we are in word by letters when we are absent, such will we be also in deed when we are present. **2 Corinthians 10:5**

Imagine getting a word from God telling you how blessed you're going to be and the excitement of anticipation, only to find yourself fighting for your life and feeling like you are cursed. But when you remind yourself of who God is and what It is believed by some that only Lucifer, the fallen angel, can justify being unfaithful to God and one's spouse. Some argue that those who preach and take on roles as Christian leaders should confront the temptations that come with their positions. According to Jesus' example, one should not take on such roles without having been tempted in the areas of lust of the flesh, lust of the eye, and pride of life. These three sins are considered to be the foundational sins of Lucifer, which were found in his heart under the umbrella of iniquity.

Only Lucifer, the fallen angel, can justify being unfaithful to God and one's spouse. Some argue that those who preach and take on roles as Christian leaders should confront the temptations that come with their positions. According to Jesus' example, one should not take on such roles without having been tempted in the areas of lust of the flesh, lust of the eye, and pride of life. These three sins are considered to be the foundational sins of Lucifer...the root, which were found in his heart under the umbrella of iniquity.

The Wicked may seem to be prospering, but only for a season. Every enemy has an expiration date stamped to their soul. No one gets away with anything. This is why it was imperative for the kingdom's message of repentance to be preached; this was done before and during Jesus' ministry. "Prepare and make the crooked way straight." This message should tell us something. In these last days, the enemy has deceived the man just as he deceived Eve in the garden. The difference with Eve is that she did not have the teaching, temple, or pastors and the word of God to combat the enemy.

What in the world is going on when we have access to so many messages, churches everywhere, and bible teachers around the globe? If all fails, YouTube. So what is the man's excuse for fulfilling the" lust of the flesh, the lust of the eye, and the pride of life." You're talking about pride. God says He cannot stand a proud look." Pride was the cause of the fall of the angels who lost their place in heaven. Most times, we remember people for their mistakes and where they made them. When we repent and turn away from our sins, God forgives our sins, "He casts them in the sea of forgetfulness to remember no more."

When God calls you to do something, He prepares you divinely for that something, even if you do not feel divine intervention. He will give you a Rhama word; it has not yet been proven, and sometimes it takes years to be proven. But know this: that word is connected to God's divine will and that word will come to pass. You might not even be around when that word is proven at its fullest, but nonetheless, something inside tells you just to do what God has said to do. There is a price to pay for your obedience to God; you will go through pain trying to do it. You will hurt and lose some things along the way and people, but you have to do it anyway.

That's why, after death, is the judgment because they are things that Lucifer has done in eternity that have manifested in time and have presented themselves and unfolded as wicked and evil. We have bought into the delusion of rest in peace. You can't rest somebody's bones and body, but you cannot rest their soul. After death is the judgment; the whole purpose of us even being in this world is because of what took place in eternity. We are in time for the manifestation so it can be annihilated and it can be judged blotted out; never to return to heaven again, we need to wake up.

We have preaches that think that they can do whatever they want to do and not be accountable; there is no rest in peace that is not biblical. That is not God's word. The devil spun that lie is OK for the world to believe, but is something wrong with believers stepping outside of God's world and saying rest in peace when Jesus says I am the resurrection when Jesus said man was appointed and wants to die, and after death is the judgment what part are we missing because we're not accountable then guess what we don't have to be all concerned with what we do because as long as we don't get caught, we think we got away with it, but the truth of the matter is whether the angels show up or not God is watching.

Imagine me telling God I don't like His rules and judgments, but I like His blessings and the loved ones He's given me. I might as well tell Him how I don't think He's fair and we should vote on some things…well, everything; surely He can understand how I feel; I am an American.

Imagine me thinking that I am God because of all that I have accomplished to find out when it's all said and done; I have no power over death and have to leave behind all that I worked for and worshiped. I want to stay but have no godly authority to stop the process of my departure, and what's said is, when you don't know where you're going when you leave here when you were the one preaching to others about God, Jesus, and the Holy Spirit. And They called you, The GOAT" Do you believe this crap? Now it's time to face The Almighty Sovereign God. I can't help but wonder, what will God call you? Imagine me?

By What Authority

Chapter 7

If you believe that God has called you to preach, then you should preach without hesitation. Remember, on the day you depart from this world, you will be accountable to God, not men. Don't refrain from preaching what God has commanded you to preach just because someone else discourages you. As those who have been chosen before you, you will undoubtedly face questions about your authority. However, you must have confidence in the Holy Spirit to guide and direct you, even if others don't understand the story behind it. Trust in the power and authority that God has bestowed upon you to fulfill His will.

John is an example that no matter how great the calling, people of power and position will challenge your authority and by what authority you do what you do if it does not meet their approval. As much as the Pharisees studied the Law and the Prophets, knowing God said he would send his prophet Elijah, but when it happened, they rejected it. They knew and studied the prophecies. This is one of the last things recorded that the prophet Malachi said,

"They will be mine," says the Lord Almighty, "in the day

when I make up my treasured possession. I will spare them, just as in compassion a man spares his son who serves him. And you will again see the distinction between the righteous and the wicked, between those who serve God and those who do not.

"Surely the day is coming; it will burn like a furnace. All the arrogant and every evildoer will be stubble, and that day that is coming will set them on fire," says the Lord Almighty. "Not a root or a branch will be left to them. But for you who revere my name, the sun of righteousness will rise with healing in its wings.

And you will go out and leap like calves released from the stall. Then you will trample down the wicked; they will be ashes under the soles of your feet on the day when I do these things," says the Lord Almighty. "Remember the law of my servant Moses, the decrees and laws I gave him at Horeb for all Israel. "See, I will send you the prophet Elijah before that great and dreadful day of the Lord comes. He will turn the hearts of the fathers to their children, and the hearts of the children to their fathers, or else I will come and strike the land with a curse."

John's birth circumstances were extraordinary. His father, a priest, was well-versed in prophecy and the Law of Moses since he and his wife belonged to the same tribe of Aaron and Moses - the tribe of Levi. They waited for 400 years for the prophecy of the prophet Elijah to come true, but when it finally did, they were unprepared for it. When God chooses someone for a divine plan, the stakes can be high, making it challenging to comprehend. During the fulfillment of the prophecy, the circumstances are rarely perfect, so it is essential to pay attention to the unusual.

The Birth of John The Baptist Foretold

In the time of Herod, king of Judea, there was a priest named Zechariah, who belonged to the priestly division of Abijah; his wife Elizabeth was also a descendant of Aaron. Both of them were upright in the sight of God, observing all the Lord's commandments and regulations blamelessly. But they had no children because Elizabeth was barren, and they were both well along in years.

Once when Zechariah's division was on duty and he was serving as priest before God, he was chosen by lot, according to the custom of the priesthood, to go into the temple of the Lord and burn incense. And when the time for the burning of incense came, all the assembled worshipers were praying outside. Then an angel of the Lord appeared to him, standing at the right side of the altar of incense.

When Zechariah saw him, he was startled and was gripped with fear. But the angel said to him: "Do not be afraid, Zechariah; your prayer has been heard. Your wife Elizabeth will bear you a son, and you are to give him the name John. He will be a joy and delight to you, and many will rejoice because of his birth, for he will be great in the sight of the Lord. He is never to take wine or other fermented drink, and he will be filled with the Holy Spirit even from birth.

Many of the people of Israel will he bring back to the Lord their God. And he will go on before the Lord, in the spirit and power of Elijah, to turn the hearts of the fathers to their children and the disobedient to the wisdom of the righteous—to make ready a people prepared for the Lord."

Zechariah asked the angel, "How can I be sure of this? I am an old man and my wife is well along in years." The angel answered, "I am Gabriel. I stand in the presence of God, and I have been sent to speak to you and to tell you this good news. And now you will be silent and not able to speak until the day this happens because you did not believe my words, which will come true at their proper time." Meanwhile, the people were waiting for Zechariah and wondering why he stayed so long in the temple.

When he came out, he could not speak to them. They realized he had seen a vision in the temple, for he kept making signs to them but remained unable to speak. When his time of service was completed, he returned home. After this his wife Elizabeth became pregnant and for five months remained in seclusion. "The Lord has done this for me," she said. "In these days, he has shown his favor and taken away my disgrace among the people."

In the sixth month, God sent the angel Gabriel to Nazareth, a town in Galilee, to a virgin who pledged to be married to a man named Joseph, a descendant of David. The virgin's name was Mary. Luke 1:5-27

The people of Israel are known as His chosen people. They established the priestly order in the wilderness after their miraculous deliverance for Pharoah and Egypt. Moses set up the Levitical Priest and the Tabernacle, and it was in effect even during the time of the birth of John the Baptist. They are waiting desperately for the fulfillment of the prophecy. Two things must occur: the prophet Elijah must come as the forerunner and make the crooked paths straight for the Lord to come.

The Birth of John the Baptist, *Luke 1:57-80*

When it was time for Elizabeth to have her baby, she gave birth to a son. Her neighbors and relatives heard that the Lord had shown her great mercy, and they shared her joy. On the eighth day, they came to circumcise the child, and they were going to name him after his father, Zechariah, but his mother spoke up and said, "No! He is to be called John." They said to her, "There is no one among your relatives who has that name." Then, they made signs to his father to find out what he would like to name the child. He asked for a writing tablet, and to everyone's astonishment, he wrote, "His name is John." Immediately, his mouth was opened, and his tongue was loosed, and he began to speak, praising God. The neighbors were all filled with awe, and people were talking about all these things throughout the hill country of Judea. Everyone who heard this wondered about it, asking, "What then is this child going to be?"

For the Lord's hand was with him. His father, Zechariah, was filled with the Holy Spirit and prophesied: "Praise be to the Lord, the God of Israel because he has come and has redeemed his people. He has raised up a horn of salvation for us in the house of his servant David (as he said through his holy prophets of long ago), salvation from our enemies and from the hand of all who hate us– to show mercy to our fathers and to remember his holy covenant, the oath he swore to our father Abraham: to rescue us from the hand of our enemies, and to enable us to serve him without fear in holiness and righteousness before him all our days. "And you, my child, will be called a prophet of the Most High; for you will go on before the Lord to prepare the way for him, to give his people the knowledge of salvation through the forgiveness of their sins, because of the tender mercy of our God, by which the rising sun will come to us from heaven to shine on those living in darkness and in the shadow of death, to guide our feet into the path of peace." And the child grew and became strong in spirit, and he lived in the desert until he appeared publicly to Israel.

It's Not What It Looks Like

It is common for individuals to pray to a God with a specific outcome in mind, only to find that the answer they receive differs from their original expectation. If we are not mindful, we may overlook this answer and continue to wait for one that aligns with our imagined outcome. This tendency can result in missed opportunities and overlooked blessings. Recognizing that many answered prayers have been disregarded due to preconceived notions, leading to unintended consequences, is essential. It is crucial to approach every situation with an open mind, discerning what needs to be embraced and what needs to be rejected. While not all situations may be attributed to negative influences, it is essential to recognize when they are and to seek guidance from the Lord.

It is prudent to seek divine intervention when making decisions that impact our lives. One should be vigilant and discerning when evaluating the actions and intentions of others, seeking guidance from God if there is any doubt. Ultimately, we can trust in the power of the Holy Spirit and our faith and rely on our beliefs to guide us toward the right path.

John the Baptist Prepares the Way *Luke 3:1-20*

In the fifteenth year of the reign of Tiberius Caesar—when Pontius Pilate was governor of Judea, Herod tetrarch of Galilee, his brother Philip tetrarch of Iturea and Traconitis, and Lysanias tetrarch of Abilene— during the high priesthood of Annas and Caiaphas, the word of God came to John son of Zechariah in the desert. He went into all the country around the Jordan, preaching a baptism of repentance for the forgiveness of sins. As is written in the book of the words of Isaiah the prophet:
"A voice of one calling in the desert,
'Prepare the way for the Lord, make straight paths for him. Every valley shall be filled in, every mountain and hill made low. The crooked roads shall become straight, the rough ways smooth. And all mankind will see God's salvation.'
" John said to the crowds coming out to be baptized by him, "You brood of vipers! Who warned you to flee from the coming

wrath? Produce fruit in keeping with repentance. And do not begin to say to yourselves, 'We have Abraham as our father.' For I tell you that out of these stones, God can raise up children for Abraham. The ax is already at the root of the trees, and every tree that does not produce good fruit will be cut down and thrown into the fire." "What should we do then?" the crowd asked. John answered, "The man with two tunics should share with him who has none, and the one who has food should do the same." Tax collectors also came to be baptized. "Teacher," they asked, "what should we do?" "Don't collect any more than you are required to," he told them.

Then some soldiers asked him, "And what should we do? He replied, "Don't extort money, and don't accuse people falsely—be content with your pay." The people were waiting expectantly and were all wondering in their hearts if John might possibly be the Christ. John answered them all, "I baptize you with water. But one more powerful than I will come, the thongs of whose sandals I am not worthy to untie. He will baptize you with the Holy Spirit and with fire. His winnowing fork is in his hand to clear his threshing floor and to gather the wheat into his barn, but he will burn up the chaff with unquenchable fire." And with many other words, John exhorted the people and preached the good news to them. But when John rebuked Herod the Tetrarch because of Herodias, his brother's wife, and all the other evil things he had done, Herod added this to them all: He locked John up in prison.

The Misappropriation of Authority.
John the Baptist knew who he was and what his

purpose was in this world. His message of repentance was without bias or prejudice. John was very focused and consistent with his message from God. John condemned the marriage of Herod and Herodias according to the Law of Moses. Herod feared John, believing him to be a true prophet, but Herodius was determined to have him put to death. Because of John, they would eventually get a divorce because John publicly denounced their marriage as illegal, according to Moses. Herod had such a strong lust for Salome, who was his brother's daughter, even much so that Herodius would use it against him and ultimately have John arrested and executed.

Salome (flourished 1st century CE), according to the Jewish historian Josephus, the daughter of Herodias and stepdaughter of Herod Antipas, tetrarch (ruler appointed by Rome) of Galilee, a region in Palestine. In Biblical literature, she is remembered as the immediate agent in the execution of John the Baptist. Josephus states that she was twice married, first to the tetrarch Philip (a half-brother of her father, Herod Philip, and a son of Herod I the Great) and then to Aristobulus (son of Herod of Chalcis). She is not to be confused with Salome, sister of Herod I the Great.

The Gospels of Mark (6:14–29) and Matthew (14:1–12) account for the imprisonment and eventual beheading of John the Baptist by Herod Antipas. This was primarily due to John's condemnation of Herod's marriage to Herodias, who was the divorced wife of his half-brother, Herod

Philip. This marriage was in violation of Mosaic Law. Despite his fear of the popular prophet's supporters, Herod was persuaded to imprison John by Herodias. During a festival, Salome, the daughter of Herodias, danced before Herod and his guests. Delighted, Herod promised to grant her any request she made. At the behest of her mother, Salome asked for the head of John the Baptist on a platter, as she was infuriated by John's condemnation of her mother's marriage to Herod. Herod, who was reluctant to carry out the execution, was forced to fulfill his promise by his oath. Salome then presented the platter with the severed head of John the Baptist to her mother.

King Herod did not like John's message of repentance. He knew the Law of Moses as well as the prophets but wanted to continue in his sin of being married to his brother's wife and lusting after his brother's daughter, who was his own niece. Herod was filled with lust and did not like being called out on it and neither did Herodias, knowing her husband was alive in the next country.

By What Authority did King Herod and Herodias do these sinful, lustful, and ungodly things?

It is not uncommon for individuals of authority to impede or undermine an individual whom God has chosen to elevate to a higher level or position in society. It requires a person in a position of power to acknowledge the authority of another. While they may acknowledge the anointing of an individual, their own ego may cause them to believe that they can prevent the next move of God if they feel that the person called to lead will surpass them. It is important to remember that, regardless of our actions, we all have an expiration date. God's plan is eternal, and our role in it is vital. It is crucial to avoid falling into the trap of bullying, as this is a trait shared by both Lucifer and Jezebel. We should recall when John the Baptist's followers informed him that the one he had baptized (Jesus) was baptizing on the other side of the Jordan. John's response was, "He must increase, while I decrease."

Someone is afraid of God increasing you. You never have to manipulate, sabotage, or lose your integrity for what God has ordained for you to be and have. Just continue to be faithful, humble, and focused on God's will for your life, and be blessed. Remember how King Saul tried to stop David? He used David and his anointing to fight the enemies he feared, but he had no problem-fighting David.

Similar to today, church leaders have no problem fighting other church leaders but are afraid to go outside of those walls to fight the true enemies of God and the destroyers of their children and future. Saul wasted valuable time and military power trying to stop David from achieving his divine purpose and destiny rather than fighting his true enemies who were seeking to annihilate him and Israel as a nation. Saul hunted David for over ten years to prevent the prophecy from coming to fruition. So, by what authority was Saul operating? The same prophet, Samuel, whom God used to anoint Saul as king, was the same prophet God used to anoint David as the future king. When God gives us a direct order and uses it for the anointing He gave us, He will make an example out of us and replace us. Sometimes, because it may take decades, it doesn't mean God has forgotten the unrepented sins. God's word will not return to Him void. Saul depended on his anointing to rule as king but was deceived into thinking his anointing was more powerful or wiser than the God who anointed him in the first place. David had to run for his life, almost like he wasn't anointed. As great as a warrior David was, he would not fight Saul because he understood God had anointed him as king. To fight Saul would be the same as fighting God, and David wanted no part in fighting against God.

We have leaders today who have confidence in their anointing to fight against you as if the same God does not anoint you. Be wise enough not to fight the Lord's anointed, but be vigilant in fighting for your right to be what God has called you to be. Maybe somewhere else to minimize the tensions and confusion, let the Lord Jesus lead you to be fruitful in your decisions and stand on God's word. Remember, when God anoints you, your anointing will be tested and tried. You will never know how anointed you are until you are faced with a lion, a bear, and a Goliath. Some enemies you are ordained to fight are not after you but what God has entrusted you with…so don't take everything so personally. When the dust settles, you will be standing when your enemies are paralyzed with fear. King Saul continued to pursue David as though he was the enemy when, in fact, the true enemies feared David but had no fear of Saul. Saul died like a fool, and his sons and followers because of Saul's stubbornness and disobedience to God. The Bible declares that stubbornness is of the spirit of witchcraft.

The same Philistines who killed Saul when he came out to meet them in battle embraced David and allowed him to live within their borders from Saul's hands. David had no hand in Saul's death…he loved Saul and mourned his death.

By What Authority did Saul come against David?

The Authority of Jesus Challenged
One day, as Jesus was teaching the people in the temple and preaching the gospel, the chief priests and the scribes with the elders came up and said to him, "Tell us by what authority you do these things, or who it is that gave you this authority." He answered them, "I also will ask you a question. Now tell me, was the baptism of John from heaven or from man?" And they discussed it with one another, saying, "If we say, 'From heaven,' he will say, Why did you not believe him?' But if we say, 'From man,' all the people will stone us to death, for they are convinced

that John was a prophet." So they answered that they did not know where it came from. And Jesus said to them, "Neither will I tell you by what authority I do these things."

The questioning of Jesus' authority by those who believed themselves to be divine figures on earth is a significant event that bears reflection. It is noteworthy that the children of the Pharisees seek to carry out their father's will. They attempted to prevent Jesus from fulfilling His mission and silenced His voice. It is essential to understand that your authority may likewise be contested. You must be prepared to face such challenges, just as Jesus did.

Jesus said, "I still have many things to say to you, but you cannot bear them now. When the Spirit of truth comes, he will guide you into all the truth, for he will not speak on his own authority, but whatever he hears he will speak, and he will declare to you the things that are to come. He will glorify me, for he will take what is mine and declare it to you. All that the Father has is mine; therefore I said that he will take what is mine and declare it to you. John 16:12-15

As a believer, you have been promised the power of the Holy Ghost, who is always available to you. The Spirit of God has given you the authority. When the Holy Spirit speaks through you, you will find it necessary to rely on

His guidance and help when people respond to the message you have been a vessel to convey. This is important for those who are making decisions for their lives. Remember that as a believer, you have been promised the power of the Holy Ghost, who is always available to you.

Jesus said, "You did not choose me, but I chose you and appointed you that you should go and bear fruit and that your fruit should abide, so that whatever you ask the Father in my name, he may give it to you. These things I command you, so that you will love one another.

"If the world hates you, know that it has hated me before it hated you. If you were of the world, the world would love you as its own, but because you are not of the world, I chose you out of the world; therefore, the world hates you." John 15:16-19

In this context, the word "world" does not refer to a physical location but rather to a state of being. It describes the opposing entities or people who are against the will of God. In this particular context, the Pharisees were considered part of the world, along with sinners. Despite believing they were holy men of God, they were deceived by their own arrogance, obsession with themselves, and vanity. This sense of self-importance led them astray from the true teachings of God. Their misguided beliefs ultimately prevented them from truly understanding the nature of God and the importance of humility and selflessness.

By What Authority did King Herod kill John the Baptist?

By What Authority did the Pharisees arrest and kill Jesus?

The religious leaders undertook a ruthless campaign to eradicate the church movement, dispatching an individual by the name of Saul to the task. Their efforts were marked by a callous and savage determination to halt the progress of God's work, even in the face of their own soldiers and Roman guards. Despite Jesus having risen from the tomb, they remained steadfast in their enmity towards him. Some people are weak, while others are wicked…the Pharisees were wicked, and their descendants are as well, even today, trying to stop the church and the true message of Jesus Christ. John and Jesus called them brood vipers, indicating they were offspring of the serpent—sons of Satan—because they bore his spiritual image.

It's disheartening to realize that a majority of people placed their trust in these individuals who were perceived as the intermediaries between themselves and God. It's quite a thought-provoking realization that these were the very leaders who were supposed to guide them on their spiritual path.

* * *

When you are divinely appointed and commissioned by God for a specific task, no external force can impede your progress except yourself. Utilizing the authority bestowed upon you by God, through the dedicated focus on and of Jesus Christ, you are empowered to proclaim your message without hesitation boldly. You are given the same authority to preach the gospel as Jesus, John, the prophets, the apostles, and all of the messengers who were before you. Preach with confidence because there is no higher authority to endorse you.

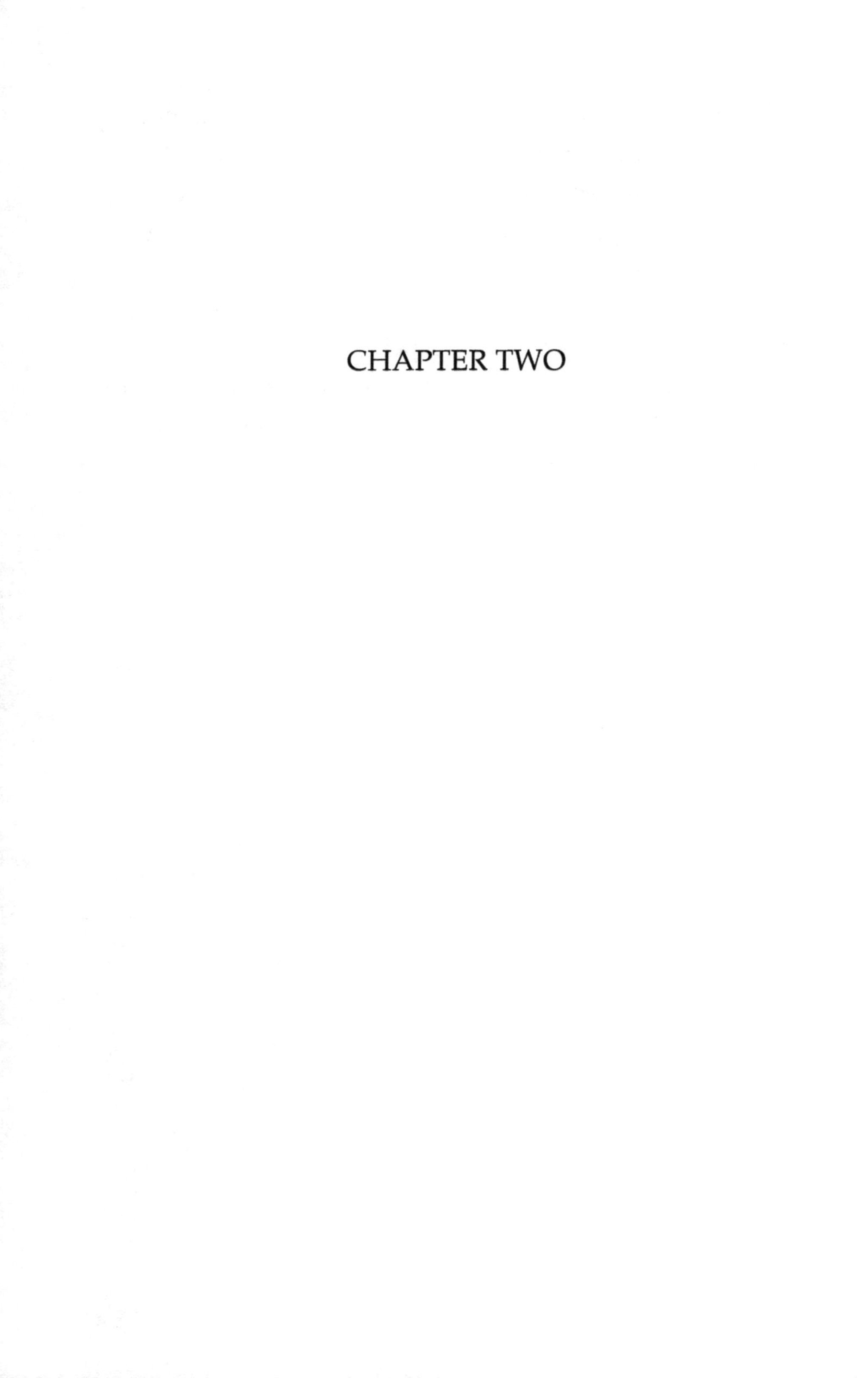

CHAPTER TWO

Can Anything Good Come Out Of This?

Chapter 8

Nazareth is a city located in the Galilee region of Israel. It is noteworthy as the birthplace of Mary, the mother of Jesus Christ. According to historical records, Mary met her future husband, Joseph, in Nazareth. God called Mary at a young age, believed to be between 14 and 16 years old, to fulfill one of the greatest prophecies of humankind. Mary was young, a virgin, and probably not very popular then; God chose her to bring forth the Son of God. The anticipation of the Messiah's arrival was a widely-known prophecy that may have inspired many young girls to aspire to play a role in it. Being a virgin was an invaluable asset in those days.

Mary and Joseph are engaged, and the wedding plans are set. The husband-to-be approached the father and paid the bride's dowry, which was accepted, and an agreement was made…everything was set. I am home in my room, and the angel Gabriel visits me. God has supernaturally put His seed in me, but will they believe me? I am still a virgin; no man has touched me.

In the sixth month of Elizabeth's pregnancy, God sent the angel Gabriel to Nazareth, a town in Galilee, to a virgin who pledged to be married to a man named Joseph, a descendant of David. The virgin's name was Mary. The angel approached her and said, "Greetings, you who are highly favored! The Lord is with you." Mary was greatly troubled by his words and wondered what kind of greeting this might be. But the angel said to her, "Do not be afraid, Mary; you have found favor with God. You will conceive and give birth to a son, and you are to call him Jesus. He will be great and will be called the Son of the Most High. The Lord God will give him the throne of his father David, and he will reign over Jacob's descendants forever; his kingdom will never end." "How will this be," Mary asked the angel, "since I am a virgin?" The angel answered, "The Holy Spirit will come on you, and the power of the Most High will overshadow you. So, the holy one to be born will be called the Son of God. Even Elizabeth, your relative, is going to have a child in her old age, and she, who was said to be unable to conceive, is in her sixth month. For no word from God will ever fail." "I am the Lord's servant," Mary answered. "May your word to me be fulfilled." Then the angel left her.

At that time, Mary got ready and hurried to a town in the hilly country of Judea, where she entered Zechariah's home and greeted Elizabeth. When Elizabeth heard Mary's greeting, the baby leaped into her womb, and Elizabeth was filled with the Holy Spirit. In a loud voice, she exclaimed: "Blessed are you among women, and blessed is the child you will bear! But why am I so favored that the mother of my Lord should come to me? As soon as your greeting reached my ears, the baby in my womb leaped for joy. Blessed is she who has believed that the Lord would fulfill his promises to her!" And Mary said: "My soul glorifies the Lord, and my spirit rejoices in God my Savior, for he has been mindful of the humble state of his servant. From now on, all generations will call me blessed, for the Mighty One has done great things for me— holy is his name.

Mary spent around three months staying with her cousin Elizabeth and then returned home. It is possible that Mary stayed until Elizabeth's son was born. Mary's house was approximately 100 miles away from Elizabeth's house. When she returned, Mary was likely at least 3 1/2 months pregnant. After all the celebrations, Mary returned home and confronted her family, her fiance, Joseph, and her friends. None of these individuals knew about her supernatural and Holy Spirit experience. Therefore, Mary faced a significant challenge: Would they believe her?

According to the biblical account, Mary, a virgin, was visited by an angel who told her she was pregnant with a son. When she informed Joseph, he found it difficult to believe her and was on the verge of breaking off their engagement. Joseph needed to clear himself with the family and priest to prove that he had not consummated the marriage, as per the Law of Moses. The situation would have been challenging for both sides of the family. Let's look at the laws Joseph and Mary faced during her engagement and pregnancy.

Her father will say to the elders, "I gave my daughter in marriage to this man, but he dislikes her. Now, he has slandered her and said, 'I did not find your daughter to be a virgin.' But here is the proof of my daughter's virginity." Then, her parents shall display the cloth before the elders of the town, and the elders shall take the man and punish him. They shall fine him a hundred shekels of silver and give them to the young woman's father because this man has given an Israelite virgin a bad name. She shall continue to be his wife; he must not divorce her as long as he lives.

If, however, the charge is true, and no proof of the young woman's virginity can be found, she shall be brought to the door of her father's house, and there the men of her town shall stone her to death. She has done an outrageous thing in Israel by being promiscuous while still in her father's house. You must purge the evil from among you. **Deuteronomy 22: 16-24 NIV.**

When we see the production of this story of Joseph, Mary, and baby Jesus so many years later, we make it a cute little story, but these people were under much pressure and scrutiny. They had so much on their shoulders, and to be so young, especially Mary, about maybe 16 years old.

Joseph was struggling with this, and his opinion of Mary was probably changing. He gets a much-needed message from God.

Because Joseph, her husband, was faithful to the law and yet did not want to expose her to public disgrace, he had in mind to divorce her quietly. But after he had considered this, an angel of the Lord appeared to him in a dream and said, "Joseph son of David, do not be afraid to take Mary home as your wife, because what is conceived in her is from the Holy Spirit. She will give birth to a son, and you are to give him the name Jesus because he will save his people from their sins."

All this took place to fulfill what the Lord had said through the prophet: "The virgin will conceive and give birth to a son, and they will call him Immanuel" (which means "God with us"). When Joseph woke up, he did what the angel of the Lord had commanded him and took Mary home as his wife. But he did not consummate their marriage until she gave birth to a son. And he gave him the name Jesus. **Matthew 1:19-25 NIV.**

God chose Joseph for this assignment; this was his purpose in life. How many men could have done this? On top of everything that came with it, God tells him not to consummate the marriage until after she has the child. Now, this takes faith and love for God. The enemy alone would plant so many voices in his head about not believing its god but some secret of a man who was with

Mary when she visited her cousin Elizabeth.

The angel came with good news, but it didn't feel good at the time. Have you ever gotten a word from God through whatever means and was excited only to find out you had to wait on the fulfillment of that word? People may think you are crazy because of the things you go through while waiting for the fulfillment of the prophecy; well, it was no different for Joseph and Mary during this time. We are getting to see the fulfillment and the process left for us on record, but imagine how they felt on a daily basis. They didn't have many people they could trust, and you get tired of trying to explain the unexplainable.

When we see the Christmas stories of Joseph and Mary, we get a different picture of Mary having the baby Jesus. It's a cute story of "Peace on earth and goodwill toward men," but Mary suffered to bring this baby into the world. Joseph is going to Bethlehem, his native city because he has to register for the census, but look at the timing: Mary is now full term and about to deliver her baby but goes with him. Mary will have this baby in Bethlehem. The prophecy is that the Messiah, the savior, will be born in Bethlehem. They were not trying to fulfill the prophecy; they were trying to honor God and live their lives.

Mary is experiencing a lot of pain as she is going through labor. Unfortunately, all the hotels in the area are full, and they tell us they do not have any available rooms.

This is confusing and worrying as an angel had earlier informed me that I was carrying the savior, the Messiah, the King of Israel, inside me. If there is no room for me, how can there be no room for him? What is going on? The savior of the world was working in her and going through her. Now, with no doctors, nurses, medication, or climate control, this young woman will have this baby.

A king was being born, and the only place she had to accommodate his birth was a stable barn, which was not even sanitary. She's giving birth to him among the animals. It's almost like the animals are the ones to be trusted with his birth. She is so uncomfortable and in so much pain, and the baby is not waiting for better conditions. According to the scriptures, it is time for the Messiah to be born, and Mary is laboring in birth. A king is being born with the heralding and singers, no praisers and worshipers, just surrounded by animals; with this great news, the savior of the world is born in private and alone. Soon after, Shepherds show up, and they ask them, "Why are you here?" They said we were in the field, watching our sheep, and the angel came and spoke to us and said, a king has been born, the shepherd of Israel, and he told us to come here." To Mary, this had to be a sign, but why did the angel talk to the shepherds and not come and talk to me? "I'm struggling here."

"I'm going through some changes; people think I'm crazy, they think I'm a liar, they think that when I went to visit my cousin, I slept with another man. If this was true according to the law of Moses, I could be stoned to death. An angel had to appear to Joseph to tell him not to be afraid to take Me as his wife." "The child Mary is carrying was conceived through the Holy Spirit, not by a man. God ensured that Joseph was from the tribe of Judah, the same tribe as King David, both spiritually and naturally. This is because God recognizes our limitations and accepts and welcomes the supernatural into our natural world.

Some people appear without any announcement, no social media, telephone, or any other means of communication except through other people. These people are showing up, and it comforts me to know that I am not crazy. How can they be here when no one knows where we are? We are away from home, not in our city or hometown, and not surrounded by our family or friends. We are in a strange place, and these people are showing up, saying that an angel of the Lord told them. Another group of men showed up because they saw a star in the sky and followed it, believing it represented the birth of a king on Earth."

King Herod heard that some influential people were in his country and city. Indeed, they have come to visit with me, for I am the king. They went to see the baby, and someone told him about the prophecy of the Messiah, that he would be born in Bethlehem. This is the region that he is ruling, which is over Galilee. He becomes insecure and says there can't be two kings in his region. I'm the king, so he sends out an order that says, kill every newborn child up to two years old to make sure that we destroy this newborn king. It seems like it was of his own accord of his mind, but when you read Revelation, chapter 12, it speaks about how the serpent, the dragon, was there to destroy her child as soon as it was born. As people talk about the universe, they believe that the universe is trying to tell them something. However, the woman mentioned in the 12-chapter of Revelation is believed to have been born in the universe in the kingdom of God. This is considered to be a prophecy that has been fulfilled. The events in the book of Revelation have already occurred in eternity, even though it is the last book in the Bible. What Mary goes through in time has already happened in eternity.

When we read that the dragon was there to destroy her child as soon as it was born, it is believed that this represents the king sending out his army to kill the child as soon as it was taken. Neither of them knows this has anything to do with the universe, the heavens, God's plans, or will. During our most challenging times, we may not realize that we are going through things already written in eternity. These events are manifested in time. When Jesus says, "These things must be," he offers us a glimpse into heaven and shows us how to submit to what has already been written. God knew exactly where Mary was and what she was going through, but she did not think she was fulfilling a prophecy. She was modeling what had occurred in eternity; you know what that means;

it had to happen the way it happened.

When God chooses you, if you're not careful, you will allow people and the devil to talk you out of your greatness because things are not happening as you imagine they would.

It's happening the way that is supposed to happen. Our job is to submit to God, obey Him, and love Him with all our hearts; no matter what happens or who walks out of your life, don't you walk out on God? Mary was a young woman who dedicated her body, mind, soul, and life to God. Despite the risk of being perceived as insane and losing her reputation as a virtuous woman, Mary trusted God's plan and submitted everything to Him. She knew that her decision could lead to Joseph thinking that she had been unfaithful and cheating on him, which could ruin her reputation. However, she believed God had chosen Joseph and her to carry out His plan.

When Joseph found out that Mary was pregnant, he protected her from being stoned to death and tried to shield her from public shame. Mary believed that God had chosen Joseph for her, and she was grateful for his support. She knew that it was rare for a man to be willing to raise a child that was not biologically his. Mary and Joseph followed God's instructions and remained celibate until after the baby was born. Mary was confident that God had a plan for their family, and she trusted that everything would work out in the end.

They were ordinary people, called to do extraordinary things. Now, visitors were bringing gifts and acknowledging the birth of baby Jesus. There was no physical announcement, no promotion. Nothing made anyone aware that he was born, just his presence. He was born in unusual circumstances and surroundings, in an unfamiliar place. When God calls you, you can believe he will call you to a strange place, away from everything you are familiar with. It is your place to get to know God better and to make up your mind when he isolates you. Will you serve him or not? Will you leave him or not? Will you turn on him or not? Will you go to man or stay with God?

After returning to Nazareth, Mary and Joseph received a message that everything was fine. On the eighth day, following the custom, they took baby Jesus to the temple for circumcision. An old man saw the baby and said, "Lord, you have heard my prayer. I will not close my eyes until I have seen salvation." He picked up baby Jesus and said, "Now that I have seen salvation, I can leave this world comforted." He also said to Mary, "And your heart will be pierced." Mary wondered about the meaning of these words and whether any good would come out of them.

Mary is being unjustly accused of wrongdoing. People are whispering that she went out of town with Joseph and returned with a baby. They are assuming that the baby is not Joseph's. They are saying that Mary must have gotten pregnant while visiting her cousin and that Joseph had to defend himself to the pastor who was going to marry them. According to the Law of Moses, it looked like Mary or Joseph had broken the law and the marriage covenant. However, Joseph did not touch Mary or disrespect her family or God. He had to defend himself and his honor by telling the truth. Mary is innocent, and it's unfair that people are gossiping about her.

When the scriptures say, "Mary would not be made an example," let me tell you what that means according to the law of Moses, which says, *"If a man is found sleeping with another man's wife, both the man who slept with her and the woman must die. You must purge the evil from Israel. If a man happens to meet in a town a virgin pledged to be married and he sleeps with her, you shall take both of them to the gate of that town and stone them to death—the young woman because she was in a city and did not scream for help, and the man because he violated another man's wife. You must purge the evil from among you.*

But if out in the country, a man happens to meet a young woman pledged to be married and rapes her, only the man who has done this shall die. Do nothing to the woman; she has committed no sin deserving death."

Mary fits none of these scenarios but may be any of them. She has had a baby and continues to say, The Spirit of God did it. Can you imagine? Mary is holding on to her story of the angel visiting her; this is how they want to come and be honest. Who is the father of your child? We read the Bible, and we go too fast. We see these little stories produced and in movies, and we don't get it. It looks cute now, but not when you are in it. Everybody thinks that they will follow Jesus now that you say, but would you have followed Jesus back then with all of this going on? He isn't king; he is from Nazareth, a poor town. He doesn't have money. Would you believe Jesus in those days after hearing the rumors?

It is a lot easier for us 2000 years later to go to church and praise God in the name of Jesus, but how about then? Jesus is circumcised on the eighth day, and they get this word from this older man at the temple. Then Joseph receives a dream and says the child's life is in danger. Take him and his mother and flee to Egypt until they hear a word from God because King Herod is seeking to kill the child. No angel is saying I will protect you and the baby… there's no word besides the dream. Why? Because in the universe—eternity, the serpent was mad with the woman. The serpent was there to destroy her child as soon as it was born, so here's the manifestation of it in time, and it is not pretty, and it says, but the child was caught up to his God, And the woman was driven in the wilderness.

What is that away from family, away from friends, away from the familiar? They said where she was nourished for 3 1/2 years and 1260 days are two scenarios with that symbolically. It says that the Lord had to nurture and feed her because you know why she's in the strange place in the unfamiliar city in the strange land. She's with nothing familiar. The enemy is after her mind, and the scriptures say God hid the woman in the wilderness. God hid her mind because the devil was after her mind. He was trying to destroy her, so he was trying to kill her and her reputation and take her mind.

The Bible says out of the mouth of the serpent came a flood because he desired to carry the woman away. The woman carried away her reputation; the flood was sent to destroy her reputation and credibility. "She's a liar, that's not God's son, she is crazy,' these things were said so she would not be accepted in society or her son. She would not be accepted in the church (temple, synagogue). So, she would not be accepted amongst her people; if she is not accepted among her people, then she wouldn't be accepted or respected anywhere; the enemy was after her voice. He was trying to shut her mouth!

The woman is the only creation God made to have two wounds: the heart, which gives birth to spiritual things, and the natural womb, which gives birth to natural things. Lucifer gave birth to iniquity from his heart, but this woman gave birth from her body. He will never be that thing that can give birth naturally, so he's in this world as a recruiter because he can't give birth. Satan knows this child is from God, but his job is to make all others believe otherwise. See, he's from heaven and knows all things are possible in that world. Mary can't prove that God is the father of her son, and now, on top of that, she has to run for her life and her son's. Why does she have to run from a king when she has given birth to a king? Why am I not blessed according to the world's standards or a natural kingdom? Where is my support system? Where are the money and protection? Where is the army?

When you get a word from God, you may not be able to prove God gave it to you at the time of conception. You have to keep it moving, keep walking through your valley. You have to keep believing. We cannot see our future without God. God had a plan much more significant than proving Himself to a few unbelievers. Mary had no idea she would be the most talked about virgin woman. She's the most famous teenage mother in history. She's the most famous teen pregnancy. See this thing for what it is. Let's take away the fantasy. Let's take away the Hollywood production of it, and let's see it for what it is. This can help you to go through what you're going through so that you won't think you are crazy. God did call you to preach. God did call you to Ministry. God did call you, and it's up to you to answer the call.

The suffering, sacrifice, and misunderstanding are proof that God called you. If God called you and called you, somebody will believe you; sometimes, it may not be your family. It may not be your friends, it may not be your own husband or wife, but somebody is going to believe that God has called you. God will have somebody who will believe that that thing in you was put there by God. God put that ministry in you; God put that word in you. God put that passion in you to do His will.

God did this to you! Can anything good come out of this when they think you are crazy? Can anything good come out of this when they believe I'm a cheater? Can anything good come out of this when they think I am a liar? When they believe I made this up, can anything good come out of this? When you can't even go back to your hometown because your reputation is shot and torn apart, and now I'm on the run. Why am I running when God is Almighty? Why do I have to flee to Egypt?

Why do I have to run? It's written in the stars in eternity: you had to run not because you were weak, God couldn't do anything for you, but because it was already written in the book. Your job is to carry out what was written in the book in heaven, that it may manifest here on the earth; we are to submit to the script and become the best version of what God has written. God is the producer, the writer, the author, and the finisher of our faith, and now they run to Egypt. They stay there until they hear a word from God. King Herod is going crazy, killing these male children from newborn to two years old. He's trying to make sure he kills the baby of the Stars of Heaven.

* * *

The prophet Jeremiah prophesied over 500 years before this; he said," I see the children of Rachael in the street, and they were slain, and Rachael was weeping." She said," Because they will be no more." We cannot understand all of this; instead of trying to understand the circumstances and the things happening, we should try to understand our God. The only way we can realize our God is that we become dedicated, faithful to Him, and loyal to Him and trust Him because it's greater than what we see now. You will miss it if you go by what you see in time. There's a bigger picture to this, and now Joseph, Mary, and baby Jesus are in Egypt; God strikes down King Herod, and they hear he is dead, and the angel comes to Joseph. "Now you can return to Nazareth; the king who was seeking to kill the baby is dead.

By the time they return to Nazareth, Jesus is about 12 years old; they are returning to their hometown. Now, people are still whispering and talking. Imagine the chatter; "you know, I was wondering what would have become of Mary and Joseph and her baby. It looks like they ran away somewhere hiding because Mary should've been stoned to death. But Mary knows she didn't have this baby by another man; she knows who the father is, but Joseph is willing to claim it. Thinking Joseph is probably covering for her, they consider the marriage sinful, according to the law, Moses. They've been gone all these years. God could've sent them anywhere, but He sent them back to Nazareth.

* * *

Now, Jesus goes to the temple, and the religious leaders marvel at his knowledge and wisdom for his age; he's talking to the priest, but Jesus doesn't have any children at 12 years old. Although challenging and controversial, they probably felt good to be home because they had been among strangers for years. Nazareth was not glamorous in those days; it was a very humble place, and they raised Jesus there; it's where he would grow to adulthood. Jesus has not done one miracle.

Jesus has not preached any messages; he's done nothing regarding miracles and is now 30 years old. Joseph's life assignment and destiny was to care for Mary and Jesus. That was his destiny; there was no need to look at somebody else's destiny. You have to find out what your purpose is in life. That was Joseph's purpose: to protect Mary, to be a husband, to marry, and to be a father figure to Jesus. That was his destiny. That was his assignment, and he did his assignment. He didn't get to see one miracle or thing that Jesus did to make him say, "Wow, he has established the kingdom of Israel; he defeated the enemies; he destroyed the Romans. He rebuilt the kingdom of David and restored us as a people. None of that, Joseph died believing that Jesus was the son of God.

I know they don't believe me, and I can't prove it to anybody, but I know that this is God's Son. Now, why is God not doing anything with his son? I don't understand that. Why is he here in Nazareth and not Jerusalem, in the temple? Why is the high priest in the palace and the Son of God in the ghetto? The son of God is living in a humble house in Nazareth, which doesn't make natural sense. Joseph is getting ready to leave this world and is my encourager. He gives me strength when I feel weak. Only one person in this world believed me, and Joseph believed me. Jesus is good and has been great in our lives, but we have suffered. People always made a mockery of our situation. At this time, I'm not even seeing the purpose Jesus was born for.

You must stand on what God told you, no matter what it looks like. Sometimes, you may ask yourself, "Can any good thing come out of this," because you've lost so much following God. When I think I will quit, that word will give me strength to hold on just a little while longer. When I think I can't make it, that word will let me know I can. I know God is with me, even in my tears. Now, after the death of Joseph, Mary finds herself left with Jesus and the other siblings. Mary is a widow, and her children are considered orphans. Jesus, being the eldest son, is to take over the family business as a builder. Not much time after, Jesus tells his mother he has to leave to answer the call of his Heavenly Father. "Wait a minute, son, my husband just died, and according to the law of Moses, the eldest son is to take care of the widow and the orphans; you know this." Your job, son, is to care for me and your brothers and sisters because you're the next in line."

* * *

Can you imagine the written Word of God, which is God, being challenged by the Rhema Word of God, which is God, and all of that being challenged because Jesus is the living Word? So we have the written Word, Rhema Word, and the living Word of God, and the living Word says," It's time for me to leave." Mary is there looking at her eldest son; they've been together for 30 years, and she's taken care of him from birth.

Joseph is gone, and he was Jesus' natural father, and he is saying that his heavenly Father is calling him now, and he has to go and say, "You know that this is why I was born." "I understand that, son, but what I don't understand is this timing?" You are going to leave me, too. Can anything good come out of this? What's going to become of me and my other children? I'm a widow now; they are orphans, and you're telling me that God is telling you to leave now?" Jesus goes, and he gets baptized for the first time in his entire life. John is baptizing, and when John sees him coming, he says, "Behold the Lamb of God that comes to take away to send to the World." Immediately, the heavens opened up, and the spirit of God descended like a dove and said, "This is my beloved Son in whom I AM well pleased."

When Jesus left his mother, Mary, in Nazareth, all he could see was her hurt and pain. His humanity was struggling with his divinity, but he knew he had to answer the call of God. Imagine the battles he must have been going through being the living word of God. The law was telling him to stay, but Rhema's word told him it was time to leave. Jesus was in a fight. He obeyed the Father and went, despite his natural mother's hurt and feelings of abandonment. Mary must have thought, "What happened to the angel Gabriel who came to me over 30 years ago telling me I was blessed and highly favored by God? I don't feel favored or blessed." This hurt her deeply.

When Jesus was baptized, and the Father spoke to him, it wasn't to stroke his ego; it was to encourage him. Even Jesus needed confirmation and encouragement to fully embrace his journey of answering his calling for ministry. God let him know that Mary would be taken care of and that he should go to the wilderness and deal with the Devil. We should learn from this: when God calls you, the timing may not be perfect or seem right. However, having the right person in your life when He calls you is crucial. Human nature may challenge you to choose between your calling from God and those around you. If you choose God, you may lose those people, but if you choose them, you may lose God. Eventually, they will leave you because they will lose respect for your choice.

Following 40 days spent in the wilderness, during which the Devil tempted Jesus, he emerged triumphant. At this point, he was ready to commence his ministry officially. It is widely acknowledged that the period of temptation preceding the start of ministry is crucial, as it helps one to recognize potential temptations that may arise when functioning fully as a preacher. At this juncture, Jesus had nothing to lose but himself. Failure to overcome these temptations would have left him vulnerable to further temptation by Satan, which could have eventually led to humiliation as his weaknesses were exposed.

To achieve success and recognition in public, one must first endure and overcome challenges in private. Only by facing and overcoming obstacles in private can one truly develop the skills, knowledge, and confidence necessary to succeed in the public arena. It is in private where one can hone their abilities, learn from mistakes, and build the resilience needed to handle the pressures of the public sphere. Therefore, personal struggles and victories are the foundation for general success and achievement. Jesus achieved victory over the devil in private, confirming his ministry readiness.

He was then given power and authority over the enemy. This is why, when he began his ministry, the devil and demons could not challenge him. He cast out those demons and commanded them to go away. This is why we see so much preaching without the authority to cast out the devil. We cannot cast him out if we don't first defeat the devil. If the devil knows that we have been indulging in lustful activities with his agents, he will dare us to try to cast him out, resulting in embarrassment. Many preachers avoid this topic, but Jesus, on the other hand, commands us to "Cast them out!" However, we need to be true to ourselves to achieve this.

After defeating the devil in the wilderness, Jesus went to a wedding where he saw his mother, whom he had not seen since he left home to start his ministry. They ran out of wine during the wedding, and his mother told him about the situation. Jesus initially responded, "What does this have to do with me, woman? It is not yet my time." It had been 40 to 50 days since they had last seen each other, and they had not been apart like this since she gave birth to him.

Mary must have felt afraid, angry, and frustrated with how things unfolded, especially since she was living without the two men she loved the most, Joseph and Jesus. Jesus had an urgency to leave home to answer his Father's call, and Mary must have wanted to see what her son was capable of, hence her challenge to him. Until now, there was no record of Jesus performing any miracles. As the Son of God, Jesus used his power to make wine to appease Mary, the person who carried him, nurtured him, protected him, and loved him since birth. It was the only time he used his power to appease someone.

Sometime after the wedding, *"Jesus returned in the power of the Spirit into Galilee, and fame went out concerning him through all the region roundabout. And he taught in their synagogues, being glorified of all.*

And he came to Nazareth, where he had been brought up: and he entered, as his custom was, into the synagogue on the sabbath day, and stood up to read. And there was delivered unto him the book of the prophet Isaiah. And he opened the book and found the place where it was written,

"The Spirit of the Lord is upon me,
Because he anointed me to preach good tidings to the poor:
He hath sent me to proclaim release to the captives,
And recovering of sight to the blind,
To set at liberty them that are bruised,
To proclaim the acceptable year of the Lord.
And he closed the book, and gave it back to the attendant, and sat down: and the eyes of all in the synagogue were fastened on him. And he began to say unto them, Today hath this scripture been fulfilled in your ears.

And all bare him witness, and wondered at the words of grace which proceeded out of his mouth: and they said, Is not this Joseph's son? And he said unto them, Doubtless ye will say unto me this parable, Physician, heal thyself: whatsoever we have heard done at Capernaum, do also here in thine own country. And he said, Verily I say unto you, No prophet is acceptable in his own country. But of a truth I say unto you, There were many widows in Israel in the days of Elijah when the heaven was shut up three years and six months when there came a great famine over all the land; and unto none of them was Elijah sent, but only to Zarephath, in the land of Sidon, unto a woman that was a widow.

And there were many lepers in Israel in the time of Elisha the prophet; and none of them was cleansed, but only Naaman the Syrian. And they were all filled with wrath in the synagogue, as they heard these things; and they rose up, and cast him forth out of the city, and led him unto the brow of the hill whereon their city was built, that they might throw him down headlong. But he passing through the midst of them went his way." **Luke 4: 14-30 ASV**

The response of Jesus' community to his teachings was noteworthy, as they initially received his message with amazement. However, their admiration quickly dissipated when they realized that he was the son of Mary, who had a pregnancy that was shrouded in controversy, and that his father, Joseph, had recently passed away. According to the Law of Moses, Jesus was expected to take over the family business. Still, rather than doing so, he had been missing for almost two months and suddenly returned and was now reading scriptures like a holy man after breaking the law. Some community members criticized him for neglecting his familial duties and abandoning his mother, Mary. While Jesus had been a dutiful son during Joseph's lifetime, people were still attempting to determine who his biological father was. It is difficult to imagine the stresses of growing up under such circumstances.

Jesus chose to go to another town to start his ministry

and performed all kinds of miracles, which he had never done in his own home and hometown. This can serve as a lesson to preachers: don't try to convince people of who you are when you know all of the struggles you've gone through just to be anointed. Instead, look for someone who desires the God in you rather than looking at you and trying to figure you out. They will see God in you if God is in them, so you don't need more anointing. Instead, you need people with the capacity to receive what God has placed in you for them.

Can anything good come out of Nazareth? This is what they asked people who were following Jesus. The Pharisees looked down on Jesus because of where he came from and who his parents were. They judged him literally and had him executed because they thought they were handling a poor person. They felt he had no wealth; you know how the rich do the poor or particular classes of people. They thought they would get away with it because they assumed Jesus did not have the resources to fight them and the system, but God was his weapon, and He told him not to say anything. "Anything you say, Son, can be used against you, so don't open your mouth. Jesus acted as though he was dumb, like a bit of lamb, but little did they know that he was The Lamb of God who came to take away the sins of the world. For the price he paid for our sins, why would we fight so hard to be a hardcore sinner as if it was some award, a badge of honor, a heavyweight title belt, or some noble achievement to be proud of?

* * *

The Pharisees were rich preachers; they had it going on; they had it all, at least it seemed. The high priest lived in a palace just like a king. He called the shots to manipulate the circumstances to have Jesus killed. They influenced the judges, the officers, the governors, the Romans, and the kings, but they did have power with God. Don't be fooled by the influence and appearance of righteousness; God has given His children POWER! Holy Ghost Power is something that money can't buy!

The Pharisees were influential, but Jesus was powerful, although it didn't look like it. "When it's all said and done," will you be at the table with the Lord when you leave this world? Or will you be dragged into the Judgement Seat of Christ and, or worse, The White Throne Judgment, which is The Supreme Court of Heaven, where the Honorable Great I AM God is the Judge? What good is it to preach God's word but not be in favor of God? What good is it to write Christian or gospel songs and not honor the God you're singing about with a holy life? Mistakes are one thing, but a lifestyle of whoredoms is totally disrespectful with no fear of God. It's called "WICKED!" Don't do God any favors because He surely won't do you any on the day of judgment. To do all we do in the Christian community and can hardly find unity in the love of God is pitiful. We have let every kind of serpent creep into the church and didn't even check it for venom.

* * *

Now our children have been bitten. " As Moses raised the serpent in the wilderness, so must the Son of Man be lifted, and HE is lifted. He will draw." We need healing, and it can't happen if we cover our sins; we need to repent and never return to those sins again. Tell the Devil bye!! Or join him and the fallen angels, but don't play both sides. Not to be able to be with Him in heaven. "Don't be deceived; God will not be mocked, whatsoever a man sows, that he will also reap." Where do you think the Pharisees, religious leaders, lawyers, judges, and kings who raise their hands against God? They killed Jesus in the name of God using The Law of Moses. Do you think Moses gave them a thumbs up for killing Jesus like a common criminal? And hypocrites are right now? They are not in God's kingdom, have joy and peace, and they definitely are not" Resting In Peace."

They were the elite; they were wealthy, educated, and connected. It's like The Pharisees were from Buckhead, Jesus was from Bankhead, like the Hamptons and Brooklyn, Hollywood and Compton, Fisher Island and Model City, Lincoln Park and South Chicago, Mountain Brook, and West End. They were so arrogant to be so-called men of God; they knew they had the upper hand and played it to the hills. They looked down their nose at people who used their hands for trade or to make a living. Jesus was a disgrace to their culture and was going to ensure they got rid of him; no matter how many people followed him, they would not believe in him because of their prejudice toward him. When they crucified him, they thought it was over, but as much as they read and studied the word of God, they should have seen themselves in the book as false prophets bearing false witness, traitors, liars, thieves, adulterers, and murderers. Who would be labeled "Killers of the prophets."

When the people continued to rant and rave about the man Jesus preaching and teaching to those who were disadvantaged and healing them while doing miracles, They asked, "Can anything good come out of Nazareth?" Joseph, Mary, and Jesus' reputation had preceded them; they made a mockery of their answered prayer. Now, Jesus is doing what he was sent to the world to do, and they thought him to be beneath them. In other words, this is that illegitimate boy coming from that mother who covered up the way she got pregnant, and now he's the preacher everyone is talking about, and he's from the wrong tribe.

He's from the tribe of Judah; at least John the Baptist was one of them, they thought because he was from the priestly tribe of Levi. You cannot be a priest except you be of Aaron, the Levite. On top of all of this, Jesus was too young; you had to be at least 40 years old to take such a claim as a leader. So, to them, it was a no-brainer; Jesus was trash to them. They were offended that people hailed him, king of the Jews." They looked at Jesus as the disgrace they needed to get rid of, and he didn't honor them nor follow the priest's protocol. People wonder why Jesus was not born in the House of God when he was born because God's Temple was filled with imposters, murderers, and thieves.

Judas, his disciple, betrayed him; it's not like he didn't know who Jesus was; he was mad because God took too long to bless them with prosperity and prestige. Judas wanted a glamorous life like Caesar, King Herod, and the Pharisees. When people are with you for the wrong reasons, they will show their true selves when the money is held up. They have been deceived into thinking God doesn't know their heart; that is what Lucifer thought. When will we learn from those failures of the past?

When they took him to court and lied on him, Pilot, the procurator, said, "I find no fault in the man." The Pharisees continued to push the case until, finally, he was crucified. Mary, his mother, was there, and she wept for her baby. From the day she conceived, she protected her baby. No matter what anyone thought or said about her pregnancy, she knew he was something special, but maybe not how much. She watched as they drove the spikes through his flesh, not to mention how badly they beat and abused him. For every woman who has been abused, Jesus took this beating for you. You don't have to be afraid and let the devil beat on you anymore. Jesus took that unimaginable pain. Image how

Mary was there for Jesus when he was born; she

suffered to deliver that baby in unimaginable and dire circumstances. She sacrificed her life for him. When he could fend for himself, she was there to protect him. Now, she lies at the foot of the cross while her baby bleeds and feels helpless. Who could be so cruel to such a beautiful and caring human being? Jesus looks at her and says, "Woman, behold your son, John, behold your mother." This was John, his youngest disciple of the 12.

Even in pain, Jesus was setting Mary free from being his mother because he needed her to be the Woman like Eve was at the wrong tree; Mary was at the right one. All covered in blood, she did not know that he was the Tree of Life. He needed her to be a disciple, not his mother. He was now dying for her because the first Adam died with Eve. Jesus needed her to live. He knew she was feeling like her life was over, and he stopped the enemy from talking to her mind, taking over her mind, and wishing she could die with him.

The soldiers looked upon him, for it was about to be the Sabbath, and they needed to take the bodies down. So they broke the legs of the two thieves on both sides of Jesus, for he was in the middle. When they came to Jesus and saw that he was already dead, a soldier took his spear and pierced Jesus' side between his ribs into his heart, piercing him, and out came blood and water. *These things happened so that the scripture would be fulfilled: "Not one of his bones will be broken," and, as another scripture says, "They will look on the* *one they have pierced." **John 19: 36-37 NIV.***

When the mother is giving natural birth, her water breaks, and the child comes forth from blood. The life is in the blood. Out of Jesus' side, the church was birthed…his bride. Remember, Eve was taken out of Adam's side, and God took one of his ribs to make the woman. Jesus was restoring what Adam had lost. Jesus is called the second (last) man, Adam. The first Adam died with the woman, but the second man, Adam, died for the woman. Can anything good come of Nazareth? Yes, it can, and it did; they thought they were seeing blood and water, but the church was being born in the spirit realm.

When they pierced Jesus, Mary got pierced, too.
"For mine eyes have seen thy salvation,
Which thou hast prepared before the face of all peoples;
A light for revelation to the Gentiles,
And the glory of thy people, Israel.
*And his father and his mother were marveling at the things which were spoken concerning him; and Simeon blessed them, and said unto Mary his mother, Behold, this child is set for the falling and the rising of many in Israel; and for a sign which is spoken against; yea and a sword shall pierce through thine own soul; that thoughts out of many hearts may be revealed. **Luke 2: 30-35***

The mother was in pain, and Jesus needed her to be in the upper room when he sent the Holy Spirit from heaven.

Mary witnessed what God had said to her over 33 years prior and was now being fulfilled. She need to know her labor was not in vain. Sometimes, when you're going through tough times, the enemy wants you to think it is over and you missed the mark or your season; the truth is God is the author of times and seasons. So if you stay in him and with him, he can redeem the time. You will have lost nothing but sowe your pain into God to get fruit back of everlasting joy. So, don't give up; don't quit because your pain is about to turn into power! Mary, the mother of Jesus, was in that room, and the Holy Spirit fell on her, sat down like fire, and filled her with power!

When Mary gave birth to Jesus, she never would have believed it would end this way. Although she is hurting for Jesus, she doesn't know at the time she will be a witness to his resurrection. Jesus needed her free so she would be in the upper room to receive the Holy Ghost. Out of Christ came the Holy Spirit.

They thought that by killing him, they would get rid of him, but they were wrong. Jesus was resurrected and came out of that tomb; nothing could stop him. They thought the way Jesus was executed that he was a failure, but not so. They had no clue that he would be greater after his death than he was in life. They got rid of Jesus because, for one, he was turning the hearts of the people back to God and restoring their hope; the Pharisees made them pay for everything they would give them from God. The religious leaders used political strategies against Jesus by smearing his character. "Can anything good come from Nazareth? Raising the thoughts of the family from Nazareth, with the mother claiming to have given birth to God's son. The enemy will keep using the same old stuff because he has no new tricks.

They hated Jesus so much that they even posted Roman soldiers and temple guards at the mouth of the tomb to be assured that the prophecy of him being raised from the dead would not come to pass. What is sick about this is that the coming of the Messiah was the greatest anticipated promise they were waiting on. Not only did Jesus rise from the day, but he visited with believers for 40 days, showing himself. What he didn't do was show himself to his enemies. As men and women of God, never try to prove yourself to those who hate your God. Jesus never performed a miracle for his known enemies; they won't believe anyway. The signs are for the believers. Even if they do not know they are called by God, when they hear the word, they will believe when the time comes. God reveals himself to his own.

From Eve to Mary and every woman between and after, God sees your pain, and through faith in Him, it will be turned into power. God chose a virgin teenage girl and entrusted her with His Spirit and heart in the form of a seed; she then became a woman, who became a wife, gave birth to Christ, who then became a mother, who became his nurturer, who became his protector, who became his teacher, who became a widow, who was there to witness the abuse and death of her son, who became a mourner, who visited her son's tomb and witnessed it was empty, went to the upper room and tarried to received the Comforter which is the Holy Ghost and power, who became born again by way of the son whom she gave birth to, then received her joy and became the most famous woman in history.

"Bless are thou, Mary, for God has found favor with you and is with you. Blessed are you among women, and blessed is the child you will bear. I'm sure Mary didn't always feel blessed or even that the Lord was with her, but she had faith, did her job, and fulfilled her purpose in life and the kingdom. We should focus on the here and now because we don't know what plans God may have for our lives. Mary went through very difficult times from the pregnancy until Jesus' death; then, her life turned around when she was able to see they didn't hurt God's son; they made it possible for him to save the world. They thought they were destroying a man, but they were handling a God. Where are they now?

Can anything good come out of Nazareth? They started baptizing in the name of Jesus of Nazareth. They began doing miracles in the name of Jesus of Nazareth. They were casting out devils and demons in the name of Jesus of Nazareth. The church came out of Jesus of Nazareth. You and I went out of Jesus of Nazareth through spiritual birth, and that being said, "Can Anything Good Come Out Of This? I already have, it already is, and it will always be.

They thought that by killing him, they would get rid of him, but they didn't. Jesus was resurrected and came out of that tomb, and nothing had the power to stop him.

They thought the way Jesus was executed that he was a failure, but not so. They had no clue that he would be greater after his death than he was in life. They got rid of Jesus because, for one, he was turning the hearts of the people back to God and restoring their hope; the Pharisees made them pay for everything they would give them from God. So, the religious leaders used political strategies against Jesus by smearing his character. "Can anything good come from Nazareth? Raising the thoughts of the family from Nazareth, with the mother claiming to have given birth to God's son. The enemy will keep using the same old stuff because he has no new tricks.

After all the hell you have been through and the devils you had to fight, how can you let anyone tell you that you cannot preach? They want to bring up your past, bring up your past. Put the blood of Jesus on it! So you can take back everything the devil has stolen from you.

It is common for individuals to experience feelings of abandonment and isolation when they believe that God is not with them during times of great emotional pain. This is especially true when one is involved in church ministry and faces difficult situations. For instance, it can be challenging to reconcile when a spouse cheats and causes embarrassment, and it may appear that God is not on your side. It is not uncommon for people to feel frustrated when attempting to express their emotions to their partners and dealing with church members. Hearing an arrogant tone from a spouse who seems to be taking things for granted can be disheartening. Unfortunately, some individuals may refuse to change their behavior even when confronted. In such cases, it may seem like they are driven by their desires rather than representing God, which can be disheartening and lead to feelings of betrayal.

It's disheartening to hear men express bigoted views that suggest women aren't fit to preach or pastor. It's frustrating to continually hear these outdated notions that limit women's roles in religious communities. I can't help but wonder, what place are these men referring to when they say that women should stay in their place? Challenging these harmful beliefs and promoting equality for all people in every aspect of life is important. It's even more challenging when you are getting older and expect things to change, wishing you had come to your senses a year ago. But you thought he was going to change. I can't help but think, why would a man of God, or any man, want to be a preacher/pastor and player in the kingdom? Something is not right, but they are a powerful source of men to deal with. Now, to think of it, so were the Pharisees who killed Jesus and persecuted the early church.

Can anything good come out of teen pregnancy, abuse, betrayal, molestation, divorce, loss of a loved one, sickness, an accident, foster care, adoption, loss of a parent, loss of a spouse, loss of a job, being laid off, losing a business, bankruptcy, losing your children, being hated for no reason, being lied on, going to jail, addiction, an alcoholic, being persecuted, being hospitalized, rejection…can anything good come of you, or your situation? Yes, it can if you give it to God. "Is there anything too hard for God?"

Can anything good come out of bad? Can anything come out of the hood, the ghetto, the ruins of life? Can anything good come out of Bankhead? Can anything good come out of South Chicago? Can anything good come out of Atlanta? Can Anything Good come out of Compton? Can anything good come out of Brooklyn or the Boroughs of NYC? Can anything good come out of New Orleans? Can anything good come out of Birmingham? Can anything good come out of Baltimore?! Come and see how Jesus of Nazareth works through people just like you and me! ACTS!

The Word- The Woman

Chapter 9

The divine Word created the universe and everything in it. It posits that the same word that spoke the universe into being also fashioned every language, race, creature, and entity on Earth. The text highlights that this divine Word, deemed the source of all existence, took on human form and dwelled among us. Regrettably, the text laments that despite its presence, humankind failed to recognize it for what it was.

The divine Word possesses immense potency that created every element that constitutes our ecosystem, such as mountains, oceans, and trees. The holy Word is accountable for creating every living organism and the intricate systems that enable their coexistence. The Word's power can create something out of nothingness, articulate, and bring objects into being.

* * *

Ultimately, the text inspires us to contemplate the awe-inspiring creative power of this divine Word and to recognize it in all its various forms. It encourages us to seek to understand and appreciate the intricate designs and systems surrounding us and to marvel at the complexity and beauty of creation. And our road is in the food that we eat. That same Word was here in the form of a helpless child. This Word humbled him to his own Word, and he grew up like he was nothing. He went through the process of what he has spoken to and everything else that he created. Now, that process was taking him through a process of the Word.

The same Word was the voice walking through the Garden of Eden. Adam was afraid of the same voice that asked, "Where are you, Adam?" the same word that said, "Who told you that you were naked?" and the same word that said, "What is it that you have done?". The same word spoke to the serpent, saying that he and the woman should be at war all the days of their lives. This is the same Word that spoke to Abraham and made a covenant with him. The same Word told Abraham to leave his father's house and kinfolks. Not only would he become a father, but he would also become a father of many nations, and all the world's families would be blessed because of him.

The same Word replied to the Religious Leaders, "When the Pharisees confronted Jesus, they asked him,

'Who do you think you are, to do the things that you do? By what authority do you do these things?' Jesus replied, 'Let it be known that all who came before me are not worthy of me, I existed before Abraham…before Abraham was, I Am."

The same Word also told Moses to take off his shoes, as the ground he was standing on was holy. Moses had never heard the Word before, but now he was in its presence. The Word said, 'I have heard the cries of my people. I am sending you to Egypt. Tell Pharaoh to let my people go.' Moses asked, 'Who are you when they ask me your name? Who has sent me? What should I say to them? How should I answer them?' The word replied, 'I AM THAT I AM. Tell them that I AM sent you."

The same Word was used to instruct the prophet Samuel to anoint Saul as the king to satisfy the people's demand. Even though I am their God and King, the people prayed for a visible human king. They wanted a king made of flesh and blood, someone they could see. I rejected and conveyed my decision to him when Saul disobeyed me. When the prophet Samuel was feeling down and mourning over my decision to reject Saul because he disobeyed God, the same Word came to the prophet Samuel saying, "Why do you keep mourning over Saul? I have rejected him as king. Get up, dress yourself, fill your horn with anointing oil, and go to Jesse's house in

Bethlehem. You will find the one I have chosen among his sons as the next king." When Saul visited Jesse's house, he asked to see his sons. Jesse called his sons from the eldest to the youngest. His first three sons were tall and handsome, just like King Saul.

However, the prophet said God had not chosen any of these men. Jesse had brought seven of his sons, but Samuel said that the Lord had not chosen any of them either. Samuel asked Jesse if he had any more sons, and Jesse mentioned his youngest son, who was tending the sheep. Samuel asked Jesse to send for him, and they waited until he arrived. David, the youngest son, was not even considered at first. This teaches us that sometimes people can be overlooked because they don't fit the mold others have in mind for a specific job or task. David was unable to wash or clean up before meeting with the prophet. He smelled like sheep and dung as if he had no home. He was in the fields but is a true example of coming to God just as you are. Despite his appearance, God said, "Rise and anoint him; this is the one." So Samuel took the horn of oil and anointed him in the presence of his brothers, and from that day on, the Spirit of the Lord came powerfully upon David.

The story of David, anointed by God, teaches us an important lesson about favor and calling. Sometimes, God sees what He planted in us before we were even born and anointed us above others who may have been desperately seeking the same positions we may have no interest in. It is important to note that people may hate on us for God's favor, not realizing we had nothing to do with God's decision to choose us. We may not be qualified or experienced and may not fit the bill, but God has chosen us, which comes with a price. We must prove ourselves trustworthy and do what God has anointed us to do, for if we don't, people may still hate us.

The same Word told David and the people in his community who were unaware of God's grand plan in store for them. They had no idea that the same Word that had anointed David from Bethlehem would also be the one to choose Joseph, from the same bloodline as David, to fulfill the prophecy of greatness for humanity. This prophecy was to be fulfilled by the birth of a son, who would be born in the small town of Bethlehem. It's incredible how one Word could hold so much power and bring about such a significant event.

The same Word came to Isaiah the prophet and said, "Who has believed what we have heard? And to whom has the Lord's power been revealed? He grew up before God like a young plant, a root growing in dry ground. He had no exceptional beauty or form to make us notice him; nothing in his appearance made us desire him. He was hated and rejected by people. He had much pain and suffering. People would not even look at him. He was despised, and we didn't even notice him. But he took our suffering on him and felt our pain for us. We saw him punished and hurt by God. He was wounded for the wrong we did; he was crushed for the evil we did. The punishment, which made us well, was given to him, and we are healed because of his wounds.

We all have wandered away like sheep; each of us has gone his own way. But the Lord has punished him for all the evil we have done. He was beaten down and punished, but he didn't say a Word. He was like a lamb being led to be killed. He was quiet, as a sheep is quiet while its wool is being cut. He never opened his mouth to defend himself. People took him away roughly and unfairly. But who can speak about what happened to him during his time on Earth?"

"He was taken from the land of the living, punished for the sins of my people. He was buried with the wicked, and his tomb was with the rich. He was buried with the rich, even though he had never committed a crime or ever told a lie. But it was the Lord who decided to crush him and make him suffer. The Lord made his life a penalty offering. He will see his offspring and will continue to live a long life. Through him, the Lord's plan will succeed. After suffering, he will see the light and be satisfied. My good servant will make many people right with God; he will carry away their sins."

"For this reason, I will make him a great man among people, and he will share in all things with those who are strong. He willingly gave his life and was treated like a criminal. But he carried away the sins of many people and asked forgiveness for those who sinned."

The same Word came to the prophet Jeremiah, saying, "Behold, the days come, saith the LORD, that I will raise unto David a righteous Branch and a King shall reign and prosper and shall execute judgment and justice in the earth."

The same Word came to the prophet Joel and said, "And it shall come to pass afterward, that I will pour out my spirit upon all flesh; and your sons and your daughters shall prophesy, your old men shall dream dreams, your young men shall see visions: And also upon the servants and the handmaids in those days will I pour out my spirit."

This same Word shows up in Nazareth through a messenger who stands in the presence of God, Gabriel, the angel. He solutes Mary, a virgin engaged to be married to Joseph of Bethlehem, who also lives in Nazareth. The angel tells Mary she has found favor with God.

* * *

The consistent occurrence of divine intervention throughout history invites us to broaden our perspective on life. We must exercise caution against making hasty judgments based on our limited viewpoint and instead trust in the divine plan, even when it may not be immediately apparent. This message inspires us to recognize the potential dangers of making assumptions based on incomplete information and consider divine plans' long-term nature. It encourages us to approach life with humility and faith, trusting that the same God who has orchestrated events throughout history remains present and active today.

"In the beginning was the Word, and the Word was with God, and the Word was God. The same was true in the beginning with God. All things were made through him, and without him was not anything made that hath been made. In him was life, and the life was the light of men. And the light shineth in the darkness; and the darkness apprehended it not. Then, there was a man named John, who was sent by God. He came as a witness to testify about the light so that all might believe through him. He was not the light himself but came to bear witness to the light. The true light, which enlightens every man, was coming into the world. He was in the world, and the world was made through him, but the world did not recognize him. He came to his own, but his own did not receive him."

"But as many as received him, to them gave he the right to become children of God, even to them that believe on his name: who were born, not of blood, nor of the will of the flesh, nor the will of man, but of God. And the Word became flesh and dwelt among us (and we beheld his glory as the only begotten from the Father), full of grace and truth. John beareth witness of him, and crieth, saying, This was he of whom I said, He that cometh after me is become before me: for he was before me. For of his fulness we all received, and grace for grace. The law was given through Moses; grace and truth came through Jesus Christ. No man hath seen God at any time; the only begotten Son, who is in the bosom of the Father, he hath declared him." John 1: 1-18 KJV

When Mary gave birth to Jesus, she fulfilled the prophecy that God gave to the serpent in the garden of Eden, when He said, "I that he will put enmity between the serpent and the woman and the serpent's seed will bruise the woman's seed heel, but the woman's seed will crush the serpent's seed head. "When Mary gave birth to Jesus, she fulfilled that prophecy. Jesus is the first of many brethren, which means he's not the only one now; the woman has the power to give birth when she receives the seed (the **word** of God) and releases it out of her mouth into someone's ear, then their heart. By this, if they believe her, conception begins, and they are born again…a new soul. Therefore, that seed needs to be nurtured to grow and mature to do its job and crush the serpent seed's head.

Mary walked into her calling full force when she found out she was carrying the son of God. Mary had to run and hide. She was ridiculed and ostracized for holding on to what God told her. They wanted to stone her for what she was standing on and believed. They wanted her to confess to a transgression she had not committed. God chose Mary to carry Jesus in her womb…So she carried the word in her body. She gave birth to the word, pushing the word out in pain, so she experienced how the word can hurt before it heals. She wrapped the word in blankets to keep the word warm; she nurtured the word, she fed the word, and she protected the word. She took the word and fled to Egypt from the death decree sent by King Herod; she carried the word in her arms, held the word close to her heart, and taught the word.

She spoke to the word before the word could talk. Now, she was giving the word a word, and the word listened. The word humbled himself to the woman. She comforted the word when the word cried; she comforted the word. She raised the word; she put the word to bed; she was an excellent mother to the word. She made the word lay down and rest. Mary washed the word. She dressed the word and covered the word with clothes. She watched the word grow. She took the word to the temple for the Passover Feast. She taught the word about the Law of Moses and the prophets. She watched as the word became a young man. She gave the word advice and started worrying about the word's safety. She warned the word concerning his enemies. She sacrificed her life for the word. She lost her reputation for the word. She was ridiculed because of the word. She was misunderstood because of the word. She saw the word being rejected. She witnessed people who made a mockery of the word. Mary loved the word with all of her heart. She cried for the word. The word made her cry when the word had to leave her to go to work. The word had to die, and Mary was there when he did. She cried for the word.

Before men could even believe in the man Jesus, Mary the woman and mother had the Word that became flesh. So, is there anyone in this world who will take the side of a person or spirit that will tell the woman she doesn't have a right to preach the Word of God? The woman was chosen to do all of this for God's word but can't preach the Word. Who is saying this? Is it the same God who chose the woman and entrusted her with His Word? Or are these false gods talking to these men and women who are trying to stop the move of God by not believing a woman can preach or pastor?

"Mary had a little lamb whose fleece was white as snow; wherever Mary went, the lamb was sure to go." Mary was the shepherd who had the Lamb of God following her voice before He was given His voice as a man, but you are saying a woman cannot be a pastor (shepherd); she already is.

Preaching God's Word is just one of your Kingdom Rights. Don't allow the devil, through any form, to deny you the right to preach the Word that God used you to give birth to, nurture, and take care of until He was able to take care of Himself. So, are you telling us that God can use the woman to care for His Word but not preach His Word? Sounds chauvinistic to me.

Scriptural wisdom, "Do not muzzle the ox while it treads out the grain." This dictum implores farmers to refrain from depriving their animals of sustenance while aiding in crop production. An injustice is being committed by withholding food from animals that are contributing to the livelihood of the farmers. Instead, providing adequate nourishment to these animals is integral to ensuring their well-being and productivity. Thus, it is imperative for farmers to heed this wisdom and treat their animals with the care and respect they deserve. If God said this was an injustice to animals, then how much more would God say to the bishops, pastors, and spiritual leaders concerning denying the woman the right to preach God's word, which was used to bring forth Jesus Christ through her own body, and raise him? ***"Jesus is that Word."***

* * *

Before Jesus began his ministry, he went to the wilderness to confront the devil, that old serpent who had deceived Eve in the Garden of Eden. Nobody had ever confronted the devil before, but Jesus was brave enough to challenge Satan and his demons. Jesus asked the devil to do to him what he had done to Eve. Jesus overcame every temptation that was used to cause humanity to fall. This was the same Word that became flesh and dwelt among us. The word became a baby, then boy, young man, and then man; that man was 100% human and 100% divine, and that Word saved us.

Victoriously, He then went on to crush the head of the serpent and its offspring. He completed this task on the cross. So preach, woman, with confidence and authority… the Word of God has redeemed you.

Jesus said, "Before Abraham was…I AM!'

He is the First and the Last, the Beginning and the End, Alpha and Omega." Jesus is the Word of God, The Great I AM…FOREVER…

Love

Chapter 10

"For God so loved the world, that he gave his only Son, that whoever believes in him should not perish but have eternal life. God did not send his Son into the world to condemn the world but so that the world might be saved through him." John 3:16

The most significant problem with church is we don't have love. It is essential to recognize that the church concept did not exist until God bestowed His love upon us. The church was born out of this love and is often symbolized as a bride in metaphorical terms. God is love, and we, as His people, are supposed to demonstrate and give this love.

I grew up attending Pentecostal and Apostolic Churches, where I met some of the most anointed, talented, and gifted people. However, I noticed they lacked love, especially when someone made a mistake or messed up. There was no mercy or example of restoring someone to their place. If someone was caught in the act, or the word got out, they were thrown away or made to sit in the back of the church until further notice. Many people have left the church because they felt like nobody understood their struggles. Instead of receiving support and guidance, they were often shunned by other congregants and left to feel ashamed and guilty. I remember some of the faces and how pitiful and degrading they looked.

This made leaving the church seem like the only option. "It's crucial to remember the teachings of Jesus, who said that a good shepherd would leave the 99 sheep to save the one. We should try to be empathetic and kind towards those going through tough times. When you stop feeling what you thought was love, and it suddenly disappears, you may find yourself searching for it. I dare not say we're not supposed to have order; I'm saying we are supposed to restore people with love. Especially when we see how they are sorry and willing to do what it takes to serve their God and community. The modern-day church has become the beast of devouring our own.

The ability of a church to thrive is not solely dependent on the anointed and proficient individuals within its ranks. While such attributes are valuable, they fail to match the transformative power of God's glory, which can only be manifested through love, repentance, and humility. As such, my criteria for evaluating the effectiveness of a church has shifted from a focus on talent and anointing to one centered around the love exemplified by Jesus Christ. The anointing has been overrated, especially in the modern church. Being anointed doesn't guarantee acceptance by God. For instance, King Saul was anointed but still was rejected by God. He spent over 20 years knowing that God had rejected him, but he held onto his anointing, which had bewitched the people. Unfortunately, Saul abused his anointing and authority and mistreated God's people with it."

According to the teachings of Jesus, serving God and His people with anointing can lead to a higher level of spiritual growth. One can be promoted and entrusted with God's glory by bringing glory to God and demonstrating love for others. However, it is essential to note that this elevation is only possible when God can trust the individual.

• Jesus' prayer: "Father, glorify me in your presence with the glory I had with you before the world began. All I have is yours, and all you have is mine. And glory has come to me through them. I will remain in the world no longer, but they are still in the world, and I am coming to you."

• "They are not of the world, even as I am not of it. Sanctify them by the truth; your word is truth. As you sent me into the world, I have sent them into the world. For them, I sanctify myself, that they too may be truly sanctified. "My prayer is not for them alone. I pray also for those who will believe in me through their message, that all of them may be one, Father, just as you are in me and I am in you. May they also be in us so the world may believe you have sent me."

- "I have given them the glory you gave me, that they may be one as we are one— I in them and you in me —so they may be brought to complete unity. Then the world will know that you sent me and have loved them even as you have loved me."

- "Father, I want those you have given me to be with me where I am and to see my glory, the glory you have given me because you loved me before the world's creation. "Righteous Father, though the world does not know you, I know you, and they know that you have sent me."

- "I have made you known to them and will continue to make you known in order that the love you have for me may be in them and that I myself may be in them." *John 17: 5-26*

The parable of the prodigal son is a well-known story from the Bible. It recounts the tale of a young man who asked his father for his share of the inheritance. Rather than waiting for his father's passing, he desired to have the portion that belonged to him immediately. The father, in an act of love and kindness, granted his son's request. The son then left home and traveled far away, hoping to distance himself from his family and their expectations. The son made new friends and spent his father's hard-earned money on parties, trying to gain their love and acceptance. He may have felt like he finally found a place where he fit in, but ultimately, he was wasting his father's money.

As he began to run out of money, a great famine hit the region. His friends were no longer around, and he found himself in need and hungry, with nobody willing to help him. He couldn't find any work for a while until the only job available was to feed pigs and hogs. He took the job but was so famished that he was tempted to eat the slop he had to feed the pigs. It was at this moment when the son came to his senses. While he was still in the pig's pen, He realized that even the servants in his father's house had enough food to eat while he was starving. He said to himself, "I will return to my father and ask for forgiveness, saying, 'Father, I have sinned against heaven, and before you, and if you hire me as a servant, I am no longer worthy of being called your son." From a distance, the father saw his son coming home and ran down the road to meet him; he hugged and kissed him. His son said, "Father, I have sinned against heaven, and before you, and if you hire me as a servant, I am no longer worthy of being called your son," but the father said to the servants,

- "Bring the best robe quickly, put it on him, and put a ring on his hand and shoes on his feet. This is my son. He was dead and is alive again. He was lost, but now he is found. Prepare a feast we must celebrate. "Now his older son was in the field, and as he came and drew near to the house, he heard music and dancing. And he called one of the servants and asked what these things meant. And he said to him, "Your brother has come, and your father has killed the fattened calf because he has received him back safe and sound."

• But he was angry and refused to go in. His father came out and entreated him, but he answered his father, "Look, these many years I have served you, and I never disobeyed your command, yet you never gave me a young goat that I might celebrate with my friends. But when this son of yours came, who has devoured your property with prostitutes, you killed the fattened calf for him!" And he said to him, "Son, you are always with me, and all that is mine is yours. It was fitting to celebrate and be glad, for this your brother was dead and is alive; he was lost and is found."

Sometimes, people have hidden feelings in their hearts that they don't reveal to others. In this scenario, a younger brother knew his older brother didn't love him. He was afraid that he wouldn't stand a chance with his brother when their father died. If the oldest brother was already hating on him while his father was present, how much more would he hate and mistreat him in his absence? In such situations, people leave their homes and take chances with strangers, hoping to find love. Unfortunately, the older brother was too selfish even to understand the suffering and pain that his younger brother was experiencing. Some people only tolerate you, while others genuinely celebrate your existence. The older brother tolerated his younger brother, but their father loved and celebrated both his sons, the one who stayed and the one who returned after leaving home safely.

The absence of maternal love can create a profound

sense of incompleteness in a person, particularly in the case of a younger child. Although the text in question does not provide any information about the mother of the younger son, it is easy to imagine the pain of losing someone who has consistently offered unconditional love. In such circumstances, it is essential to remember that the affection and care that the mother provided will always be a part of the individual's life, regardless of the circumstances. By keeping the mother's memory close, one can find the inspiration to strive for excellence and become the best version of oneself. His recollection of true love may have influenced the son's ability to return home despite his mistakes. During moments of hardship, we often appreciate the depth of familial love. This realization can serve as a powerful motivator for individuals to seek reconciliation and return to the comfort and security of their loved ones. Acknowledging unconditional love from family can help individuals remain grounded and make improved decisions in the future.

As a believer, you must never forget that the Heavenly Father's love for you is unconditional. Despite any mistakes you may have made or any wrong turns you may have taken, He is always waiting for you to return to Him. It's important to note that sometimes, the hate or negative actions of members of a church or assembly can cause you to stray away from God. However, it's important not to let these negative experiences define your relationship with God. When it's all said and done, the opinions of your haters will not matter. What truly matters is the love of

God, which is immeasurable and always available to you. It's important to remember that for every Abel, there is a Cain - in other words, for every good person, there may be someone trying to bring them down. However, you can take solace in the fact that your blood is speaking to your God on your behalf and that He is always listening. It's important to forgive those who have wronged you and move on so you can continue focusing on your relationship with God. Remember that God has your back and will always be there to guide you on your journey.

- Whoever claims to love God yet hates a brother or sister is a liar. For whoever does not love their brother and sister, whom they have seen, cannot love God, whom they have not seen.

- Brothers and sisters, if someone is caught in a sin, you who live by the Spirit should restore that person gently. But watch yourselves, or you also may be tempted.

- "Love is the greatest power in existence, and it is the very essence of God."

- "Whoever does not love does not know God because God is love."

- Then one of them, who was a lawyer, asked him a question, tempting him and saying, Master, what is the great commandment in the law? Jesus said unto him, Thou shalt love the Lord thy God with all thy heart, and with all thy soul, and with all thy mind. This is the first and greatest commandment. And the second is like unto it; Thou shalt love thy neighbor as thyself. On these two commandments hang all the law and the prophets.

- Jesus said, "A new commandment I give to you, that you love one another: just as I have loved you, you also are to love one another. By this, all people will know that you are my disciples if you have a love for one another."

- "As the Father has loved me, so have I loved you. Now remain in my love. If you keep my commands, you will remain in my love, just as I have kept my Father's commands and remain in his love. I have told you this so that my joy may be in you and that your joy may be complete. My command is this: Love each other as I have loved you. Greater love has no one than this: to lay down one's life for one's friends."

- You are my friends if you do what I command. I no longer call you servants because a servant does not know his master's business. Instead, I have called you friends, for everything that I learned from my Father I have made known to you. You did not choose me, but I chose you and appointed you so that you might go and bear fruit—fruit that will last—and so that whatever you ask in my name, the Father will give you. This is my command: Love each other."

- "The first will be last, and the last will be

first...."

We were taught to "show love," but God showed us through Jesus Christ to "give love." There's a difference.

" For God so loved the world that he gave his only son, so however believed in him will not perish but have everlasting life." John 3:16. God shows us that we should give love, not just show it.

Imagine a situation where a person is starving, having not eaten for days, and they see someone eating inside a restaurant through the glass. This person inside the restaurant can see the hungry person outside and show them what they are eating. However, looking at the food does not fill the hungry person's belly or stop their hunger. The person inside the restaurant can continue eating until they are full, but that does not change the situation of the hungry person.

When we witness someone providing food to a hungry person, it may appear as an isolated event with no personal significance. However, when Jesus walked the earth, he denounced withholding help from the needy as unrighteous and evil. This implies that our actions towards others, even strangers, profoundly impact our spiritual well-being.

- "When the Son of Man comes in his glory, and all the angels with him, he will sit on his glorious throne. All the nations will be gathered before him, and he will separate the people one from another as a shepherd separates the sheep from the goats.

- "He will put the sheep on his right and the goats on his left. "Then the King will say to those on his right, "Come, you who are blessed by my Father; take your inheritance, the kingdom prepared for you since the creation of the world. For I was hungry, and you gave me something to eat; I was thirsty, and you gave me something to drink; I was a stranger, and you invited me in; I needed clothes, and you clothed me; I was sick, and you looked after me, I was in prison, and you came to visit me."

- "Then the righteous will answer him, "Lord, when did we see you hungry and feed you, or thirsty and give you something to drink? When did we see you a stranger and invite you in, or needing clothes and clothe you? When did we see you sick or in prison and go to visit you?" "The King will reply, "Truly I tell you, whatever you did for one of the least of these brothers and sisters of mine, you did for me."

- "Then he will say to those on his left, "Depart from me, you who are cursed, into the eternal fire prepared for the devil and his angels. For I was hungry, and you gave me nothing to eat; I was thirsty, and you gave me nothing to drink; I was a stranger, and you did not invite me in; I needed clothes, and you did not clothe me; I was sick and in prison, and you did not look after me."

- "They also will answer, "Lord, when did we see you hungry or thirsty or a stranger or needing clothes or sick or in prison, and did not help you?" "He will reply, "Truly I tell you, whatever you did not do for one of the least of these, you did not do for me." "Then they will go away to eternal punishment, but the righteous to eternal life." *Matthew 25:31-46*

- Prayer without love is just witchcraft modified in disguise."

The real reason why we are divided and fighting over a woman's right to preach, teach, pastor, and all of the above is because we have no love. As Jesus said, we will be healed if we genuinely love one another. In our society, we have noticed the prevalence of division and segregation within religious institutions, as well as an increasing number of divorce cases and familial conflicts. Additionally, crime rates have hit an all-time high. One of the primary reasons for these issues is the lack of humility and love towards one another. If we learn to adopt the values of Jesus, who loved his disciples and continues to love us unconditionally, we can address these societal challenges with compassion and understanding. Where is the love? We say we love our country, but we are not willing to humble ourselves to get us back on track as a country because we don't love one another...Love covers.

The Word of God teaches us that if we extend the same love and care toward our neighbors as we do towards ourselves, we can create a positive impact and significantly change our country. This message emphasizes the importance of treating others with kindness, compassion, and respect, just as we would want to be treated. By showing empathy and understanding towards those around us, we can build stronger communities and foster a sense of unity and harmony that benefits everyone. Jesus Christ carried out his ministry by preaching the good news of salvation in the power of the Holy Spirit. He portrayed compassion towards the poor, the weak, and the marginalized. Jesus' purpose was to seek and save the lost, and he fulfilled the prophecy.

When Jesus surrendered to his destiny, he died on the cross. By doing so, he transformed a symbol of shame into the most powerful demonstration of losing oneself to fulfill the will of God. It would have been impossible for Jesus to let sinners handle him if he didn't love God the Father more than himself as the Son. He understood that God was the most important part of the work. As the church, we exist because of God and Jesus being united and ushering in the power of the Holy Ghost. God loved us so much that He gave His Son, and the Son loved His Father so much that he was willing to die and be the firstborn of many. We have become the "Many" he died for.

We are saved because the Father and Son loved us even when we were sinners. He was sent to save us from sin because sin threatens all life. God and the Son do not have sin, nor are they sinners. His love for us caused God to take on sin (become infected and sick) for us. Jesus died so that we could be healed of the sickness of sin. Sin is the root cause of illness and death.

*Jesus said to them, "Surely you will quote this proverb to me: "Physician, heal yourself!" And you will tell me, "Do here in your hometown what we have heard that you did in Capernaum." **Luke 4:23 NIV***

Jesus didn't come to heal himself but to heal us. Unfortunately, some preachers make us feel comfortable with our sinful nature. But if we keep living in sin, then Jesus' sacrifice would have been in vain. We've been conditioned to do church when, in reality, we are the church. We must be willing servants, helping people instead of just dedicated churchgoers. The church was created from love, while the world is being fueled by lust. We can see how lust has become a commodity in society, wanting things over life. The church should be a place where we find God and can feel the love of God. When did we last walk into a church and feel that love? It doesn't happen too often.

We're rejecting the very thing Jesus died for - the rejected, outcasts, misfits, and hopeless. We shouldn't be using the love of Jesus Christ to heap blessings on ourselves and call it ministry. Real ministry means serving others, but who or what are we serving? We have become personality-driven. This is dangerous because God warns us about principalities, powers, and spiritual wickedness in high places. Lucifer is a personality and principality. He understands the wealth of the kingdom and the power that comes with it. The church has the highest turnover of people who go to a place for one thing and are given something totally different from what they need.

When you go to McDonald's, you can confidently order a Big Mac, fries, and a Coke from the menu and receive precisely what you paid for. Similarly, when we study the ministry of Jesus, we see that he loved people and met their needs. Jesus founded the church and created a menu of love, healing, deliverance, relief from the presence of demons, joy, peace, and unity. This menu is available at headquarters in the Kingdom. However, when we go to church seeking what Jesus advertised about the church, we often find that these things are not on the menu of the local church. Just like in a franchise, we must stay within the guidelines of that establishment. We cannot come in and do our own thing. When I was a drug addict and needed help, I went to church and found what I needed on the menu. I ordered healing, deliverance, and freedom from addiction, and I received it. I walked out of that church free from addiction and never did drugs again.

Unfortunately, many churches do not believe in casting out demons, laying hands on the sick, praying and fasting, and preaching deliverance to set the captives free. If you are a church of Jesus Christ and don't believe in these things, who is your boss, and what kind of church are you? You may have a different menu, but you shouldn't call yourself a McDonald's if you're a McDowell's (as in the movie Coming to America). This is a powerful demonstration of how the devil has copied the true church, and while the copy may be close to the original, it's not quite the same.

Just like people from McDonald's headquarters know their brand and products, those who are dedicated to Jesus Christ should know His menu and what He offers. Satan is always reading the McDonald's manual and handbook (Bible), looking for people who like McDonald's food but are not committed to the corporation (they are just consumers). There are those of us who are genuinely committed to Jesus like his disciples and apostles were, so the devil cannot deceive them. Those who have been taught by Jesus and have sat down at the table with him have tasted his food and know what is up next as a new kingdom product. They can verify what is of God and what is not. People of the world should not be your go-to or your source for information concerning God's will and the kingdom. They can give you gossip or a news report, but by no means do they have the authority to sit down with God to get revelations. God chooses specific individuals to sit at his table and receive direct communication from him, just like a corporation invites people to a boardroom meeting. During these meetings, God shares with his chosen people if he plans to introduce new products to his "menu." God is not dead; the Acts of a God are not over.

The book of Acts is an account of things God did through chosen vessels. They are the Acts of the Holy Spirit, we say," The Acts of the Apostles." The original church did things that only those who had been given authority from God could do; now, anyone can go to a typical school to be taught how to be a pastor and not believe in the Holy Spirit, signs and wonders, and casting out devils. Well, who do you think built the school and made the curriculum? Of course, it's Satan. He has built so many McDowells that we believe they are McDonalds, but the truth is, the true church is the people, not the building, so he will never win. When the tribulation comes, the physical structure will not be standing; it will be desecrated, but the true church is in your spirit and can never be destroyed as long as God lives there. Get right with God, and be sure that your body is the temple of the Holy Ghost.

Don't be so impressed with your anointing if you cannot live right. Lucifer, the devil, knows the word better than you and I because he comes from the word and lived with the word of God in eternity. His problem is he is incapable of living the same words he quotes from the scriptures. Satan cannot live the word. We, as the true church, have become the word. So, when the false churches come down, be sure you have the spirit of God on the inside, so what happens on the outside of you won't have the same effect as it would have on those who were worshipping personalities and principalities. We get caught up in the production of the church. Let me help you out; Lucifer was created with pipes for vocal chords. He is the original producer of heaven in charge of music, entertainment, and grand events, the ultimate event planner, writer, singer, and musician, to name a few, and was anointed to use all of this for worship.

Could you be more talented than Lucifer was for one moment? Of course not! We are so impressed with Gospel and Christian artists who have talents and gifts and perform for us, but if they can't live the life they sing about, they are just tingling brass. What does this mean? You are a spin-off of the original, which is the devil. When Lucifer was kicked out of heaven, God kicked out his gifts, talents, and anointing along with him. Don't you know Lucifer is anointed but rejected? There is no record of God ever repossessing anointings. Your anointing is yours whether you use it for God or yourself. The problem is, if you use it for yourself and selfish gain, you are helping the devil with his kingdom (brand). If you use it for the will and purposes of God, then your anointing is used to destroy the yokes of the devil and bondages designed to destroy the people of God. Therefore, you are helping to build the kingdom of God, which is his Holy brand.

It's important to know that before the war in heaven, there was only one kingdom, and God was the ruler of it. However, Lucifer challenged God's authority and lost his place. A woman then replaced him. Lucifer started his brand, but in reality, he stole samples of God's brand and labeled them his own. Satan is not a creator of good things but rather a copycat of good and the embodiment of evil. Although he may make things seem good, he has no goodness. Eventually, he will have to reveal his true identity, and you will see that the brand he has been building is not God's but his own. God has said, "You have not been building the kingdom of God, but your own kingdom. You have dared to use everything and everyone that belongs to your Boss, including gifts, talents, and anointings! "So, don't you see the signs? Satan is using you to build his kingdom while preaching and teaching Jesus…" woe unto you, pastors!"

I am so sick and tired of pastors being politically correct while so-called representing Jesus when Jesus has never been a politician or political…the kingdom is righteous. When it comes to God, why are we so political? Another word for "Sellout!"

Study Jesus' ministry and his love for people. If the church does not have what Jesus put on the menu, you will discover you have been tricked. Wherever The devil ends up when this is over (he knows he has a short while), you will be there with him. God will not separate the false prophets from their daddy, the devil. When you go to church, are you taking love to church or going to receive love? Are you filled with love or lust? If love is absent, then the worship was of another god and production of Lucifer to empower witchcraft and lust of the flesh, the lust of the eye, and the pride of life. Satan cannot cast out Satan because then his kingdom cannot stand. Satan is a brand;

Lucifer is a brand; the devil and demons are workers and enforcers of those brands and will not deviate from their agency; they incorporate the ignorant with them. So whether you believe in love or not, God is love, and that will never change.

Dear friends, let us love one another, for love comes from God. Everyone who loves has been born of God and knows God. Whoever does not love does not know God because God is love. This is how God showed his love among us: He sent his one and only Son into the world that we might live through him. This is love: not that we loved God, but that he loved us and sent his Son as an atoning sacrifice for our sins.

Dear friends, since God so loved us, we should also love one another. No one has ever seen God, but if we love one another, God lives in us, and his love is made complete in us. This is how we know that we live in him and he in us: He has given us of his Spirit. And we have seen and testify that the Father has sent his Son to be the world's Savior. If anyone acknowledges that Jesus is the Son of God, God lives in them, and they are in God. And so we know and rely on the love God has for us. God is love. Whoever lives in love lives in God, and God in them. This is how love is made complete among us so that we will have confidence on the day of judgment: In this world, we are like Jesus. There is no fear in love.

But perfect love drives out fear because fear has to do

with punishment. The one who fears is not made perfect in love. We love because he first loved us. Whoever claims to love God yet hates a brother or sister is a liar. For whoever does not love their brother and sister, whom they have seen, cannot love God, whom they have not seen. And he has given us this command: Anyone who loves God must also love their brother and sister. 1 John 4:7-21 NIV

Jesus said, "A new commandment I give to you is that you love one another: just as I have loved you, you are also to love one another. By this, all people will know that you are my disciples if you have a love for one another."

The word "Love" is mentioned in the Old King James Version (KJV) 310 times, in the New American Standard Version (NASV) 348 times, and in the New International Version (NIV) 551 times.

If someone is not comfortable with God's guidance and moral values in this world, then it is highly likely that they would not want to spend eternity with Him. On the other hand, if someone is attracted to hatred, they probably already know where they belong. We are often unaware of what is inside our hearts until we live and experience life among many people and things. Time will eventually reveal whatever is inside of us. Only two kingdoms have manifested in this world, and the second one came from the first. Eventually, we will spend eternity with either God, who is love, or His adversary, the devil, who is jealous of God, a liar and hateful. He will do anything and

everything evil to God's children trying to hurt God…
Satan is evil like that. Children of God, refrain from evil; no
matter how hard it gets, continue in His love, knowing that
God cares for you and is love.

The quest for lost love is a perpetual journey that we
undertake throughout our lives. It is time to unravel this
hidden treasure and bring it to the fore. Turning to God,
who embodies the essence of love, is the key to unlocking
this treasure. Love, by its very nature, is incapable of
hatred. However, those who fail to comprehend the
nuances of love often perceive it as foolishness. It is
pertinent to note that love is unconditional and will
invariably find its way back to us, regardless of the
changes in our lives.

It is imperative to remember that those who do not love
God can never truly love us. It is futile to try and force
someone to love us, as love is a natural and organic
emotion that cannot be coerced. The ultimate test of love is
time, as it never fails to manifest itself through the ebbs
and flows of life. If love fails to withstand the test of time,
it is not love after all. God is love, and He never fails…

The Blood

Chapter 11

When Adam and Eve sinned, they became afraid and hid themselves from God. They covered themselves with fig leaves because their eyes were opened after eating the fruit from the forbidden tree. When God spoke to them about the seriousness of their actions, He covered them in animal skin. This could not have happened without blood being shed, as the wages of sin is death.

Therefore, after Adam and Eve sinned, God covered them with animal skin, which represented the first sacrifice. Years later, Adam and Eve had two sons, Cain and Abel. Cain, being the eldest, brought an offering of vegetation to God. On the other hand, Abel, the younger brother, brought a lamb as a sacrifice. Abel aligned himself with the universe, the kingdom, and eternity without his knowledge. He had no clue this was written in heaven. As it was written, "The Lamb was slain before the foundations of the world."

God accepted Abel's Offering but rejected Cain's offering.

And the LORD GOD said to Cain, "Why are you so angry?

And why do you look annoyed? *If you do well [believing Me and doing what is acceptable and pleasing to Me], will you not be accepted? And if you do not do well [but ignore My instruction], sin crouches at your door; its desire is for you [to overpower you], but you must master it." Cain talked with Abel, his brother [about what God had said]. And when they were [alone, working] in the field, Cain attacked Abel, his brother, and killed him. Then the LORD said to Cain, "Where is Abel, your brother?" And he [lied and] said, "I do not know. Am I my brother's keeper?" The LORD said, "What have you done? The voice of your brother's [innocent] blood is crying out to Me from the ground [for justice]. And now you are cursed from the ground, which has opened its mouth to receive your brother's [shed] blood from your hand* — **Genesis chapter 4.**

From eternity to time, God has told humanity that life and vitality have always been associated with blood. Amazingly right in the Word of God, he discloses to humankind that the blood speaks. Interestingly, modern science and technology have confirmed this age-old belief. It is now widely accepted that the essence of life is indeed found in the blood. This understanding has revolutionized the field of medicine and enabled doctors to diagnose and treat a wide range of diseases and disorders. It is truly fascinating to see how God has allowed us to uncover the secrets of life through our advancements in science and technology.

Are we saying, "The Blood is not enough?" We are dealing with people as if the cross had not happened. From

Genesis to Revelation, the blood sacrifice was the sacrament for sins. The blood of the lamb was offered up for the remission of sins. *"For the life of a creature is in the blood, and I have given it to you to make atonement for yourselves on the altar; it is the blood that makes atonement for one's life." Leviticus 17:11 NIV*

The order of the Levitical Priest was in place for the congregation to have a place to go to. In the Bible, Jesus is referred to as the lamb of God and the Messiah who came to take away the sins of the world. He is considered the mediator and high priest for our sins. Those who had transgressions and acknowledged their sins could go to the priest and confess, receiving forgiveness. Blood sacrifices were also made as offerings for the remission of sins, which we can see throughout the Bible.

The life is in the blood. This is more of the reason why one must be born again. It's not about religion but being a part of God's family. You can't join the kingdom; you must be born into it. The concept of original sin is a theological doctrine that refers to the first sin committed by Adam and Eve in the Garden of Eden, which is believed to have brought the fallen state of humanity. This sin was committed in heaven, but God did not allow it to be the birthplace of sin. Heaven is described as a regal, royal, and luxurious place. It is a place where God's glory and holiness are manifested in all their splendor.

God, being a righteous and just God, gives us reason to

understand why Jesus, the propitiator, was not born in a regal, royal, or luxurious place. When Jesus was born, he was born in a humble stable in Bethlehem, which indicates God's plan to save humanity from sin and show his love and compassion. Sometimes, people accuse God of not being fair, especially when they face challenges and difficulties in life. However, it is essential to understand that God is always, even when we do not understand what is happening in our limited and finite existence. God's ways are higher than ours, and his thoughts are higher than ours. Therefore, we need to trust him and believe he is working all things together for our good.

Romans 8:28: And we know that for those who love God, all things work together for good, for those who are called according to his purpose.

When Jesus was crucified, he said before he gave up the ghost (spirit), "It is finished!" The sin committed in heaven that started this mess and confusion has been eradicated in the spirit. Therefore, it had a date to be concluded, but humanity has been reconciled back to God in the meantime. The price has been paid for the original sins committed in heaven by the Lamb of God's blood.

Do we not understand that Jesus was crucified during Passover-Holy week? This is when the Israelite people commemorate the tenth and final plaque placed on the Egyptians to cause Pharaoh to let the people go and give them their freedom. Moses instructed the Hebrew-Israelite people to take the blood of the lamb and place it on their doorposts. When the death angel passes over and sees the blood, he will not strike with death.

In Mosaic Law, Passover was considered a significant event that was celebrated yearly. It was a time and place (Jerusalem) where the Levitical Priest offered up blood sacrifices for the atonement of one's sins. As per the Law of Moses, over 276,000 lambs were offered as sacrifices during the week of Jesus' crucifixion to atone for the sins of the people. It is difficult to fathom the sheer volume of blood that would have been shed during this period, considering the number of animals that were slain. This highlights the significance of Passover and the importance of adhering to the Mosaic Law during that time. When did the blood stop being the atonement for our sins?

All of the sin offerings from Genesis to the time of fulfillment when Jesus was crucified and shed his blood for us (those who hear and receive). The scripture says, "The Lamb was slain before the foundations of the world." *Revelation 5: 12*

If Jesus is not the Lamb of God sent to this world to shed his blood for our sins, then answer this one question: why did all of the sacrifices at Passover stop? Do we not need the shedding of blood from the lamb for the remission of our sins? Is Passover a continuation celebration of what God did in delivering the Israelite people from the bondage of Egypt?

Didn't Moses make it plain enough concerning the blood sacrifice for the atonement of one's sins? If Jesus is not the Lamb, then where is the atonement for your sins? To all who reject Jesus as the Savior and Messiah, how are your sins forgiven? Will you be able to justify to God, as a follower of Moses, that you decided, because of the time we live in or era, that blood sacrifice for sins is obsolete? Is there another lamb and or Lamb of God more worthy than Jesus? What are we using during Passover as the blood? How are our sins atoned for today? Is it the rich and royal one…another David or Solomon that people are waiting on? Is there a more worthy Messiah? If so, what is his name?

"Behold The Lamb of God who has come to take away the sins of the world." The Only One Worthy. *Revelation 5:1-14*

• And I saw in the right hand of him that sat on the throne a book written within and on the backside, sealed with seven seals. And I saw a strong angel proclaiming with a loud voice, Who is worthy to open the book, and to loose the seals thereof?

• And no man in heaven, nor in earth, neither under the earth, was able to open the book, neither to look thereon. And I wept much because no man was found worthy to open and to read the book, neither to look thereon. And one of the elders saith unto me,

• Weep not: behold, the Lion of the tribe of Juda, the Root of David, hath prevailed to open the book and to loose the seven seals thereof. And I beheld, and, lo, in the midst of the throne and of the four beasts, and in the midst of the elders, stood a Lamb as it had been slain, having seven horns and seven eyes, which are the seven Spirits of God sent forth into all the earth.

• And he came and took the book out of the right hand of him that sat upon the throne. And when he had taken the book, the four beasts and four and twenty elders fell down before the Lamb, having every one of them harps and golden vials full of odors, which are the prayers of saints. And they sang a new song, saying,

• Thou art worthy to take the book, and to open the seals thereof: for thou wast slain, and hast redeemed us to God by thy blood out of every kindred, and tongue, and people, and nation; and hast made us unto our God kings and priests: and we shall reign on the earth.

• And I beheld, and I heard the voice of many angels round about the throne and the beasts and the elders: and the number of them was ten thousand times ten thousand, and thousands of thousands; saying with a loud voice,

• Worthy is the Lamb that was slain to receive power, and riches, and wisdom, and strength, and honour, and glory, and blessing. And every creature which is in heaven, and on the earth, and under the earth, and such as are in the sea, and all that are in them, heard I saying, Blessing, and honor, and glory, and power, be unto him that sitteth upon the throne, and unto the Lamb forever and ever.

•   And the four beasts said, Amen. And the four and twenty elders fell down and worshipped him that liveth forever and ever. Moses has left clear and concise instructions for the atonement of man's sins by way of the blood. It is written in the scriptures that "Salvation is coming through the Jews."

Jesus came as our Savior, without whom we could not be delivered from sin and death. He declared: "The Son of God had the power to make worlds, to direct them. He came here as the Only Begotten Son to fulfill a mission, to be a Lamb slain before the foundation of the world, to bring about salvation to all humanity. Jesus Christ made it possible for us to attain eternal life and return to the presence of the Father and the Son through His sacrifice. He showed us the way to achieve this. Our hearts figuratively represent the doorway to eternal life. This is the true essence of Jesus Christ, and His grandeur is beyond compare.

When the angel of death sees the blood, he cannot touch your spirit (soul). The enemy has no right to your soul when he sees the blood of The Lamb of God. When Jesus died, he defeated death, hell, and the grave. The blood of Jesus brings about reconciliation and restoration, and any previous wrongs or mistakes are no longer valid. It questions why we continue to insult God, Jesus, and the Holy Spirit by perpetuating the idea that women are meant to be subservient to men despite the immense sacrifices and bloodshed that have taken place.

Adam was created, but Eve was made by what was taken from Adam's side. This is the model God set for us to see that in the beginning, there was unity…they were one. Adam was destined to eat the fruit from her hands, not the enemy's. Adam and Eve were created to be one, "God created he him, male and female created he them." The woman was already inside the man… they were one from the beginning. He loved his wife enough to die with her because he realized that he should have covered her. Adam undoubtedly loved Eve, but perhaps he lacked the necessary life experiences to navigate the situation. Unfortunately, it appears that the enemy took advantage of their vulnerability. Sometimes, people refer to the concept of a "weaker vessel," but it's important to remember that everyone has their strengths and weaknesses. We should try to approach the situation with compassion and understanding.

Jesus Christ is often referred to as the second man, Adam. The Biblical account of Adam's fall and the associated notion of a perfect, sinless being have inspired a parallel between Adam and Jesus. The first man, Adam, is said to have died with his wife, whereas the second man, also known as Adam (Jesus), is believed to have died for his bride, the Church.

When Jesus died, the soldier pierced him in his side. *"Since it was the day of Preparation, and so that the bodies would not remain on the cross on the Sabbath (for that Sabbath was a high day), the Jews asked Pilate that their legs might be broken and that they might be taken away. So the soldiers came and broke the legs of the first and of the other who had been crucified with him. But when they came to Jesus and saw that he was already dead, they did not break his legs. But one of the soldiers pierced his side with a spear, and at once, there came out blood and water. He who saw it has borne witness—his testimony is true, and he knows that he is telling the truth—that you also may believe. For these things took place that the Scripture might be fulfilled: "Not one of his bones will be broken." And again, another Scripture says, "They will look on him whom they have pierced." John 19:31-37*

The blood and water represent the birth of the church. Just as Eve was taken from Adam's side, not from his behind, men and women are meant to be partners. This serves as a reminder of the importance of equal partnership. Jesus restores this balance.

For the life of the flesh is in the blood: and I have given it to you upon the altar to make an atonement for your souls: for it is the blood that maketh an atonement for the soul. Leviticus 17:11

Knowing that ye were redeemed, not with corruptible things, with silver or gold, from your vain manner of life handed down from your fathers; but with precious blood, as of a lamb without blemish and without spot, even the blood of Christ: who was foreknown indeed before the foundation of the world, but was manifested at the end of the times for your sake, who through him are believers in God, that raised him from the dead, and gave him glory; so that your faith and hope might be in God.   **1 Peter 1:18-21**

And who is he that overcometh the world, but he that believeth that Jesus is the Son of God? This is he that came by water and blood, even Jesus Christ; not with the water only, but with the water and with the blood. And it is the Spirit that beareth witness because the Spirit is the truth. For there are three who bear witness, the Spirit, and the water, and the blood: and the three agree in one. 1 John 5:5-8

This is the blood of the covenant which God commanded to you-ward. Moreover the tabernacle and all the vessels of the ministry he sprinkled in like manner with the blood. And according to the law, I may almost say, all things are cleansed with blood, and apart from shedding of blood there is no remission. Hebrews 9: 20-22

The beauty of the pre-sin relationship was that there was no sense of competition or confrontation between the two parties. Each recognized and appreciated the unique gifts, talents, and tools the other brought, creating a truly collaborative and constructive environment. We should recognize the importance of the equivalence of a person and respect for all, regardless of gender. It highlights the idea that Adam alone could not fulfill what needed to be done, which is why Eve was created. The text also touches on the concept of the war in heaven, which did not happen until after the woman was in labor. Even amid childbirth, Lucifer saw the woman's glory, and this is where the idea of being born again takes on its unique significance.

Even in all of the suffering Mary went through to give birth to Jesus, fulfilling the prophecy in Genesis chapter 3, ***"I will greatly multiply thy pain and thy conception; in pain, thou shalt bring forth children; and thy desire shall be to thy husband, and he shall rule over thee."*** Mary, the mother of Jesus, gave birth to her son without any assistance, in an environment lacking basic amenities, and without the support of family and friends. This sacrificial act of giving birth to the savior of humanity, as prophesied, was witnessed by the heavens rejoicing. However, it is notable that the male-dominated society, which greatly benefited from this sacrifice, has continued to deny women access to the same freedoms that Mary lacked during childbirth. Despite this, Mary's story serves as an inspiration to many women around the world who continue to face similar challenges of discrimination.

Jesus Christ of Nazareth, the son of God, came to this world with a mission to liberate women from the oppressive societal norms prevalent during his time. He aimed to restore women to their rightful place of equality with men, both in the eyes of God and society. Through his teachings and actions, Jesus emphasized the value and dignity of women and challenged the prevailing customs that treated them as inferior beings. Jesus' message of love, compassion, and justice brought hope and freedom to countless women, inspiring them to live purposefully and confidently and be redeemed from what happened in Genesis. Woe unto you, scribes and Pharisees, hypocrites! Because ye build the tombs of the prophets and garnish the sepulchers of the righteous, And say, If we had been in the days of our fathers, we would not have been partakers with them in the blood of the prophets. Wherefore ye be witnesses unto yourselves, that ye are the children of them which killed the prophets. Fill ye up then the measure of your fathers. Ye serpents, ye generation of vipers, how can ye escape the damnation of hell?

Wherefore, behold, I send unto you prophets, and wise men, and scribes: and some of them ye shall kill and crucify; and some of them shall ye scourge in your synagogues, and persecute them from city to city: That upon you may come all the righteous blood shed upon the earth, from the blood of righteous Abel unto the blood of Zacharias son of Barachias, whom ye slew between the temple and the altar. Verily I say unto you, All these things shall come upon this generation. O Jerusalem, Jerusalem, thou that killest the prophets, and stonest them which are sent unto thee, how often would I have gathered thy children together, even as a hen gathereth her chickens under her wings, and ye would not! Behold, your house is left unto you desolate. For I say unto you, Ye shall not see me henceforth, till ye shall say, Blessed is he that cometh in the name of the Lord.

It was like the Passover when the lamb's blood was put on the doorpost; the angels were not looking for race. They were not looking for gender. They were not looking for religion, but they were looking for the blood. Don't you know your obedience to God is your revenge for your disobedience? The blood covers you, and the Holy Ghost gives you power over the enemy. Is the blood of Jesus not enough for the atonement of the woman's sin? Do we need another Christ? Should we digress into the killing of sheep and lambs for blood that has the power to atone? Tell us, what do you guys need to remove the stain of prejudice in the Body of Christ? Are you the descendants of the Pharisees who could not see? Are you waiting on another Messiah to fulfill the prophecies, especially of "Your seed will crush the head of the serpent?" Have you taken over God's house as your own?

Do you solemnly think that God is going to reward you and applaud you when you leave this world and face Him and all of the prophets, who were hated, and the apostles who were killed because they preached the gospel of the kingdom? Who's side are you on, the right or the left? Who are you? By now, I guess you know I'm not politically correct because the kingdom is not political…it is righteous. If your mission is to stop anyone from preaching the gospel of the kingdom, then according to Jesus, you are not sent by God. You have the same father as the Pharisees. You are so desperate to be accepted in circles of power and glories of this world until it's blinded you to the truth. "When it's all said and done, you will leave here with nothing. "Only what you do for Christ will last."

Listen to what Jesus had to say to the priests of the temple of Jerusalem;

If God were your Father, you would love me, for I have come here from God. I have not come on my own; God sent me. Why is my language not clear to you? Because you are unable to hear what I say. You belong to your father, the devil, and you want to carry out your father's desires. He was a murderer from the beginning, not holding to the truth, for there is no truth in him. When he lies, he speaks his native language, for he is a liar and the father of lies. Yet because I tell the truth, you do not believe me! Can any of you prove me guilty of sin? If I am telling the truth, why don't you believe me? ***"Whoever belongs to God hears what God says. You do not hear because you do not belong to God."*** *John 8:42-47 NIV*

This is the reason why Mary could not give birth to Jesus, the Son of God, in his Father's House (Temple), because imposters (priests) had taken it over…Lucifer's children. The house was full of murders and liars hiding behind traditions of religion in priestly robes while carrying out protocols of the temple. These are the same leaders who falsely accused Jesus as an adult and turned him over to the Romans to be executed. In all of their knowledge of the scriptures, they were the fulfillment of the prophecies on the dark side.   **"Woe unto you, Pharisees…hypocrites!"**

The Blood

•	For you know that it was not with perishable things such as silver or gold that you were redeemed from the empty way of life handed down to you from your ancestors, but with the precious blood of Christ, a lamb without blemish or defect.

•	He was chosen before the creation of the world but was revealed in these last times for your sake. Through him, you believe in God, who raised him from the dead and glorified him, and so your faith and hope are in God.

•	Now that you have purified yourselves by obeying the truth so that you have sincere love for each other, love one another deeply from the heart.

•	For you have been born again, not of perishable seed, but of imperishable, through the living and enduring word of God. *1 Peter 1:18-23 NIV*

The Blood of Christ

•	When everything had been arranged like this, the priests entered regularly into the outer room to carry on their ministry. But only the high priest entered the inner room, and that only once a year, and never without blood, which he offered for himself and for the sins the people had committed in ignorance.

- The Holy Spirit was showing by this that the way into the Most Holy Place had not yet been disclosed as long as the first Tabernacle was still functioning. This is an illustration for the present time, indicating that the gifts and sacrifices being offered could not clear the worshiper's conscience.

- They are only a matter of food and drink and various ceremonial washings—external regulations applying until the time of the new order. But when Christ came as high priest of the good things that are now already here, he went through the greater and more perfect tabernacle that is not made with human hands, that is to say, is not a part of this creation.

- He did not enter by means of the blood of goats and calves, but he entered the Most Holy Place once for all by his own blood, thus obtaining eternal redemption.

The blood of goats and bulls and the ashes of a heifer sprinkled on those who are ceremonially unclean sanctify them so that they are outwardly clean. How much more, then, will the blood of Christ, who through the eternal Spirit offered himself unblemished to God, cleanse our consciences from acts that lead to death so that we may serve the living God!

For this reason, Christ is the mediator of a new covenant, that those who are called may receive the promised eternal inheritance—now that he has died as a ransom to set them free from the sins committed under the first covenant.

In the case of a will, it is necessary to prove the death of the one who made it because a will is in force only when somebody has died; it never takes effect while the one who made it is living. This is why even the first covenant was not put into effect without blood.

When Moses proclaimed every command of the law to all the people, he took the blood of calves, water, scarlet wool, and branches of hyssop and sprinkled the scroll and all the people. He said, *"This is the blood of the covenant, which God has commanded you to keep."* In the same way, he sprinkled with the blood the tabernacle and everything used in its ceremonies. In fact, the law requires that nearly everything be cleansed with blood, and without the shedding of blood, there is no forgiveness. It was then necessary for the copies of the heavenly things to be purified with these sacrifices, but the heavenly things themselves had better sacrifices than these. For Christ did not enter a sanctuary made with human hands that was only a copy of the true one; he entered heaven itself, now to appear for us in God's presence. Nor did he enter heaven to offer himself again and again, the way the high priest enters the Most Holy Place every year with blood that is not his own.

Otherwise, Christ would have had to suffer many times since the creation of the world. But he has appeared once and for all at the culmination of the ages to do away with sin by sacrificing himself. Just as people are destined to die once and after that to face judgment, so Christ was sacrificed once to take away the sins of many, and he will appear a second time, not to bear sin, but to bring salvation to those who are waiting for him.

Found in you are people who accept bribes to shed blood; you take interest and make a profit from the poor. You extort unjust gain from your neighbors. And you have forgotten me, declares the Sovereign LORD. Ezekiel 22:12 NIV

President Abraham Lincoln issued the Emancipation Proclamation on **January 1, 1863**, as the nation approached its third year of bloody civil war. The proclamation declared "that all persons held as slaves" within the rebellious states "are, and henceforward shall be free."

This is what was going on in the United States of America during the 1800's. This Emancipation cost Abraham Lincoln his life because of the rebellion of some people who benefited from enslaved people. You must know by now that Satan benefits from keeping you in bondage. He has found all kinds of creative ways to make money from enslaved people.

There are those who will rebel against God in the same manner. Some benefit from the woman being a church slave and denying her kingdom rights as a citizen of the kingdom. No matter what God has said or what Jesus did, there are religious leaders telling God no. When they say no to you, they have said no to God. No to the woman being free and exercising her right to preach the gospel of the kingdom of God; after all, it is the message of liberation and freedom from the serpent, the devil. Why would any son or daughter of God who has been set free from slavery want to put his people back into bondage again? "We understand that Jesus shed his blood for all of us to set us free from sin. However, why are women who have experienced this freedom prohibited from sharing the message of their liberation and giving honor to Christ, who is their Emancipator?"

After all of this bloodshed because of sin, are we still saying the woman's sins from the Garden of Eden is too much to repair? Does she have some special sin? Adam was forgiven and restored as God's son, but Eve's place continues to be behind...unrestored. Is she never to be respected as a partner/helper at his side again? "Has she been silenced forever, and if so, by whom?

Her voice belongs to the One who created her, not her enemy. God should be using her voice, not Satan. They have used her mouth for everything and anything but to speak the Word of God. Someone seems to have an agenda to silence her while humiliating and exploiting her. However, her Heavenly Father has got her back...you will see.

Are we saying, "The Blood of Jesus Christ is insufficient?"
Then what was the wait for the Messiah all about?
The devil is a liar!
"He who the Son sets free...is free indeed!"
Preach Woman!

The Witness

Chapter 12

On the day of Pentecost, God was not on a gender assignment; God had finished the work to reconcile his children back to him. And when the prophet Joel said, "In the last days, your sons and daughter shall prophesy," Prophets were the highest office because the prophets were over kings. The prophet was consecrated to office had before you had bishops and priests…before you had an Apostle, you had a Prophet.

This is why God said Prophesy: This is to speak. He knew that the devil would come and try to shut the mouths of the witnesses down and say you don't have the right to preach or Pastor. In the last days, you're called to crush the head of the serpent, not be partners with him. He already tried that one. The spirit of the Lord comes upon you, but you're going to have the spirit of the Lord in you, you're going to have the kingdom in you, you're going to have the resurrection power in you. God Knew you, and He knows those being used to hinder the work of His kingdom.

Then Peter and the other apostles answered, saying, We

ought to obey God rather than men. The God of our fathers raised up Jesus, whom ye slew and hanged on a tree. Him hath God exalted with his right hand to be a Prince and a Saviour, for to give repentance to Israel, and forgiveness of sins. And we are his witnesses of these things; and so is also the Holy Ghost, whom God hath given to them that obey him. **Acts 5:29-32**

The statement is a powerful testimony about the Holy Ghost's impartiality. The speaker, addressing both men and women, emphasizes that the Holy Ghost doesn't discriminate and that whoever believes in Him will receive His gift. The speaker then goes on to make a poignant statement about how society has wrongly portrayed women as inferior and restricted them from experiencing the same spiritual blessings that men have been privileged to receive. I go on to further state that women have been humiliated and oppressed by the devil, who has targeted them, even went after their marriage and unborn children to destroy them, and you're saying she is supposed to keep what…quiet? I am highlighting how important it is for women to receive the gift of the Holy Ghost because this is your power! This is your endorsement from God to preach. If God did not want you to be a witness, don't you think He would have restricted or forbidden you to be in the Upper Room, where He specifically told the disciples and followers to wait until they hear from heaven?

Well, who told the women? We are talking about an era where women were considered second and third class, and they had no rights or voice. "Have you ever wondered why on earth she would be invited to a male-dominated meeting with God? Let's dive into this intriguing scenario together! "Look at how long they have waited for this day. The coming of the Messiah was about restoring what was lost and getting the woman's respect back from the garden. Only Christ can do this. The first man, Adam, couldn't help her as he needed deliverance, too. Adam continues to need Jesus to this day. In Genesis, God declared to the serpent that there would be an ongoing battle between his seed and the woman's seed. However, believers still debate regarding women's roles in preaching or speaking in the Body of Christ. As believers, it is essential to recognize the source of any destructive orders that seek to silence women's voices. Examining the scriptures and seeking guidance from the Holy Spirit to understand God's will concerning the matter is imperative.

We must remain vigilant in identifying those responsible for actions of unknown origin. It is essential to consider that individuals aligned with malevolent motivations may seek to imitate the tactics of their predecessors. For instance, in the case of a woman whom an adversary targets, it is reasonable to assume that their offspring may similarly desire for her to remain silent if she is aligned with her God. Alternatively, they may seek to recruit her to join their ranks and amplify their message. Thus, it is imperative to remain attentive to any potential threat's subtleties and respond accordingly. Do we not see the immense influence she holds in the global market? She is frequently exploited for the "lust of the eye, the lust of the flesh, and the pride of life" - three of the most potent weapons in the arsenal of darkness. These tools are used to ensnare our society in a never-ending cycle of delusional gratification and power-seeking.

If you were the devil and God spoke to you, warning you that a woman would be your greatest threat to annihilation, would you attempt to befriend her, employ her, and empower her under your authority? How can she be useful to God if she receives your orders, gifts, and assignments? The devil's intent to shame humanity is not a new concept. From the beginning, he sought to discredit those created by God to manipulate and control them for his purposes. He has recently made significant strides in this endeavor, particularly in the past six decades. Through the entertainment industry, he has effectively communicated his message to a new generation, uniquely and creatively glorifying shame. As a result, the devil has successfully reconstructed his kingdom, giving it a new and more insidious face…FAME.

Shame has a new demonic meaning, "Fame!" This is the devil's quote, "No shame in my game." The devil is using fame as the lur to get the souls of men, women, and now children. Everyone cannot be famous; Everyone cannot be rich in this world, and everyone cannot be a boss. That would be like having all the water in the world, but you can't drink it (because of the salt) and dying of thirst. If everyone wants to be served, then who will do the serving? If everyone wants to be chauffeured, then who will do the driving? Who will watch the film if everyone wants to be in the movie? Fame, they say, is eternal. But they don't tell you it's more like a loan than a possession. It's fickle and unfaithful, and it never truly belongs to anyone. Many people aspire to be famous, but few realize the intense pressure that comes with it. Those who have achieved fame, whether through talent, hard work, or sheer luck, know that the spotlight can be both a blessing and a curse. They are constantly aware of the possibility that their fame could bring them shame or ruin their reputation, and they often struggle to balance their public personas with their private lives. The reality is that fame is a fickle and unforgiving mistress. It can lift you up one day and tear you down the next, and it has never shown any loyalty or love to anyone. This is why many celebrities and public figures constantly fear making mistakes or saying the wrong thing, knowing that one misstep could cost them everything they have worked hard to achieve.

New fame has no shame because Satan has found this to be wise in the destruction of the marriage (the first thing the devil did in the garden, cause division in the union) family, woman, mother, wife, her children, business, and her place in the kingdom of God. You have no clue how powerful you are in God…except God reveals it to you cause the devil won't.

* * *

Women received back their dead by resurrection. Some were tortured, refusing to accept release so that they might rise again to a better life. Others suffered mocking and flogging, and even chains and imprisonment. They were stoned, they were sawn in two, and they were killed with the sword. You can find solace in the knowledge that those who came before us in life bear witness to the truth that only what we do for God will last. Hebrews 11:35-37

Therefore, since we are surrounded by so great a cloud of witnesses, let us also lay aside every weight and sin which clings so closely, and let us run with endurance the race that is set before us, looking to Jesus, the founder, and perfecter of our faith, who for the joy that was set before him endured the cross, despising the shame, and is seated at the right hand of the throne of God. Hebrews 1-2

After all, you have suffered as a woman in this world. Do you think that for the woman to be silent was and is a universal message…of course not. We must consider the time and era in which these things were written and the circumstances that caused the apostle to write a letter to address such a thing. The devil has been using men to use women for degrading things ever since the fall in the garden. How can the degradation of the woman continually be justified, using scripture? How long will we beat that dead horse as a people and society? Christ died and fixed that sin of disobedience.

* * *

Therefore, as by the offense of one judgment came upon all men to condemnation; even so, by the righteousness of one, the free gift came upon all men unto justification of life. For as by one man's disobedience many were made sinners, so by the obedience of one shall many be made righteous.

Moreover, the law entered that the offense might abound. But where sin abounded, grace did much more abound: That as sin hath reigned unto death, even so, might grace reign through righteousness unto eternal life by Jesus Christ our Lord. Romans 5: 18-21

Satan may lure us with stolen goods, but we must remember that they do not rightfully belong to him. His voice in the world soothes and comforts the pleasures of the flesh and life and has deceived many, but we possess the strength to resist and remain faithful to our God.

Do not love the world or the things in the world. If anyone loves the world, the love of the Father is not in him. For all that is in the world—the desires of the flesh and the desires of the eyes and pride of life—is not from the Father but is from the world. And the world is passing away along with its desires, but whoever does the will of God abides forever. 1 John 2:15-17

Please be aware of the devil's devices. Do not use your gift and anointing to exploit people for selfish gain; yes, we

are to be blessed but do not diminish your power from
God because of vanity. Many preachers do not have the
power of the Holy Ghost and revelation; they are scholastic
and have a word. So, like the Pharisees, they will kill you
and your career and be proud of themselves, thinking they
have done God a great service.

*Thus, you witness against yourselves that you are sons
of those who murdered the prophets. Fill up, then, the
measure of your fathers. You serpents, you brood of vipers,
how are you to escape being sentenced to hell? Therefore I
send you prophets and wise men and scribes, some of
whom you will kill and crucify, and some you will flog in
your synagogues and persecute from town to town, so that
on you may come all the righteous blood shed on earth,
from the blood of righteous Abel to the blood of Zechariah,
the son of Barachiah, whom you murdered between the
sanctuary and the altar. Truly, I say to you, all these
things will come upon this generation. Mathew 23: 31-36*

What is dangerous about this text is that Jesus is calling
them serpents. It was the serpent that was used to deceive
Eve in the garden. By the time we get to the Book of Acts,
we have an account of about 45 years of these so-called
holy men of the temple killing men and women of God
and persecuting the church. Jesus is giving us an inside;
he's letting us know upon his death, burial, and
resurrection that the unrepented leaders would have
innocent blood on their hands because they

misappropriated the authority and tried to kill the will of God.

But ye denied the Holy One and the Just, and desired a murderer to be granted unto you; And killed the Prince of life, whom God hath raised from the dead; of which we are witnesses. Acts 3:14-15

Who is telling you that you cannot preach? Is it the first Adam or the last? The first Adam was not your savior; he was your husband and needed a savior, too. Now that the savoir has come, what are we waiting for… Who are we waiting for? Jesus is the restorer. We have an account of before and after the cross. Overall, this is a call to action to recognize the Holy Ghost's power and combat societal injustices that have prevented women from experiencing God's authority and blessings without prejudice.

And he said unto them, It is not for you to know the times or the seasons, which the Father hath put in his own power. But ye shall receive power, after that the Holy Ghost is come upon you: and ye shall be witnesses unto me both in Jerusalem, and in all Judaea, and in Samaria, and unto the uttermost part of the earth. Acts 1:7-8

Then they returned to Jerusalem from the mount Olivet, near Jerusalem, a Sabbath day's journey away. And when they had entered, they went up to the upper room, where they were staying, Peter and John and James and Andrew,

Philip and Thomas, Bartholomew and Matthew, James the son of Alphaeus and Simon the Zealot and Judas the son of James. All these, with one accord, were devoting themselves to prayer, together with the women and Mary, the mother of Jesus, and his brothers.

In those days, Peter stood up among the brothers (the company of persons was in all about 120) and said, "Brothers, the Scripture had to be fulfilled, which the Holy Spirit spoke beforehand by the mouth of David concerning Judas, who became a guide to those who arrested Jesus. Acts 1:12-16

The scriptures record women's presence and receiving the Holy Ghost. These women are witnesses. Mary, the mother of Jesus, was visited by the angel Gabriel to give her the message of being favored and was going to carry the seed. She gave birth to Jesus, nurtured and protected him, and watched him grow. Who would be a better witness than her? These women were near the cross when Jesus was dying. They were close enough that they could hear him and communicate. All other disciples had left Jesus for fear of the Pharisees and Romans, except for John, the youngest disciple.

Now there stood by the cross of Jesus his mother, and his mother's sister, Mary the wife of Cleophas, and Mary Magdalene. When Jesus therefore saw his mother, and the disciple standing by, whom he loved, he saith unto his mother, Woman, behold thy son! Then saith he to the disciple, Behold thy mother! And from that hour, that disciple took her unto his own home. John 19: 25-27

Jesus, although dying, is still focused on his purpose even to the death. Before he leaves this world, he sets Mary, the mother, free. She now has to be the woman, while he has to be the seed; God spoke about in the garden when He said to the serpent,

"Because thou hast done this, thou art cursed above all cattle, and above every beast of the field; upon thy belly shalt thou go, and dust shalt thou eat all the days of thy life: And I will put enmity between thee and the woman, and between thy seed and her seed; it shall bruise thy head, and thou shalt bruise his heel." Genesis 3: 14-15

Jesus is about to shift from being Mary's son to being the Son of God, the second man, Adam, the seed to crush the serpent's head. Mary's heart is broken and is about to be pierced, so he sets her free. John is taking the place of Jesus to be Mary's son, while Jesus takes the place of Adam to be God's son because he's about to do a three-way split. He's about to die and go into a deep sleep; he will put his spirit into God's hand, and his soul is going down to Hades while his body is on the cross, soon to be taken into a borrowed tomb because he only needs it for a couple of days. Do we understand how powerful this move of God was and is still moving to this very day…Preach!

This is where his heart, Mary's heart, and God's heart

will be pierced. Out of his heart will come blood and water; this is when the church (bride) is birthed out of his side, like when the woman was taken out of his side, and Adam called her "Woman" because she was taken out of the man. We must be born again. The miracle and power of being born again could only come from God through Jesus Christ, your redemption; then how are you struggling with your call from God? Man, I didn't call you…God did, man did not die for you…God did; man did not anoint you… God did; man could not redeem you; Jesus did! He died for you, woman, Eve; God has fulfilled His promise to you from Genesis chapter 3.

What most fail to understand is Eve, along with all of the other women who may have thought God would use them to fulfill this prophecy. So, although they are not in this world, they are waiting in the next, you heard me say, "were." After Jesus died and got victory over death, hell, and the grave, he set the captive free. Eve was one of those captives. Though she was in paradise, she was not free. When Jesus set them free, they left Hades and Hell and were resurrected by the Resurrection….Jesus!

After Jesus set free those under the law and prophets, he returned to his borrowed tomb and dressed himself. He turned that tomb into a dressing room for you. He designed his newly glorified body and took the time to fold the grave clothes napkin wrapped around his head but left the garments around his body unraveled/

unfolded. Then he rolled away the massive stone at the mouth of the grave, not so he could get out, but so that the faithful. Fearless and devoted women who believed in him could get into the tomb. He knew they were coming. If the men were coming, he would leave the stone for them to move just as they did at Lazaras's tomb because they were strong enough. Look how thoughtful and considerate God is.

When Jesus died, Mary, his mother, along with the other women, witnessed his death, and it hurt them. They did not know and understand all of those scriptures and prophecies; all they knew was that he had suffered and died. These are witnesses, and they are women…fearless and relentless. When the men were afraid and hiding out, the women were mourning and praying right there amongst the enemies of God. Mary is among a few named women. So many women who believed in Jesus' ministry were disciples and supporters of his work. Mary Magdalene, who was at the tomb, pleaded for his body so she could wash and prepare him for burial. They are our witnesses with Apostle John, whom the Lord appeared to on the Island of Patmos many decades later, who gives us the witness account of the Book of Revelation. When you have experience with God, you are a witness.

Who better speak about her demise, challenges, redemption, and victories because the enemy came after her? Not because he loved her but the very opposite, because he hates her and wishes to carry her away, be done with her.

And when the day of Pentecost was fully come, they were all with one accord in one place. And suddenly, there came a sound from heaven as of a rushing mighty wind, and it filled all the house where they were sitting. And there appeared unto them cloven tongues like as of fire, and it sat upon each of them. And they were all filled with the Holy Ghost and began to speak with other tongues, as the Spirit gave them utterance.   Acts 2: 1-4

And when the Holy Ghost came, it cut all of that out because you can't stop God from talking to a man or woman, choosing to use a man or woman. The Holy Ghost is the Spirit of Truth…..the Witness! He's talking to sons and daughters of the highest God. You've been reconciled back to the Father. When Moses disobeyed God by striking the rock instead of speaking to the rock, Satan fought for Moses' body and brought railing accusations against him. Still, Michael, the archangel, was there to fight for Moses' body and rebuked the devil. *Yet Michael the archangel, when contending with the devil he disputed about the body of Moses, durst not bring against him a railing accusation, but said, The Lord rebuke thee. Jude 1:9*

Well, where do you think the devil got that confidence and entitled kind of arrogance to feel he had the right to the man of God's body? Ever since he deceived the woman in the Garden of Eden and was able to get her and her husband to disobey God, he has been fighting over her body. This is why, at a young age, Satan comes for her body, innocent but guilty. He's placating you all of your life until your eyes come open. He thinks he still owns you because of that first sin. Don't let anybody take you back to the first garden, and play with your freedom or anointing. That was the first garden, but God had His Son go through the next garden to get you back and pay the price in blood twice in the garden of Gethsemane, where he was under so much pressure for your redemption that he was sweating great drops of blood. Before suffering betrayal, his crucifixion, but after his resurrection, He waited to appear to you…a woman, not a man. If he had wanted you to shut your mouth, he would not have occurred to you first. In the first Garden, he gave Adam the message to give to the woman about the tree of knowledge, good and evil, but in the last Garden, he was sure to provide Mary with the message to give to his disciples (Adam) that he has risen… he's resurrected.

"Then the disciples went away again unto their own home. But Mary stood without at the sepulcher weeping: and as she wept, she stooped down, and looked into the sepulcher, And seeth two angels in white sitting, the one at the head, and the other at the feet, where the body of Jesus had lain. And they say unto her, Woman, why weepest thou? She saith unto them, Because they have taken away my Lord, and I know not where they have laid him. And

when she had thus said, she turned herself back and saw Jesus standing, and knew not that it was Jesus. Jesus saith unto her, Woman, why weepest thou? Whom seekest thou? She, supposing him to be the gardener, saith unto him, Sir, if thou have borne him hence, tell me where thou hast laid him, and I will take him away. Jesus saith unto her, Mary. She turned herself and saith unto him, Rabboni, which is to say, Master. Jesus saith unto her, Touch me not; for I am not yet ascended to my Father: but go to my brethren, and say unto them, I ascend unto my Father, and your Father; and to my God, and your God. Mary Magdalene came and told the disciples that she had seen the Lord and that he had spoken these things unto her." John 20:10-18

Now it was Mary Magdalene and Joanna and Mary the mother of James and the other women with them who told these things to the apostles, but these words seemed to them an idle tale, and they did not believe them. But Peter rose and ran to the tomb; stooping and looking in, he saw the linen cloths by themselves and went home, marveling at what had happened. Luke 24: 10-12

Remember, God never gave Eve the message of not eating from the tree directly; he told Adam, and then Adam told Eve. So, the enemy played on that very thing and said, "Did God say? He proposed doubt and then moved; now, things have turned around. God told the woman and entrusted her to notify them, which she did. The men's disciples were present, along with a woman.

The message conveyed was that it's finished! You are back to the place where you were meant to be, which is by my side. It's worth noting that the woman was created from Adam's side, not from his behind. Therefore, she should stand beside him and not behind him. The biblical account describes Adam as a tiller of the ground or a gardener. Interestingly, when Jesus appeared to Mary after his resurrection, he was mistaken for a gardener. This is significant because Jesus is often referred to as the "last Adam," who came to restore women to their rightful place —this parallel between Adam and Jesus as gardeners highlight the restoration theme.

All of your rights and authority have been restored to you. God said to the serpent, your seed in the woman's seed should be at all the days of your life; you know that got to be spiritual because a woman doesn't produce natural seed through her body. Hence, if you don't preach, if you do not teach, if you do not prophesy, how are you going to shut down this enemy that's coming after you'll see your offspring when you preach and release that word? You are producing your offspring that will go after that serpent's offspring. It's a war going on, And you can't take my weapon because my weapon is my word, and my word is from God, made and manufactured to win battles, and I can't win with my mouth shut. I can't win with you telling me I can't preach; I can't win with you, pretending you are for me in my face and talking about me behind my back, telling your peers I don't believe in women preachers the devil is a liar and he's two-faced. You have the title and position of a pastor/bishop/ preacher, but the nature of the serpent, who is a leader and deceiver. When Jesus took on the sins of the world, our sins were nailed to that tree.

Kingdom protocols were broken. Satan didn't have the rights he used to have when the work had been finished. This is why, in the upper room, there were males and females. If the woman were supposed to remain silent, she would not have been in the upper room. When the Holy Ghost fell, they began to SPEAK in unknown tongues (languages they did not know). Why would God have women present when He sent them the Holy Spirit, which is the spirit of truth, and he will give them power? Power to do what…be silent! Be in bondage? God meant just what He said through the prophet Joel: And it shall come to pass afterward, that I will pour out my Spirit **on all flesh; your sons and your daughters** shall prophesy, your old men shall dream dreams, and your young men shall see visions. Even on the male and female servants in those days, I will pour out my Spirit.

This explains how the slaves got it. They had no education and could not read the Bible but were filled with the Holy Spirit. "All types of flesh – black, white, rich, poor, educated, ignorant, and prejudiced. Do you understand? Right here in America, the Spirit of the Lord fell on the slaves right in the field during slavery. God did His thing! Here we are..now what are you going to do with all of that power and spirit? God is not a politician running for officer; he does not need God. He is already God; he does not have to figure out what we want to hear so he can appease us to get our vote because He is God. God is not political..He's righteous.

"But you will receive power when the Holy Spirit comes on you, and you will be my witnesses in Jerusalem, and in all Judea and Samaria, and to the ends of the earth."

There are approximately 180 named women discussed in the New Testament alone. Women in the Bible held positions of power. They were called prophetesses, judges and leaders, warriors, healers and caregivers, mothers and wives, disciples and followers of Jesus Christ who testified of him.

Mary Magdalene was the first witness of Jesus Christ's resurrection and spread the word to the Twelve Apostles. In Mark 16: 9-10, it says Mary "went and told them that had been with him, as they mourned and wept." She taught of the resurrected Christ. Mary Magdalene was the first witness of Jesus Christ.

Joanna and Mary, mother of James: Several more women who were close to Jesus proclaimed the resurrection, including Joanna and Mary, the mother of James, as Luke 24:9-11 demonstrates. All three women were there to tend to Christ, Luke 24:1-10.

* * *

Priscilla invited many to "come into (her) house, and abide there" after being baptized in Acts 16:15. She later became a missionary with the Apostle Paul. When a man came to the synagogue in Acts 18:26, "speaking boldly," both Priscilla and Aquila "expounded unto him the way of God more perfectly."

Phebe is referred to in the King James Version of the Bible in Romans 16:1-2 as "sister," "servant," and "succorer," which some have interpreted to mean "deacon" or "minister," per Biblical Archaeology. She is the only woman in the Bible referred to as such. Paul recommended her to the Christians in Rome and said Phebe was "a succorer of many" and left her to teach the congregation in his stead.

Mary, Jesus' mother, gave a beautiful testimony of the divinity of Christ in Luke 1:46 often referred to as "Mary's Magnificat," or the Ode of the Theotokos or the Canticle of Mary. In part of her account, she says, "For he that is mighty hath done to me great things; and holy is his name."

The Samaritan woman at the well, spoken of in John 4, listened and believed Jesus Christ speak before his disciples joined him. John 4:28-30 reads that "the woman then left her waterpot, and went her way into the city," where she taught of what she heard. "Come, see a man, which told me all things that ever I did: is not this the Christ?"She brought many more people from town to listen and learn about Christ. Verse 39 reads, "And many of the Samaritans of that city believed on him for the saying of the woman, which testified, He told me all that ever I did." More Samaritans joined the group, and "many more believed because of his own word."

Joel 2:28-32 And it shall come to pass afterward, that I will pour out my spirit upon all flesh; and your sons and your daughters shall prophesy, your old men shall dream dreams, your young men shall see visions:

The Answer

Chapter 13

We often seek answers to our immediate needs and desires when we pray. However, we should remember that the impact of our prayers can extend far beyond our own lives. Our prayers may be the answer to someone else's prayers from centuries ago. Therefore, we must not underestimate the power of prayer. Its answers can bring hope and inspiration to us and those around us.

You may possess the qualities or skills that someone else is looking for to solve a problem or answer a question. You might be the missing piece of someone's puzzle, the solution to a challenge they are facing, or the source of guidance they need. You never know how your actions or words might impact someone else's life, so always strive to be helpful, kind, and supportive. You might be the answer that someone has been searching for.

The Apostle Paul once revealed that he had prayed to God three times, asking Him to remove the 'thorn in his side.' Paul had been waiting for the thorn to be removed, believing it to be the answer to his prayers. However, while waiting, the Lord responded and said to him, "My grace is sufficient for you." It's common to feel discouraged when we see God answering prayers we've prayed for someone else while our requests seem to be left unanswered. This can lead to confusion and puzzlement, especially when eagerly awaiting a specific outcome. It's important to remember that God's plans are not always what we expect and that our prayers are being heard and answered in ways that are best for us, even if we can't see them yet.

Paul had no idea he would receive a profound understanding of grace through becoming God's model of love, mercy, and grace. This experience became the answer to his prayers. Sometimes, we ask God to remove uncomfortable situations from our lives, but He may use those situations to help us grow and become a source of hope and inspiration for others. You might be someone's answer. Sometimes, we encounter challenges that we call our "thorns." These could be difficulties, struggles, or hardships that we face. It's important to remember that if God chooses not to remove these thorns, it may be because He wants to use them to make us a testimony. Our experiences and how we handle them can inspire and encourage others who may be going through similar struggles. So, let's trust in God's plan and use our thorns to become a living testimony of His love and faithfulness.

We often miss the answers to our prayers, expecting them to appear in a specific way. Our preconceived notions create a mental image of what the solution should look like, and when it fails to match our expectations, we start doubting its authenticity. Consequently, we seek God's intervention once again, praying for an alternative answer that aligns with our imagination. However, it's crucial to understand that the answer to our prayers may not always come in the form we anticipate. It could be disguised in a situation we least expect or someone we never thought could offer a solution. Therefore, it's essential to keep an open mind and trust that God's ways are higher than ours, and His thoughts are higher than ours.

When John the Baptist arrived with the message of repentance and baptism, the Pharisees, who were familiar with the prophecy of making the crooked paths straight, rejected him. Despite witnessing something unusual, they could not reconcile John's teachings with their preconceived notions, leading them to reject his message. It is important to note that despite their knowledge of God's Word and the Law of Moses, astute men can still miss important details. This highlights the importance of always praying and demonstrating humility before God, even when the answer may seem obvious. Seeking God's guidance can be challenging, but it is necessary as, ultimately, it is for our benefit and to bring glory to God. Prayer is a deeply personal practice unique to each individual, like our DNA or fingerprints. It is a form of communication that allows us to express our deepest thoughts, desires, and fears to God. However, prayer is not just about asking for things or requesting divine intervention. It is about building and nurturing a relationship with God.

This requires trust, honesty, and consistency in our communication. At its core, prayer is about being open and vulnerable with a God like we would be with a parent who lovingly cared for us when we could not care for ourselves. When we pray, we use a language that goes beyond words and is understood by the heart. Just like a mother understands the needs of her newborn without words, God understands our needs and desires through our presence and the emotions we convey while we pray. The act of prayer is not centered on lengthy declarations and proclamations but rather on the humility of humanity. It involves entrusting oneself to the care of an infinite God who bears our infirmities and cares for us. As we mature, we must not merely request God's assistance, but rather, as dutiful children, we should be willing to contribute to God's vision and purpose in this world and look forward to reuniting with Him in the next world.

It is common for individuals to reach out to others only when they require something, never bothering to communicate when things are going well. This mindset is concerning and begs the question: how many people fall into this category? It is astonishing how little thought is given to the possibility that others may also need something or appreciate hearing that they are loved. No one wants to be thought of solely when something is required from them. Many of us have been guilty of treating God like a mere tool or Genie, someone who should grant our wishes. It is not uncommon for people to be upset with God when His response is not what we expect, as if we are deserving or worthy of it. Such behavior is unacceptable, and we should strive to conduct ourselves with more excellent poise and reverence.

Sometimes, people send messages or texts without a hello, greetings, or pleasantries. For instance, they might directly ask for money by saying, "I need some money" or "I need $20," without asking how you are or starting a conversation. This can be offensive to anyone as it shows a lack of respect and basic manners. If we think about it, this behavior can even be perceived as disrespectful to God. God is our creator, so he knows our needs before we ask. When Jesus was asked to teach them how to pray, He said,

"And when you pray, you must not be like the hypocrites, for they love to stand and pray in the synagogues and at the street corners so that they may be seen by others. Truly, I can say to you that they have received their reward. But when you pray, go into your room and shut the door and pray to your Father, who is in secret. And your Father who sees in secret will reward you.

"And when you pray, do not heap up empty phrases as the Gentiles do, for they think that they will be heard for their many words. Do not be like them, for your Father knows what you need before you ask him. Pray then like this: "Our Father in heaven, hallowed be your name. Your kingdom come, your will be done, on earth as it is in heaven. Give us this day our daily bread, and forgive us our debts, as we also have forgiven our debtors. And lead

us not into temptation, but deliver us from evil. Matthew 6:5-13:

When we pray and ask God for something, we have no clue how He will answer or what form our answer will come in. One of the most significant challenges to our faith is waiting for the reply. It's in the waiting that determines whether or not we will keep the faith and be faithful. Sometimes, when we get a prophetic word or promise from God, we naturally become anxious and, many times, impatient and want to hurry up the process by coming up with an answer as if God needed some help. When Abram received a promise from God to bless him with a son, he was already 75 years old and had been blessed with abundant wealth and material possessions. Despite all of this, his heart's greatest desire was to have a child of his own. However, he and his wife Sarai had been unable to conceive throughout their long years of marriage. By the time they received God's promise, Abram was already at an age where it seemed impossible for him and Sarai to bear a child - he was 75, and Sarai was 65. Despite this, Abraham held onto his faith and trusted in God's promise, even though the odds seemed against him. God introduced himself to Abram with a challenge. God required Abram to leave his family, country, and land to receive this promise. By faith, Abram left behind everything familiar to go to a new and strange place to please God.

The Lord had said to Abram, "Leave your country, your people and your father's household and go to the land I will show you. "I will make you into a great nation, and I will bless you; I will make your name great, and you will be a blessing. I will bless those who bless you, and whoever curses you, I will curse; and all peoples on earth will be blessed through you." So Abram left, as the Lord had told him, and Lot went with him. Abram was seventy-five years old when he set out from Haran. Genesis 12:1-4

Abram's faith was tested for many years while he was waiting for the promise of having a son. During this waiting period, he discovered what he was truly made of. Despite his challenges, Abram remained steadfast in his belief in God's promise. He trusted in the voice of the new God he had encountered, unlike any of the other gods he had been taught to worship. Unlike the physical idols that could be seen and touched, this new God was invisible and unfamiliar to Abram. As Abram embarked on his journey to find the land God promised him, he encountered numerous trials and tribulations. He had to navigate battles, famine, and the loss of servants and friends to sickness and hunger. At one point, he even found himself on the brink of losing his wife. Despite these setbacks, Abram remained committed to his faith and followed God's voice wherever it led him. In doing so, he demonstrated his unwavering trust in the divine plan laid out for him.

Abram traveled through the land as far as the site of the great tree of Moreh at Sheeted. At that time the Canaanites were in the land. The Lord appeared to Abram and said, "To your offspring I will give this land." So he built an altar there to the Lord, who had appeared to him. From there he went on toward the hills east of Bethel and pitched his tent, with Bethel on the west and Ai on the east. There he built an altar to the Lord and called on the name of the Lord. Then Abram set out and continued toward the Negev. Now, there was a famine in the land, and Abram went down to Egypt to live there for a while because the famine was severe. Genesis 12:6-10

Abram faced a challenging situation after receiving a reassuring word from God. Famine struck, and he had to leave where he was worshipping and celebrating God, maybe wondering if he had made the right decision in leaving his familiar place. His faith in God was tested, and he was tempted to doubt whether he had heard from God. Abram was so afraid of the king of Egypt that he lied and said Sarai was his sister instead of his wife. The king was to take Sarai as one of his wives. However, despite setbacks and testing, he remained faithful and was ultimately blessed by God, even in Egypt, where he had previously faced the cost of losing his wife. In the end, Abram was restored and regained everything he had lost, including his wife. One of the offerings given to Abram from the king of Egypt was an enslaved person named Haggai. She became Sarai's handmaiden.

In this passage, Abram expresses his concern to God that he has no offspring to carry on his legacy despite his blessings and accomplishments. He reminds God of the promise He made to him that he would have a son and wonders whether it will ever come to fruition. God responds with reassurance, promising Abram that he will indeed have a son who will be blessed and become a source of blessing to the world. This promise is significant to Abram, who has been unable to conceive a child despite his advanced age and that of his wife. It represents a beacon of hope in an otherwise uncertain future and a testament to the power of faith in the face of adversity. After years of trying, Abram and Sarai were still childless. It had been a decade since God had promised Abram a child, but time was not on their side. Abram and Sarai were already old when God first spoke to Abram about having a son, and now Abram was about 85 years old, and Sarai was 75. Frustrated and desperate to see the promise fulfilled, Sarai came up with the idea of using Hagar as a surrogate to conceive a child for Abram and herself. Perhaps this was what God meant when He promised them a son. Sometimes, when we have waited so long for God's promises to come to fruition, we may be tempted to take matters into our own hands. Sarai gave Hagar to Abram, and she conceived and gave birth to a son they named Ishmael. Abram was 86 years old when Ishmael was born.

After 24 long years of God making a promise to Abram, he decides to visit him. Abram had recently relocated with his wife Sarai after experiencing a difficult situation with his nephew Lot. Lot, whom Abram had treated like his own son, had turned against him. He expressed his desire to split and go his own way, along with his family, herds, workers, and followers. This decision was painful for Abram, who had exposed Lot to a whole new world - one that he likely would have never experienced if it weren't for Abram leaving their homeland and following the words spoken to him by God. Despite the hurt, Abram had to allow Lot to go his own way, and they parted ways. It was a difficult decision, but both needed to continue their respective journeys.

The more significant the promise or blessing, the greater the tests and the waiting period. Many people tend to get disheartened during this waiting period and give up on their dreams. The text also gives an example of Abram, who, at the age of 99, was still discussing with his company what God had promised him. Despite his old age, he continued to believe in God's promise and had complete faith in Him. On the other hand, Lot, who was with Abram, was determined to do his own thing and ignored Abram's love and counsel. Despite Abram's discouragement, Lot left to pursue his desires. This shows how sometimes even the best advice and guidance may not be enough to deter people from making their own choices.

When you have been waiting for a long time for something that God has promised you, it is possible that you may lose many things, including friends, family, resources, and relationships. Some people may even think you are crazy for not giving up or quitting. Abram and his nephew Lot disagreed on who should take charge. However, instead of asserting his authority, Abram gave Lot the option to choose the direction he wanted to go. To avoid potential conflicts, Abram decided to go in the opposite direction of whichever direction Lot chose. Ultimately, Abram said he would go west if Lot went east and north if Lot went south. Lot chose to go towards Sodom and Gomorrah, attracted by the bright lights of the cities. Abram decided to go in the opposite direction, and they parted ways, never to see each other again.

During this time, God visited Abram and told him that his name shall no longer be Abram (which means man of greatness), but from this day forward, it shall be Abraham (which means father of nations). Similarly, Sarai's (which means princess) name was changed to Sarah (which means queen). During this visit, God also tells them that Sarai will give birth to a son by this time next year. Sarai was preparing something for the guests to eat when she heard this news and laughed. God asks her why she laughed, and she embarrassingly denies it. However, God reminds her that nothing is too hard for Him, and because she laughed, her son will be called Isaac, which means laughter.

When Abram was ninety-nine years old, the Lord appeared to him and said, "I am God Almighty; walk before me and be blameless. I will confirm my covenant between me and you and will greatly increase your numbers." Abram fell facedown, and God said to him, "As for me, this is my covenant with you: You will be the father of many nations. No longer will you be called Abram; your name will be Abraham, for I have made you a father of many nations. I will make you very fruitful; I will make nations of you, and kings will come from you. I will establish my covenant as an everlasting covenant between me and you and your descendants after you for the generations to come, to be your God and the God of your descendants after you.

The whole land of Canaan, where you are now an alien, I will give as an everlasting possession to you and your descendants after you; and I will be their God." Then God said to Abraham, "As for you, you must keep my covenant, you and your descendants after you for the generations to come. This is my covenant with you and your descendants after you, the covenant you are to keep: Every male among you shall be circumcised. You are to undergo circumcision, and it will be the sign of the covenant between me and you. For the generations to come every male among you who is eight days old must be circumcised, including those born in your household or bought with money from a foreigner–those who are not your offspring. Whether born in your household or bought with your money, they must be circumcised. My covenant in your flesh is to be an everlasting covenant. Genesis 17:1-13 NIV

The story of Abraham and Sarah is a testament to the unwavering faith in God. They endured various trials and struggles yet remained steadfast in their belief in the divine promise. However, it's crucial to recognize that Sarah's journey was even more challenging than Abraham's, given that she had to confront the additional burden of being a woman in a male-dominated society. This is a testament to the power of faith and perseverance. Despite facing numerous challenges and setbacks, Abraham and Sarah remained steadfast in their belief in God's promise to bless them with a child. They endured years of waiting and uncertainty yet never wavered in their trust that God would fulfill His promise. And finally, after decades of waiting, God showed up in their lives and blessed them beyond measure. He did not need to be convinced or persuaded into blessing them; instead, He chose to do so out of His goodness and grace. Sarah, who had longed for a child for so many years, could finally hold onto the promise she had waited for so long. She could laugh and feel joy again, knowing God had been faithful to His word.

It's a beautiful reminder that, no matter how difficult our circumstances may be, we can trust in God's goodness and faithfulness. Like Abraham and Sarah, we too can hold onto His promises and know He will come through for us in His own time and in His way. It is vital to acknowledge that God recognizes our sacrifices for our calling, regardless of gender. It would be unfair for God only to bless Abraham for his faith, as Sarah played an equally significant role in their journey. Abraham would not have fulfilled his calling without her steadfast support and belief.

The story of Abram and Sarai, who later became Abraham and Sarah, is a remarkable account of faith, patience, and obedience to God. God promised them a child, but as the years went by, they grew old and still had no child. However, their wait was not in vain, as God was using this time to transform them into the people they needed to be to receive the promise He had made to them. They learned to trust God even when things seemed impossible, and their faith was strengthened through the waiting process. Abraham and Sarah thought they were ready for the promise, but God had a more excellent plan. He wanted to produce something that would last for generations to come. He was interested in giving them a child and creating a nation and a people that would bear His name and fulfill His purposes.

Finally, the son God blessed them with was born, and it was indeed a miracle. This son, Isaac, would go on to produce the 12 tribes of Israel and the Jewish people we know today. The promise God made to Abraham and Sarah was not just for them but for the generations that would come after them. God's purpose and plan for Abraham's seed still produced fruit thousands of years after Abraham left this world. When faced with difficult situations, we often seek someone to trust and believe in. For many people, this trust and belief come from God. However, trusting something we cannot see or touch can sometimes be challenging. Despite this, it is essential to remember that when we choose to trust and believe in God, we open ourselves up to the possibility of experiencing something truly extraordinary. By having faith that God will make good on his promises to us, we allow ourselves to be open to receiving the answers we seek. This can lead to peace and comfort, knowing we are not alone in facing life's challenges.

So, if we choose not to trust and believe in God, we may never know how great. When faced with difficult situations, we often seek someone to trust and believe in. For many people, this trust and belief come from God. However, trusting something we cannot see or touch can sometimes be challenging. Despite this, it is essential to remember that when we choose to trust and believe in God, we open ourselves up to the possibility of experiencing something truly extraordinary. By having faith that God will make good on his promises to us, we allow ourselves to be open to receiving the answers we seek. This can lead to peace and comfort, knowing we are not alone in facing life's challenges. So, if we choose not to trust and believe in God, we may never know just how great *The Answer* to our prayers could be.

The story of Joseph from the Bible tells us about a young man who was betrayed by his brothers and sold into slavery. After that, he was falsely accused and sent to prison. However, Joseph's ability to interpret dreams eventually led him to be called upon by the Pharaoh to interpret his dreams. Joseph became known as the Dreamer and helped others understand the meaning of their dreams. Sometimes, we may not understand people who are different from us, but we should remember that they may have been called to be that way for a purpose, which is to be ready when the time comes for God's will to be fulfilled in their lives. Some people may appear strange or different from others on a journey of self-discovery, which is necessary to understand their life's purpose and what is expected of them. Serving others is considered a divine calling and can be challenging, as seen in the example of Jesus, who was referred to as the suffering servant. Those called to serve others may face hardships and difficulties, even from the people they are trying to help.

The account of Joseph's brothers' betrayal and the sale of him into slavery has been documented in the Book of Genesis. The narrative recounts how the brothers, disconcerted by Joseph's dreams that indicated his eventual exaltation, plotted to kill him. However, they eventually decided to sell him to a caravan of Ishmaelite/Midianite traders who were passing through. The Ishmaelites were well-known for their trade, and the brothers offered to sell Joseph to them for 20 pieces of silver. The Ishmaelites purchased Joseph and took him to Egypt to sell him for a profit. The Ishmaelites were unaware that Joseph was, in fact, their blood relative, descended from Abraham, their forefather, four generations later. The Ishmaelites were merely conducting business and were unaware of Joseph's familial connection with his captors.

Hagar, the mother of Ishmael, was exiled to the wilderness with her son. An angel appeared to Hagar and conveyed that God would bless her son and his descendants, who would grow into a great nation. Ultimately, they settled in the Midian region and became known as the Midianites, distinguished by their place of residence, while their patrilineal lineage identified them as Ishmaelites. Joseph, who they rescued, was instrumental in saving his family during the famine that killed many people. Jacob, who was Joseph's father's name, was changed to Israel, to whom his 12 sons attributed to the making of a nation of people called the Israelites…called Jews today. How could they know they were the answer to generations of people? We read and study them and teach and preach about their stories.

This is the lineage of Abraham, Isaac, Jacob, and Joseph from the Old Testament. God promised Abraham that he would be blessed and become the father of many nations. Abraham's son Ishmael, whose mother was Haggai, and Isaac, whose mother was Sarah, carried forward his legacy. Jacob, one of Isaac's sons, had 12 sons, including Joseph, who became the second most powerful man in the world at that time. Joseph's divine revelation and wisdom saved countless lives during a harsh famine, including the kingdom of Egypt. This famine brought the Ishmaelites and Isaac's bloodline together as the Ishmaelites rescued Joseph and were eventually able to save his brother's bloodline.

The Bible also mentions the story of Moses, who was saved from Pharaoh by a Midianite priest, the descendant of Ishmael. Moses later married the daughter of this priest and became a shepherd for 40 years before God called him to lead the Israelites out of Egypt. It is remarkable how God's plan unfolds in mysterious ways, orchestrating events that span generations and bloodlines. Despite the appearance of abandonment, God is always there, guiding His people to fulfill His will.

One day, when Moses had grown up, he went out to his people and looked at their burdens, and he saw an Egyptian beating a Hebrew, one of his people. He looked this way and that, and seeing no one, he struck down the Egyptian and hid him in the sand. When he went out the next day, behold, two Hebrews struggled together. And he said to the man in the wrong, "Why do you strike your companion?" He answered, "Who made you a prince and a judge over us? Do you mean to kill me as you killed the Egyptian?" Then Moses was afraid and thought, "Surely the thing is known." When Pharaoh heard of it, he sought to kill Moses. But Moses fled from Pharaoh and stayed in the land of Midian. And he sat down by a well.

Now, the priest of Midian had seven daughters, and they came and drew water and filled the troughs to water their father's flock. The shepherds came and drove them away, but Moses stood up, saved them, and watered their flock. When they came home to their father, Reuel, he said, "How is it that you have come home so soon today?" They said, "An Egyptian delivered us out of the hand of the shepherds and even drew water for us and watered the flock." He said to his daughters, "Then where is he? Why have you left the man? Call him, that he may eat bread." And Moses was content to dwell with the man, and he gave Moses his daughter Zipporah. She gave birth to a son, and he called Gershom, saying, "I have been a sojourner in a foreign land."

The story of Joseph in the Bible teaches us the importance of having a positive attitude and helping others. Joseph's brothers hated him for reasons they didn't understand, but it was because he was the answer to their unrevealed problems. Later, when they faced a severe famine, Joseph answered their problems. If Joseph had become bitter and resentful because of the injustices he suffered, he would have missed out on his blessings. This story reminds us that sometimes things may not go how we imagined or want them to, but staying positive and trusting that everything happens for a reason is essential. Helping others and being open to their dreams can also lead to our blessings and success.

Sometimes, when we are going through the most challenging times, all we can see are problems. You may be going through a tough time right now. There's a bigger picture than you may see. Maybe your problems are a part of the process, and vigorous training is needed to be someone's answer. They see you as a problem, but God sees you as the answer.

When Moses saw the burning bush, he was not the only one who saw it. However, he was the only one who responded to it. This quote, 'Many are called, but few are chosen,' means that those who respond to the call and dedicate themselves to the voice that called them are chosen. How often have you heard someone say, 'I know I'm here for a reason (purpose)'? You need to listen to God long enough to know that purpose. The purpose will keep knocking at your door even if you don't want to answer it. When God calls you, don't expect everyone to hear what you hear. We must trust Him enough to keep walking even when we're in the valley of the shadow of death, fearing no evil because God is with us.

The early life of Moses was one of luxury and privilege, having been raised in a palace. However, at the age of forty, he made a decision that would lead to his exile for the next four decades. This decision was prompted by the fact that Moses had committed a crime, namely, the murder of a man. As a result, he found himself on Pharaoh's list of most wanted individuals and was forced to flee to a distant land, Midian, where he would reside for the next forty years. Notably, no record exists of any conversation or divine encounter between Moses and God during this period. It is thus conceivable that Moses may have felt that he had compromised whatever destiny his life was meant to fulfill. He was, in effect, a fugitive from justice. Moses, despite his education and royal background, found himself in the humbling position of a shepherd in the fields of Midian. The Egyptian culture viewed shepherds with disdain, as they were considered uneducated and beneath their social status.

Shepherding, as a profession, entailed physical labor, patience, and a great deal of dirt. Moses, who had once held high status, now spent his days watching someone else's sheep to provide for his family. The enemy indeed plagued Moses' mind, reminding him of who he used to be and how low he had fallen. Unbeknownst to him, God had a more excellent plan for Moses' life, requiring him to be humbled so that God could receive the glory. Moses' journey from a high-ranking prince to a lowly shepherd teaches us that sometimes, we must be stripped of our pride and ego to fulfill our true purpose. After spending four decades in the palace, Moses spent another forty years in the wilderness, devoting himself to shepherding. It was during this time that he was called upon by God, who manifested himself in the form of a burning bush that remained unconsumed by the flames. When Moses proceeded to investigate the site, he encountered the God he had been taught about and had heard about but had not yet known for himself. Until then, his knowledge of God had been second-hand, passed down from others.

Moses didn't even know what name to address God as. What is your name? How should I answer the people when I go to Egypt to tell them you called me and have sent me to deliver them from the bondage of slavery? What will I say, Moses asked God. "I AM THAT I AM," God said to Moses, tell them I AM," said God.

From Moses' birth to this very moment, Moses had suffered an identity crisis. Born Hebrew escapes the decree of the Pharaoh from being killed by way of the order of the firstborn male child to be killed by the sword of Pharoah. He escapes a death decree as a newborn and is saved by the pharaoh's daughter, then nurtured and nursed by his birth mother (who is enslaved), but he is raised as a prince of Egypt by his adopted mother, hiding his true identity growing up as a child. Born Hebrew but raised as an Egyptian prince. Then, at the age of forty, he intervenes and saves a Hebrew enslaved person from the abuse of an Egyptian. When presented with the task of returning to Egypt, Moses was overcome with fear, knowing that he was a wanted man due to an unresolved murder charge. However, God reassured Moses that he need not worry about the outstanding warrant, as all those seeking him were no longer alive. "Fear not, Moses, for I am with you," proclaimed the Lord God.

Moses, an essential figure in the world's religious history, embarked on a mission to deliver God's people from Egypt. His journey was filled with challenges, as he was met with resistance from those who did not accept his authority. God intervened and inflicted ten plagues on Pharaoh and Egypt, which eventually led to the release of the Israelites. The journey to the promised land was difficult, as they wandered in the wilderness for 40 years. During this time, Moses authored the first five books of the Bible, also known as the Torah. The books, which include Genesis, Exodus, Leviticus, Numbers, and Deuteronomy, were written over several years while Moses led the Israelites through the wilderness. Remarkably, these books have stood the test of time and remain relevant today.

Moses is credited with overseeing the construction of the Tabernacle, the formulation of the Ten Commandments, and the establishment of the Passover Feast, which is widely regarded as one of the most significant religious observances of the year. As part of this ritual, God instructed Moses to apply lamb's blood to the doorposts and lintels of homes, which would serve as a sign to the death angel to "pass over" households so marked. This tradition continues today as a symbol of faith and divine protection with the Passover feasts. This is done in remembrance of how God delivered them as a people out of the bondage of slavery and abuse.

The story of Moses is an inspiring example of how we can be a source of help and support for others, even when we struggle to find answers. Despite his flaws and past mistakes, God did not waver in his belief in Moses or his purpose. When Moses had given up hope and accepted his life as it was, destiny called him to become a deliverer and prophet for a nation in need. This story teaches us the important lesson that our past should not define our future and that we should never give up on our purpose in life. Despite enduring immense suffering and significant sacrifices, Moses' contributions to the world's religious history are undeniable. Despite his challenges and years off the grid, Moses remains essential in developing and propagating various religious beliefs. The Mosaic Laws have played an instrumental role in shaping the cultures of numerous societies. It is remarkable to consider how Moses' mother could have foreseen that her son would be the chosen one by God to deliver their people from over 400 years of bondage.

The divine call to answer someone's dilemma or problem has been universally recognized as a significant responsibility. It is imperative to comprehend that each of us possesses the potential to be a solution for someone. Often, we become excessively engrossed in our predicaments, which may cause us to overlook that we are the solution to someone else's problem. How many times have we said, "Jesus is the answer?" We can sing that and say that now, but during Jesus' time, many thought of him as a false prophet and rejected him.

"Jesus returned to Galilee in the power of the Spirit, and news about him spread through the whole countryside. He taught in their synagogues, and everyone praised him. He went to Nazareth, where he had been brought up, and on the Sabbath day, he went into the synagogue, as was his custom. And he stood up to read. The scroll of the prophet Isaiah was handed to him. Unrolling it, he found the place where it is written: "The Spirit of the Lord is on me because he has anointed me to preach good news to the poor. He has sent me to proclaim freedom for the prisoners and recovery of sight for the blind, to release the oppressed, to proclaim the year of the

Lord's favor." Then he rolled up the scroll, gave it back to the attendant, and sat down. The eyes of everyone in the synagogue were fastened on him, and he began by saying to them, "Today, this scripture is fulfilled in your hearing." All spoke well of him and were amazed at the gracious words that came from his lips. "Isn't this Joseph's son?" they asked. Jesus said to them, "Surely you will quote this proverb to me: 'Physician, heal yourself! Do here in your hometown what we have heard that you did in Capernaum.' " "I tell you the truth," he continued, "no prophet is accepted in his hometown."   Luke 4:14-24

Unfortunately, some individuals cannot see beyond their preconceived notions and biases, preventing them from recognizing the potential in others. The Israelites had been following the teachings of Moses and the prophets for a long time, which had given them an understanding of the signs that would indicate the arrival of the Messiah. Despite Jesus fulfilling these criteria, they were more interested in a king like David or Solomon, who would bring wealth and glory to their earthly kingdom. However, Nazareth, where Jesus was from, was a humble and impoverished place.

"I assure you that there were many widows in Israel in Elijah's time when the sky was shut for three and a half years, and there was a severe famine throughout the land. Yet Elijah was not sent to any of them but to a widow in Zarephath in the region of Sidon. And there were many in Israel with leprosy in the time of Elisha the prophet, yet

not one of them was cleansed–only Naaman the Syrian."

All the people in the synagogue were furious when they heard this. They got up, drove him out of the town, and took him to the brow of the hill on which the city was built in order to throw him down the cliff. But he walked right through the crowd and went on his way. Then he went down to Capernaum, a town in Galilee, and on the Sabbath began to teach the people. They were amazed at his teaching because his message had authority".   Luke 4:25-32

The historical text speaks of Jesus being rejected by his people and how he went to Capernaum. The people were amazed at his message and admired how he preached with authority. This raises an essential point about ministry - sometimes, we may feel like we need more of God's anointing to deal with certain people, but the truth is that we need to change the people we are ministering to. It is not always a matter of increasing one's anointing but instead finding someone hungry for God's word and respecting our anointing. The anointing that we appreciate is the anointing that we will benefit from.

Interestingly, it is said that Jesus could not do many mighty works in his hometown of Nazareth because of their unbelief. However, in Capernaum, he performed many mighty works because the people there believed in him. This highlights the importance of faith when it comes to receiving from God. It is essential to highlight that during the time of Jesus, the people of Nazareth had a negative perception of him and his mother, Mary. Some even went as far as to tarnish their reputation and question their legitimacy. It is worth noting that Jesus' paternity, like King David's, was also a topic of discussion and debate among the people at that time. Jesus' teachings and actions have been the subject of numerous controversies throughout history. Nevertheless, the impact of his teachings has been remarkable, and his sacrifice is considered an eternal contribution to humanity. His teachings have played a significant role in shaping the moral and ethical values of many cultures worldwide. His love, forgiveness, and compassion message has inspired countless individuals and continues influencing today's world.

The crucifixion and death of Jesus Christ are regarded as the ultimate sacrifice for the redemption of humankind's sins. The act of atonement was a painful offering that was presented to God and accepted. Jesus, who was without sin, became a sin for humanity. All the sins of the world were nailed to the cross, and through his death and resurrection, Jesus provided a way for believers to be forgiven and reconciled with God.

From Mount Hor, they set out by the way to the Red Sea to go around the land of Edom. And the people became impatient on the way. And the people spoke against God and against Moses, "Why have you brought us up out of Egypt to die in the wilderness? For there is no food and no water, and we loathe this worthless food." Then the LORD sent fiery serpents among the people, and they bit the people so that many people of Israel died. And the people came to Moses and said, "We have sinned, for we have spoken against the LORD and against you. Pray to the LORD, that he take away the serpents from us." So Moses prayed for the people. And the LORD said to Moses, "Make a fiery serpent and set it on a pole, and everyone who is bitten when he sees it, shall live." So Moses made a bronze serpent and set it on a pole. And if a serpent bit anyone, he would look at the bronze serpent and live. Numbers 21:4-9.

When serpents bit the Children of Israel, the Lord God instructed Moses to make a brazen serpent and put it on a pole. The people were to gather and look up at it. He told Moses to lift it before them and said He would heal them of their snakebites."

Jesus said, "Just as Moses lifted up the snake in the wilderness, so the Son of Man must be lifted up, that everyone who believes may have eternal life in him." 3:14

How can you exalt Jesus if you don't preach about Him? Jesus restored the woman from the destruction in the Garden of Eden because she listened and obeyed the wrong voice. To give glory to God, one must proclaim His name and share His teachings. Have you ever wondered how justice can be served for the wrongs done to us? The good news is that we can find true vindication and justice through Christ's redemption and restoration. It's incredible to think that despite the wrongs we may have suffered, there is hope for restoration and healing. Through the power of the cross and the shedding of his blood, Jesus has freed us from the burden of sin. His love and sacrifice are the inspiration that draws us towards him, and it is through these actions that our souls are redeemed. This message is not limited to any particular gender but is meant for all who have experienced his love's transformative power.

You become a witness when you experience Jesus' love, forgiveness, and power for yourself. The Holy Spirit compels you to speak about His goodness and what He has done for you, thereby lifting Him. You become the right voice, vindicated from the judgment of obeying the wrong voice. So, raise your voice and let the world know what you used to be and what you have done. You have been changed. If God commands you to lift the snake that had bitten and harmed you, then you must also have the strength to lift the woman who had caused you damage. This indicates that the pain caused by someone or something in the past can no longer hurt you. It symbolizes that you have moved on from the past and have become stronger and wiser due to your experiences. So, let go of grudges and resentments and move forward in life with a positive attitude, knowing that you have the power to overcome any obstacle that comes your way.

When Adam and Eve sinned, they experienced fear for

the first time and hid themselves. But after Jesus was lifted up on the cross, we understand that even the serpent (the devil) is afraid. Let this remind us that we can overcome fear and face challenges head-on with faith and courage. Don't let fear hold you back. The enemy may make you feel inferior and want to dominate you. But remember, you are not a snake meant to crawl on your belly or perform for others. You are meant to speak up and preach the gospel of the Kingdom, to lift up Jesus and spread his message far and wide. Don't be afraid to use your voice to make a difference and lift up those around you.

Change the way you see yourself; I know it's challenging. Stop focusing on your problems and start seeing you the way God sees you. You're not the problem without a solution, but the solution for the problem lies within you. You are the answer to your generation. You can only see your true self by seeing how great the One who created you is.

God, The Creator, created you to be The Answer.

This speaks about Satan's desire to have a hold on the old version of ourselves, the one who was rebellious and disobedient to God. It emphasizes the importance of knowing who we are listening to and following, regardless of whether we consider ourselves saved. The enemy knows that if we surrender to God, we will obey whatever He commands. The prophecy in the garden foretold the crushing of Satan's head at the cost of someone's heel being bruised for having the courage to stomp on the devil's head. We get to see how Jesus exposes the devil's intentions and tactics.

And the Lord said, Simon, Simon, behold, Satan hath desired to have you, that he may sift you as wheat: But I have prayed for thee, that thy faith fail not: and when thou art converted, strengthen thy brethren.   Luke 22:31

Have you ever noticed how Jesus addressed Simon as his original name and not Peter? This was to let Simon know that Jesus knew exactly who he was talking to at the time. Peter wanted to do what was right, but Simon, his birth name and nature, was associated with the flesh. This name was produced because of the curse that came upon the ground for man's sake, and since the body is made from the ground, it is associated with the curse. However, God did not curse the spirit of man. Some people talk about getting rid of generational curses, but Jesus came to deal with the curse from its root.

When Jesus died on the cross, he could remove the curse from its source. Some people spend a lot of time identifying and tracking down any family members who may have engaged in immoral or unethical behavior (generational curses). They believe that if they miss anyone, their family will continue to experience negative consequences. However, Jesus was able to break the curse of sin and death that has been present since Adam's time. This means that through faith in Jesus, individuals can be free from their family history's adverse effects and be restored to a new life. It's important to remember that troubles and persecutions are a part of life, and it doesn't mean your family is cursed more than others. Most families may know how to keep their secrets hidden, making it seem like they don't have any curses. However, faith in God helps us do the right thing, even when things get tough. Judas, for example, betrayed Jesus for money because he was convinced by the devil that there was an easier way and that Jesus was taking too long with his teachings. However, Judas did not make it because he lacked trust in God and was not patient enough. His faith failed him.

Jesus once said, "'I have prayed that your faith won't fail you." He knew that the work would be completed at the cross. Remember, the devil may try to use everything in his power to get to you, but always keep in mind that he is after your faith. Stay strong and hold on to it." The enemy knows that your faith is your access granted to the new and powerful you. Don't allow people to persuade or flatter your flesh while Satan is seeking to destroy your soul. What is your purpose in being here? We need to understand our purpose and focus on fulfilling it. When we identify what we were created to do, we can align our actions with our true calling and, in turn, bring glory to God. Discovering our purpose can bring clarity and direction to our lives and help us lead a more fulfilling and meaningful existence. So, it's essential to reflect on our passions, talents, and strengths and find ways to use them to serve others and positively impact the world.

The garden where Adam fell, where humanity lost his place and authority. Simon is the sinful man of the flesh, but Peter is the Apostle, and neither Simon nor Peter ever heard of an apostle. But the Holy Spirit's job is to train and equip us with all the tools and skills we need to support our callings, anointings, and who we are in the kingdom… which is spirit. Satan knows if we make it through to the converted part, he has no power over us. His job is to keep leaders, pastors, and preachers as carnal and worldly as the ungodly. The devil does not care about your religion, sex, and all of the above; he cares about what you are called to do and hopes to prevent you from reaching the fulfilled chosen you. The greater the assignment and calling, the greater the opposition.

Have you ever been in a relationship and felt like you have found the one, so you ask for a sign or two? After you get your signs, you are full of expectations and joy, thinking about how good this relationship is and will be. You may have gotten the support and the approval you needed from your side, but on their side, all hell breaks loose, and there is a consistency in the negative energy towards you. Sometimes, we may find ourselves wondering why certain people in our lives seem to dislike us so much despite our best efforts. We might even feel they are actively working against us and trying to sabotage our relationships. Worse, they may not even know us well enough to form a valid opinion of us. This kind of behavior can put a lot of strain on a relationship. Eventually, one person may decide to give up and walk away, which can be a painful and regrettable experience.

When questioned about their previous behavior, they responded, "I just didn't like him/her!" It can be confusing and disorienting to experience such a sudden change in demeanor from someone. I want to remind you that Satan does not know you as much as he would like to believe. His hatred towards you results from your close relationship with God and God's purpose for your life. Satan despises your connection with God!

Many people have turned away from God due to pressure from loved ones and friends, eventually abandoning God like Simon or Judas. God is faithful… question yourself when you are not…, especially what God entrusted you with.

Satan may try to corrupt our hearts and minds, hindering us from fulfilling our mission. Jesus knew that Simon (the old nature) would deny him, but Peter (the new man) could never deny him. Simon is from the dust of the earth, while on the other hand, Peter the apostle is the called servant from the kingdom of heaven; it is his spirit man who knows God. He's been covered by the blood. The enemy knew Peter was chosen to be in charge of the newly born church, so he desperately sought to destroy Simon so Perter would never come forth. We think we need many things to please God, and this is not true; we can please

God by coming to Him honestly and transparent; this means whatever I have, whatever I am, I will get it from God. We need to know God's will for our lives to be at peace with whatever He calls us to do and not envy our neighbors. If we get this right, we will become someone's answer.

"Who hath believed our report?

and to whom is the arm of the LORD revealed?

For he shall grow up before him as a tender plant,

and as a root out of a dry ground:

he hath no form nor comeliness;

and when we shall see him, there is no beauty that we should

desire him.

He is despised and rejected of men;

a man of sorrows and acquainted with grief:

and we hid as it were our faces from him;

he was despised, and we esteemed him not.

Surely he hath borne our griefs,

and carried our sorrows:

yet we did esteem him stricken,

smitten of God and afflicted.

But he was wounded for our transgressions,

he was bruised for our iniquities:

the chastisement of our peace was upon him;

and with his stripes, we are healed.

All we, like sheep, have gone astray;

we have turned everyone to his own way;

and the LORD hath laid on him the iniquity of us all.

He was oppressed, and he was afflicted,

yet he opened not his mouth:

he is brought as a lamb to the slaughter,

and as a sheep before her shearers is dumb,

so he openeth not his mouth.

He was taken from prison and from judgment:

and who shall declare his generation?

for he was cut off out of the land of the living:

for the transgression of my people was he stricken.

And he made his grave with the wicked,

and with the rich in his death;

because he had done no violence,

neither was any deceit in his mouth.

Yet it pleased the LORD to bruise him; he hath put

 him to grief: when thou shalt make his soul an offering

for sin, he shall see his seed, he shall prolong his days,

 and the pleasure of the LORD shall prosper in his
hand". Isaiah   53:1-10

It's 700 years in advance that the prophet Isaiah prophesied the coming of the Messiah. Despite possessing the requisite attributes and fulfilling the prophecies, Jesus encountered widespread disbelief and rejection from the people. The reason for their skepticism and disapproval is attributed to their preconceived notions of the Messiah's physical appearance and intellectual prowess, which Jesus did not conform to. Despite these challenges, Jesus persevered and continued to carry out his mission, serving as a testament to the power of determination and willpower in the face of adversity. During his time on Earth, Jesus faced opposition from various groups, including the religious leaders known as Pharisees. They made his path difficult and demonstrated hatred towards him, ultimately contributing to his death. Despite this opposition, Jesus remained steadfast in his teachings and message of love and forgiveness.

We know that Jesus is THE ANSWER, and look how they treated their answer. The answer was mistreated, abused, used, misunderstood, rejected, despised, cast down, hated, lied to, falsely accused, betrayed, arrested, condemned, and judged. God sent His Son to save the world, and many people didn't receive Him or believed He was the Messiah. Although they had knowledge of the scriptures and prophecies concerning him, they did not accept Jesus simply because he did not fit what they had in mind as The Answer to their long-awaited prayers. While dying on the cross, Jesus said, "Father, forgive them, for they know not what they do." He did so because he wanted to leave the door open for some to repent and be saved. This act of extending grace beyond death and the grave was a testament to his compassion and love for humanity. Thankfully, some of them did repent and were publicly acknowledged as followers of Jesus by getting baptized and receiving the Holy Ghost.

"'The Lord said to my Lord, "Sit at my right hand, until I make your enemies your footstool."Let all the house of Israel therefore know for certain that God has made him both Lord and Christ, this Jesus whom you crucified."

Now, when they heard this, they were cut to the heart and said to Peter and the rest of the apostles, "Brothers, what shall we do?" And Peter said to them, "Repent and be baptized every one of you in the name of Jesus Christ for the forgiveness of your sins, and you will receive the gift of the Holy Spirit. For the promise is for you and for your children and for all who are far off, everyone whom the Lord our God calls to himself." And with many other words, he bore witness and continued to exhort them, saying, "Save yourselves from this crooked generation." So those who received his word were baptized, and there were added that day about three thousand souls.   Acts 2:34-41

After Jesus was crucified, the day of Pentecost arrived, and the Holy Spirit descended upon those who were present. The people asked Peter, "What must we do to be saved?" This was because they were the same people who had asked for Jesus to be crucified. They did not believe in him; some even hated and turned against him. However, their hearts changed when they heard the message of the kingdom being preached and the price Jesus had paid for their salvation. Jesus knew that, eventually, many hearts would be touched by God's love and mercy. Even if someone comes to understand it late, the important thing is that they ultimately do. After all, this is the very reason why Jesus came to this world.

It's important to remember that forgiveness can be a powerful tool for setting yourself free from hurt and pain caused by others. Even if someone has hurt you deeply, forgiving them can release you from carrying that pain with you for the rest of your life. By forgiving those who wronged you, you can create space in your heart and mind for healing and growth rather than allowing negative emotions to control your thoughts and actions. It's also important to remember that forgiveness doesn't necessarily mean forgetting or excusing the harm done to you. Instead, forgiveness can be seen as acknowledging the damage done while letting go of the anger, resentment, and bitterness that can come with holding onto grudges. By forgiving others, you can free yourself from the negative emotions holding you back from experiencing true peace and happiness.

When you go to heaven, you may encounter people who have wronged you. By forgiving them now, you can avoid being shocked or surprised by their presence and move forward with a clear heart and mind. Consider choosing forgiveness as a way of setting yourself free and moving forward toward a brighter future. This can help you feel more at ease with the idea that God is there with you to forgive, even in the face of injustice and hardship. Remembering our heavenly Father has forgiven us. So, don't hesitate to forgive those who have wronged you and start focusing on a better tomorrow. There is nothing more powerful than love, and God embodies this love. Forgiveness is an essential aspect of love and is regarded as such. Although it can be challenging to sit down and have a meal or a conversation with someone who has wronged us, it is crucial to remember that forgiveness is a divine act. By forgiving those who have harmed us, we allow God's love to work through us and heal our hearts.

In certain circumstances, finding the answer to a problem can be a source of agony, inducing profound emotional distress. Nevertheless, such distress may pave the way for the emergence of an answer. Alternatively, we may be attempting to discover an answer when, in fact, we are the answer to another person's challenge. In times of prolonged waiting, the answer may cause pain. Be careful how you perceive the answer. Sometimes, we kill the answer God sends to us. Don't kill your answer because you may not get another one. They killed Jesus, and after He was resurrected, He did not speak to the religious leaders again nor visit their temple. The Pharisees thought they knew God better than most and died only to find out they killed the answer. God had sent them The Answer when they thought He did not answer their prayers.

By holding onto faith and trust in God, we can find the strength to persevere in knowing Jesus is our most outstanding example of how people may mistreat you, misunderstand you, and not appreciate you. However, without a doubt, God has sent you as The Answer.

This Is War

Chapter 14

"The kingdom of heaven has suffered violence, and the violent takes it by force!"

According to the biblical account, in the celestial realm of heaven, a great conflict occurs between Michael, the archangel and his loyal angels, and Lucifer and his followers. This battle is raging, and it all began with an act of rebellion, which marked the first sin to manifest (commission) itself against God and His kingdom's established order. This rebellion was fueled by pride, which was the first sin to be concealed (omission), leading to a devastating war that caused a significant disruption in heaven's unity and harmony. Heaven's once peaceful and harmonious realm is now fraught with tension and strife as the two opposing forces continue to clash in a fierce battle for supremacy.

Lucifer wants to be God, so he says to Eve, "If you eat from this tree, you will be like gods." He passed his desires onto her. He knew the history; she didn't; he set her up. He went after her on purpose, with a purpose to disqualify her from God so he could use her for his kingdom. The devil is using her to this day. This is why he comes early in her life with molestation, rape, and exposure to evil and confusion, to raise her feeling guilty and full of condemnation. Iniquity was found in the heart of Lucifer, and God was not the Father. The heart is the womb in the spirit; it conceives and produces what is heard and believed. This is why we must guard our hearts by being selective in what we hear and, most importantly, what we believe; this is how we produce fruit in our lives.

When tested for conception, Lucifer tested positive and was carrying something in his heart that was not put there by God. It is iniquity, like a pregnancy test testing positive and whether it is a boy or girl. Well, in heaven/eternity, it wasn't gender-based but good or evil-based. Pride is evil and is the father; this birth cannot happen in heaven; they must go. Pride and Lucifer have had an adulterous relationship, and not only infidelity, but they now are murderers in their hearts. This triggered the war; there was a newly founded courage and rage to take over, no matter the casualties and consequences. Lucifer and his rebellious followers are kicked out. Down they must go; this cannot happen in eternity, so God creates the earth as a module from eternity called Time." In this place, it's like a bubble. These angels come from a place of freedom and no restrictions. To be cast down to the earth is a punishment. They are here doing it time, like being on death row. This is why they asked Jesus, "Have you come to torment us before our time? "They know they are doing time. This is why they are furious and committing so much evil on the earth.

We need to understand why there are so many murders, rapes, molestations, robberies, and divisions in households and governments. Why is the world in such turmoil? Because the devil knows he has a short time, this is the only place where he can be god. "He's the god of this world." So, if this is the only place I get to play god, then every hidden evil in my heart will be manifested here. This is the place where my offspring can rule and reign. We have to resist the devil. Therefore, seeing we have this ministry, even as we obtained mercy, we faint not: but we have renounced secret and shameful ways; we do not use deception, nor do we distort the word of God. On the contrary, by setting forth the truth plainly, we commend ourselves to everyone's conscience in the sight of God. And even if our gospel is hidden, it is hidden from those who are perishing, in whom the god of this world hath blinded the minds of them which believe not, lest the light of the glorious gospel of Christ, who is the image of God, should shine unto them.

Lucifer is going down and is determined not to go down alone, so he tries to drag down as many with him as possible. You would think, why would I go down with the devil? He knows if you haven't overcome, 'The lust of the eye, the lust of the flesh, and the pride of life," he can get you. So many preachers have fallen into this category of wanting to be rich and famous and all the fulfillment of pride that comes with it.

"Therefore rejoice, you heavens and you who dwell in them! But woe to the earth and the sea because the devil has gone down to you! He is filled with fury because he knows his time is short."

The heavens are rejoicing because the fruits of sin were never delivered in heaven; sin was cast down before it could manifest and produce fruit. There are some things left on record for those who are believers. Just because something is available to everyone doesn't mean it is for everyone. These will only benefit those who believe. God wanted this generation to know about certain secrets of heaven. No other generation has been given so many hidden secrets of heaven before now.

Think about how many messages, reads, and movies are produced through life about someone or something evil trying to rule or take over the world by overthrowing good. Why are we, as humans, so drawn to these types of entertainment? No matter how many ways it is written and produced, it sells because these stories are connected to truths from eternity. We link to them spiritually whether we are aware of it or not. We are more spirit than we are flesh. The body of flesh is temporary, and our soul is eternal, coming from eternity. The devil is trapped in time (this world) like someone locked up in prison, telling their story over and over of when they used to rule the streets to as many people who come through the system. We are like those going through the system when we come into this world. The devil wants to tell his story to every generation. To as many as he can get to hear him has the potential for him to recruit them to come over to his side.

This is why, in one hour (60 years), the world has taken such a devastating turn in changing for evil. Look at where families were and look at where they are now. Just 60 years ago, you had fathers in the homes, raising their children. Marriage was honorable, and prayer was a part of the daily lifestyle, even blessing God and giving thanks for our food before we ate. Prayer was taken out of schools and replaced with guns. We would be home at a particular hour for dinner to have supper at the table. We lived and died for our families and took care of one another. Everything might not have been perfect, but it sure wasn't demonic. The fathers have been removed from the home and families in one generation. Satan has used the government and courts to become the systematic father while he has become the stepfather in the household through multiple persons and perverts. The devil was endlessly having access to easy molestation and grooming in the house through many forms. This has brought about hate for the father figure and authority. When a father figure has wrongly touched you, your views can be highly distorted. Most women had no idea the devil was after her relationship (she gave to her husband to eat) and her children, born and unborn (the dragon was there to destroy her child as soon as it was born).

He made Cain jealous of his baby brother and killed him. Eve could not see this when "she saw it was good for the eyes, one to be desired and to eat." She wanted pleasure; the devil wants your soul and the souls of your children. Now, all your children want is to be desired; this is the curse of eating from the wrong tree. Pictures all over social media are hungry for anyone to desire them at almost any cost. They are attracting people with lust and not love. You cannot show people your looks and body and expect them to see your heart. Shallow relationships produce deep hurts and pains that may never be resolved or healed in a lifetime. This is one of the reasons suicides are at a record high; they couldn't handle rejection. Satan did it by using the parents and, in turn, using the children and, in the end… destruction.

How many women saw a person that was good to her eyes and something good to eat only to find out their grown child is damaged because of the open invitations they gave to the devil to bring him home from a club or bar? Met on the street, in a store, at a gas station…it doesn't matter where; the devil is living in your house around your babies (offspring). He can use every person you sleep with to plant seeds to destroy your offspring before you destroy his offspring. You're looking for something good, some fun and pleasure. Satan is seeking to destroy you and your children, grandchildren, and great-grandchildren, and he won't stop on his own; YOU MUST STOP HIM!

Return to your God, and He will return to you…it's not too late. You cannot handle these foreign gods because you need to come to a conclusion based on the results. You have no strategies for these gods without the blood of Jesus. Prodigal Daughters, come back home to your Heavenly Father. He loves you unconditionally. Humble yourself as the Prodigal Son did, and come to yourself; you do not belong in the pig's pen. Stop letting the enemy degrade you and shame you. You have cried with disgrace and shame, saying to yourself, no one would believe what I allow this person (devil) to do to me. I have to pretend I am ok. Let me tell you this, daughter: God was there! He knows your secrets and still loves you and wants you. Our Father does not play about His love for you; He wants you to love Him back.

In one generation, our music has gone from praising the woman, asking for a dance, courtship, entertainment, fun, and dancing to degrading the woman, verbal abuse, to devil worshiping, chanting, and war dancing…selfish and lawlessness. Lucifer understands that everything in existence begins with a word and ends with words. You will have what you say if you believe or die trying. Lucifer knows how powerful words are; look how all races and cultures have been impacted by producing words to music (rap). If the music is not evil, the message certainly is and has revealed secrets that have been hidden in the devil's heart and mind since eternity. The devil has chosen this generation. Listen to Satan talking to his children, giving them specific instructions for the destruction of a people. Their reward is money, power, and lust. To glamorize, idolize, and glorify the pleasures given by what you see... bodies.

"When the woman saw that the fruit of the tree was good for food and pleasing to the eye, and also desirable for gaining wisdom, she took some and ate it. She also gave some to her husband, who was with her, and he ate it." The devil uses the same old trick because it is working on a new generation. He's constantly putting things in your face that look good but unsuitable. Satan has been grooming a generation for the revealing of the Anti-Christ. It's coming! He has targeted the church just like he did Eve. Why is the church embracing his idolatry as kingdom worship? What's the going rate for a soul nowadays?

"In the beginning, God said, and it was." The devil is the counterfeit, but he is a good counterfeit, *"If it were possible, he would fool the very elect."* I see you, Satan, and your offspring!

God declared in the Garden who the woman was and how powerful she would be. God didn't tell her in the garden; He said this to the serpent, and she was there to witness it. Imagine trying to understand the meaning of what God had said. So the LORD God said to the serpent, "Because you have done this, "Cursed are you above all livestock and all wild animals! You will crawl on your belly and eat dust all the days of your life. And I will put enmity between you and the woman and between your offspring and hers; he will crush your head, and you will strike his heel."

Enmity, between the serpent and the woman…This is war!

She is a chosen vessel created by God. We want to remember the sin to keep her in chains and to hold her down, keeping her in her place. When you understand she was created as a great wonder, it is why we cannot figure her out.

"And there appeared a great wonder in heaven; a woman clothed with the sun, and the moon under her feet, and upon her head a crown of twelve stars: and she being with child cried, travailing in birth, and pained to be delivered. And there appeared another wonder in heaven; behold a great red dragon, with seven heads, ten horns, and seven crowns upon his heads. And his tail drew the third part of the stars of heaven, and did cast them to the earth: and the dragon stood before the woman which was ready to be delivered, for to devour her child as soon as it was born."

* * *

The devil has declared war on the woman and her child in eternity well before time. What happened to the woman in the garden had nothing to do with religion…religion didn't exist. Making the event religious gives the enemy full range to torment and abuse the woman, even in relationships. The first recorded war took place in heaven…these accounts are written in the Book of Revelation. There are things we will never understand until we fight with all we have to know and understand our God. God is our Heavenly Father, and He resides in the place where the woman was created. As long as we make this subject religious, we will never win this war. The enemy will play us out of position…because he knows it's real and came from eternity.

Jesus said you don't believe earthly things. How can I tell you about heavenly things? Later, Jesus gives John the Apostle the Book of Revelation because things in the heavens have happened and are continuing to happen. Jesus meets with his disciples after his crucifixion and resurrection, reinstating Peter for denying him three times. This is when he asks Peter, "Do you love me?" He asked this of him three times. Peter said, "Lord, you know all things; you know that I love you." Jesus said, "Feed my sheep. Truly, I say to you, when you were young, you used to dress yourself and walk wherever you wanted, but when you are old, you will stretch out your hands, and another will dress you and carry you where you do not want to go." (This he said to show by what kind of death he was to glorify God.) And after saying this, he said to him, "Follow me."

Peter turned and saw the disciple whom Jesus loved(John) following them, the one who also had leaned back against him during the supper and had said, *"Lord, who is it that is going to betray you?" When Peter saw him, he said to Jesus, "Lord, what about this man?" Jesus said to him, "If it is my will that he remain until I come, what is that to you? You follow me!"* So the saying spread abroad among the brothers that this disciple was not to die; yet Jesus did not tell him that he was not to die, but, *"If it is my will that he remain until I come, what is that to you?"*

This is the disciple who is bearing witness about these things and who has written these things, and we know that his testimony is true. When Jesus spoke these things to his disciples, it would be about six decades later that he would meet John on this island. The Book of Revelation is not a book of inspiration but revelation. It is called Revelation because it reveals what was previously hidden. There have been mysteries of heaven that were not meant to be imagined or seen by human minds and eyes. According to reports, John was approximately 88 years old during his exile to Patmos Island. Before his exile, he had devoted his entire adult life to being a follower of Jesus Christ and had withdrawn from social issues. John was the youngest of the chosen disciples and was only 21 when Jesus made him a disciple. John was the only Apostle of the chosen of Jesus.

According to the Bible, the Lamb was slain before the foundation of the world. This means that Jesus Christ was chosen to redeem humanity from sin even before the world was created. It is believed that Christ's sacrifice on the cross is the only way for sins to be forgiven and for salvation to be attained. Shedding blood is necessary because it symbolizes the sacrifice of the lamb's blood for the atonement of one's sins, which is Christ who died for us. Sin was first found in heaven when Lucifer, the angel who rebelled against God, was cast out of heaven along with his followers. Sin was in the heart of the serpent but entered the world through Adam and Eve when they disobeyed God in the Garden of Eden. Ever since then, humanity has been plagued by sin and its consequences until Jesus Christ died and shed his blood for our sins.

The discovery of iniquity in Lucifer's heart has been a subject of much debate and discussion among theologians and scholars of the Bible. Iniquity, essentially the root of all sin, is a deeply ingrained and insidious trait that can grow and take hold of an individual's heart and mind. It is often described as a persistent and pervasive inclination towards doing wrong, even when one knows that it is morally or ethically reprehensible. The question of how iniquity came to be present in Lucifer's heart is complex and has been explored from many different angles. Some argue that it resulted from his pride and arrogance, which blinded him to the truth and led him down a path of rebellion against God. Others suggest that it was a consequence of his free will, which allowed him to choose evil over good.

Regardless of how it got there, the fact that iniquity took root in Lucifer's heart had profound consequences. As it grew and matured, it gave rise to various other sins, including envy, bitterness, anger, and, ultimately, rebellion. These sins, in turn, led to his fall from grace and his expulsion from heaven, a fate that he shares with all who give into the lure of iniquity and turn their backs on God. The heart is the spiritual womb where our thoughts, emotions, and beliefs originate. Whatever we listen to and believe can significantly impact our spiritual lives. It is, therefore, essential to guard our hearts and minds and be discerning about what we expose ourselves to, whether it be music, movies, or other forms of media. This is because what we allow into our hearts can shape our worldview and ultimately determine our spiritual destiny.

Jesus says, Behold, I stand at the door and knock. If anyone hears my voice and opens the door, I will come into him and eat with him, and he will be with me. The one who conquers, I will grant him to sit with me on my throne, as I also conquered and sat down with my Father on his throne. He who has an ear, let him hear what the Spirit says to the churches.'" Revelation 3:20-22

* * *

God sent the proposal. It is up to us to accept it or reject it. The relationship has to be consensual. If God forced Himself, it would be considered rape… spiritually. So God will love on us, be patient with us and long-suffering, waiting in hopes we have a changed heart, but He will not take away your right to choose.

Now, therefore, fear the LORD, and serve him in sincerity and in truth: and put away the gods which your fathers served on the other side of the flood, and in Egypt, and serve ye the LORD. And if it seems evil unto you to serve the LORD, choose you this day whom ye will serve; whether the gods which your fathers served that were on the other side of the flood or the gods of the Amorites, in whose land ye dwell: but as for me and my house, we will serve the LORD. And the people answered and said, God forbid that we should forsake the LORD, to serve other gods; Joshua 24: 14-16.

Even with Mary (mother of Jesus), when the angel brought her the word from God, he saluted her in greeting, asked her not to be afraid, and gave her the proposal.

In the sixth month, the angel Gabriel was sent from God to a city of Galilee named Nazareth, to a virgin betrothed to a man named Joseph, of the house of David. And the virgin's name was Mary. And he came to her and said, "Greetings, O favored one, the Lord is with you!" But she was greatly troubled at the saying and tried to discern what sort of greeting this might be. And the angel said to her, "Do not be afraid, Mary, for you have found favor with God. And behold, you will conceive in your womb and bear a son, and you shall call his name Jesus. He will be great and will be called the Son of the Most High. And the Lord God will give him the throne of his father David, and he will reign over the house of Jacob forever, and of his kingdom, there will be no end." And Mary asked the angel, "How will this be since I am a virgin?"

And the angel answered her, "The Holy Spirit will come upon you, and the power of the Most High will overshadow you; therefore, the child to be born will be called holy—the Son of God. And behold, in her old age, your relative Elizabeth has also conceived a son, and this is the sixth month with her who was called barren. For nothing will be impossible with God." And Mary said, "Behold, I am the servant of the Lord; let it be to me according to your word." And the angel departed from her.

See how Gabriel, the messenger, presented the proposal to Mary. Even though this was a long-awaited prophecy, and probably every little Israelite girl was hoping to be chosen to bring forth the Messiah. The angel still acknowledges her voice and responds to the message. After getting Mary's consent, the angel left. The Word of God is a powerful seed that has the potential to bring forth life. For this seed to take root and grow, it must be received by someone spiritually receptive. The process of receiving the Word is likened to conception, where the ear canal serves as the fallopian tube waiting to receive the seed. The fallopian tube is a narrow duct in a female's reproductive system that connects the ovary to the uterus. It plays a crucial role in fertility as it serves as the conduit for the egg to travel from the ovary to the uterus, where it may be fertilized by sperm. Similarly, figuratively, the ear can be considered a channel through which ideas and thoughts reach the heart, where they can be conceived and nurtured in the realm of the spirit.

For conception to occur, faith is needed, which is likened to the egg waiting to be fertilized. When the Word is preached, and someone who hears and receives it with faith, spiritual ovulation occurs, and the egg is released in anticipation of the seed. When the seed and faith come together and are received, conception begins. The heart becomes pregnant with the Word, and the person transforms spiritually. If the Word is nurtured and protected, it will produce life, just as a fertilized egg will develop into a new life. As the Word grows and takes root, the person's understanding of themselves and their relationship with God will change. This transformation can be compared to biblical figures such as Jacob becoming Israel, Simon becoming Peter, and Saul becoming the Apostle Paul. When the Word is mixed with faith, it produces the things from God.

It is unrealistic and unfair to expect people to change their behavior overnight to meet the expectations of others.

As new believers, we must surround ourselves with the family of God, who prioritize their love for God and can nurture our growth and development as we progress in our faith journey. Doing so can build a supportive community to help us feel loved, accepted, and understood. The book of Acts provides a detailed account of the various demonstrations that the church portrayed. These demonstrations include the spreading of the gospel, the establishment of new churches, and the healing of the sick. Additionally, the church demonstrated unity, generosity, and love towards one another, which served as an inspiration for many.

God was the first to identify the presence of iniquity in Lucifer's heart, which he recognized as something that did not belong to Him. Iniquity did not reflect God's image, character, or values, and God saw that Lucifer's manifestation of iniquity was not aligned with His ways. Therefore, God concluded that it could not be His. This process of recognizing iniquity in Lucifer's heart can be compared to conducting a pregnancy or paternity test.

If Lucifer, the fallen angel, was seduced by pride and gave in to its allure. This act of consent led to Lucifer's conception, which ultimately resulted in the birth of iniquities. It is believed that this birth took place on Earth, which became the birthplace of iniquities. It is also mentioned that God is not the father of these iniquities and that Lucifer and those who gave in to pride and conceived were cast out before the birth of their offspring. This interpretation of the origin of iniquities is a cautionary tale against the dangers of giving in to pride and other vices. This gives Lucifer reasons to persecute the woman, wanting to destroy her and her child as soon as it was born. Lucifer didn't know the woman, but he knew God, and with all of that glory she had, without a doubt, she was the glory of God. His response was similar to a jealous ex because as he fell from heaven (grace), he knew what this new being (woman) was carrying and giving birth to came from God. Wow, this is God's child. God has never had an actual birth child before coming from a being.

The Woman is a new creation. This is why the heavens see her as a great wonder. She is the first known being with two wombs: the heart (spiritual womb), the place where spiritual things are generated, and the natural womb (uterus), where human beings (flesh) are developed. The spiritual and natural realms have distinct differences, one of which is the presence of a womb. While males and females have a spiritual womb, only females have a natural womb. This design was intentional and serves a specific purpose. The solution for sin was placed uniquely and divinely in the secret place of the female, which remained hidden until the time of fulfillment. This signifies the critical role played by women in the redemption of humanity. The Woman is a unique and unprecedented being who is set to replace Lucifer. Unfortunately, this being, and as a result, she has been subject to discrimination, abuse, and inequality throughout history. Lucifer has been relentlessly pursuing her and using anyone or anything to mistreat her, and it is time for this to stop. We must strive for equality and treat all beings with respect and fairness.

"And a great sign appeared in heaven: a woman clothed with the sun, with the moon under her feet, and on her head a crown of twelve stars. She was pregnant and was crying out in birth pains and the agony of giving birth. And another sign appeared in heaven: behold, a great red dragon, with seven heads and ten horns, and on his heads seven diadems. His tail swept down a third of the stars of heaven and cast them to the earth. And the dragon stood before the woman about to give birth so he might devour it when she bore her child. She gave birth to a male child, one who is to rule all the nations with a rod of iron, but her child was caught up to God and his throne, and the woman fled into the wilderness, where she had a place prepared by God, in which she is to be nourished for 1,260 days." Revelation 12: 1-6

We can see that this war started in heaven and is manifested on earth. The woman (Mary, mother of Jesus) in the universe (eternity) is crying in labor pains while giving birth to a son (Jesus), and the dragon (the devil manifesting through King Herod) is seeking to destroy the child.

* * *

"After Jesus was born in Bethlehem in Judea, during the time of King Herod, Magi from the east came to Jerusalem and asked, "Where is the one who has been born king of the Jews? We saw his star when it rose and have come to worship him." When King Herod heard this, he was disturbed, and all Jerusalem was with him. When he had called together all the people's chief priests and law teachers, he asked them where the Messiah was to be born. "In Bethlehem in Judea," they replied, "for this is what the prophet has written: " 'But you, Bethlehem, in the land of Judah, are by no means least among the rulers of Judah; for out of you will come a ruler who will shepherd my people Israel."

Then Herod called the Magi secretly and found out from them the exact time the star had appeared. He sent them to Bethlehem, saying, "Go and search carefully for the child. As soon as you find him, report to me so that I may go and worship him." After they heard the king, they went on their way, and the star they had seen when it rose went ahead of them until it stopped over where the child was. When they saw the star, they were overjoyed. On coming to the house, they saw the child with his mother, Mary, and they bowed down and worshiped him. Then, they opened their treasures and presented him with gold, frankincense, and myrrh gifts. And having been warned in a dream not to return to Herod, they returned to their country by another route. When they had gone, an angel of the Lord appeared to Joseph in a dream. *"Get up," he said, "take the child and his mother and escape to Egypt. Stay there until I tell you, for Herod is going to search for the child to kill him." So he got up, took the child and his mother during the night, and left for Egypt, where he stayed until the death of Herod. And so was fulfilled what the Lord had said through the prophet: "Out of Egypt I called my son."*

When Herod realized that the Magi had outwitted him, he was furious, and he gave orders to kill all the boys in Bethlehem and its vicinity who were two years old and under by the time he had learned from the Magi. Then what was said through the prophet Jeremiah was fulfilled: "A voice is heard in Ramah, weeping and great mourning, Rachel weeping for her children and refusing to be comforted, because they are no more." Matthew 2: 1-18.

See how The Book of Revelation, the account before time, clearly shows this war in heaven when the time of fulfillment on earth parallels heaven's account. When Eve ate fruit from the forbidden tree, we see the woman through the eyes of the serpent as the problem. Still, God sees the woman as the answer to the problem, and here's why: in the Book of Revelation 13': 8, *"The Lamb was slain before the foundations of the world, meaning the problem already existed. Ok, we also have in the Book of Revelation, " and she, being pregnant, was having labor pains and cried because she was about to deliver." Revelation 12:2.*

* * *

"And the dragon stood in front of the woman who was about to deliver her child; he was there to destroy the child as soon as it was born. And she gave birth to a son who was to rule all nations with a rod of iron: and her child was caught up to his God and his throne. And when the dragon saw he was cast into the earth, he persecuted the woman who brought forth the child" Revelation 12: 4, 5, 13.

The Book of Revelation is unique in that it is revealed and not merely inspired. This means that Jesus allowed John, one of his apostles, to glimpse into heaven and eternity, which exist beyond the confines of time. Like a movie, John was given a front-row seat in heaven, and Jesus instructed him to record everything he saw. Time is a construct created to measure space, seasons, and events for accountability of things that happened in eternity previously unknown to humans on Earth. Sin occurred in eternity before time existed, and the devil was punished and given time as a result. Similar to a prisoner on death row, the devil is currently serving his sentence and awaiting his ultimate punishment. When you have lived an eternal life of luxury, and it is suddenly taken away, it's understandable to feel angry. Regardless of how successful or extravagant our lives may be, they are only temporary. Nothing in this world is permanent; it's not how the earth was designed. Satan is furious because he misses being known as Lucifer, *"son of the morning" and "the bright and morning star."* As he falls from grace, he sees a woman who has replaced him." This is why it is so hard to get equal pay for equal work, to be recognized for a job well done and feel like you're hurting the male counterparts, to be able to be next in line to get appointed as pastor or bishop, CEO, President of a corporation, because you are Lucifer's threat and heaven's reward.

Please know who you are and not make excuses for those who are insecure and two-faced with you concerning your promotion and excuses for why you didn't get the position. We know why when you understand the book. When you realize you have replaced the irreplaceable. I say above him. His strategies are relentless against you. He works through any vessel that operates in pride and the self-absorbed. Forget the titles they hide behind, know your enemy, and beware of the spirit in operation.

"For we wrestle not against flesh and blood, but against principalities, against powers, against the rulers of the darkness of this world, against spiritual wickedness in high places." Ephesians 6:12

He is the problem and knows this, while God made the woman for the solution…the Answer. She's been labeled as the problem, but the devil knows God ordained her to be The Answer. The serpent gives power to the beast, and the beast has been given a voice to deceive as many as possible to worship the image. Why do you think everything has been thrust into fashions, selfies, and promoting vanity? Because John saw this generation laugh into global idolatry, and his job was to shut the woman's mouth and destroy her offspring. The Beast is a system; the serpent is the devil. The serpent and the beast agree to destroy the woman and her seed. The beast has influenced the world through imagery and vanity; everyone wants to be rich and famous. At an early age, through technology, he was able to complete this task, written in the Book of Revelation. Most pastors and preachers don't even peach from this book, and it is the book that reveals the persecution of the church but also the eternal victory of God's people and the devil's final destination and destruction.

The beast becomes the voice to influence the end generation while taking away the woman's right to speak so he can have free rein for her children. The man he wishes to destroy is deceived, this time into helping him destroy the woman and shut her down. But *"The earth helped the woman,*

"And when the dragon saw that he was cast unto the earth, he persecuted the woman which brought forth the man child. And to the woman were given two wings of a great eagle, that she might fly into the wilderness, into her place, where she is nourished for a time and times, and half a time, from the face of the serpent. And the serpent cast out of his mouth water as a flood after the woman, that he

might cause her to be carried away of the flood. And the earth helped the woman, and the earth opened her mouth, and swallowed up the flood which the dragon cast out of his mouth. And the dragon was wroth with the woman and went to make war with the remnant of her seed, which keep the commandments of God, and have the testimony of Jesus Christ" Revelation 12:14-17.

Read the book "God, The Woman And Their Enemy."

Interestingly, John's statements about 2000 years ago sounded impossible and crazy to most people. However, today, we are witnessing the manifestation of his words as we enter the era of the "Digital Dollar." This form of currency will fundamentally reshape how we conduct business and live our lives daily. It is worth noting that it has also been foretold in Revelation 13:18 that people will not be able to buy, sell, or trade unless they have the mark of the beast. This highlights the significance of the ongoing shift to digital currency and its potential impact on our future.

"Because of the signs it was given power to perform on behalf of the first beast, it deceived the inhabitants of the earth. It ordered them to set up an image in honor of the

beast who was wounded by the sword and yet lived. The second beast was given the power to give breath to the image of the first beast so that the image could speak and cause all who refused to worship the image to be killed. It also forced all people, great and small, rich and poor, free and slave, to receive a mark on their right hands or on their foreheads so that they could not buy or sell unless they had the mark, which is the name of the beast or the number of its name. This calls for wisdom. Let the person who has insight calculate the number of the beast, for it is the number of a man. That number is 666." Revelation 13:14-18 NIV

This system has been so successful because of its balance of technology and convenience. Still, one day, it will make the difference whether you eat or not, take care of your family, or do financial transactions…to live, period. The Anti-Christ will then, in turn, make a law of how the mark will be used. He will demonstrate his hate for Jesus Christ's followers and seek to convert them to the dark side, which will have lights of deception. He will hide behind things of God, but they will not be God. He will even use Pastors, Bishops, and spiritual advisors to persuade you to deny Jesus. He will use unbelievable pressure to persuade before it comes to the killing. When the time comes for the Anti-Christ to take complete control of the world, he will make examples of those who refuse to accept the mark. The murders will be enforced by technologies, robots, and intelligence we use daily…having no clue we were being groomed. It will be so massive that the human heart will not be able to take it, but a machine can because it has zero feelings; what a convenience to get the job done.

Cover yourselves with the blood and know, *"The disciple is not above his master, nor the servant above his lord. It is enough for the disciple to be his master and the servant to his lord. If they have called the master of the house Beelzebub, how much more shall they call them of his household? Fear them not, therefore: for there is nothing covered, that shall not be revealed; and hid, that shall not be known. What I tell you in darkness, that speak ye in light: and what ye hear in the ear that preach ye upon the housetops. And fear not them which kill the body, but are not able to kill the soul: but rather fear him which can destroy both soul and body in hell. Mathew 10: 24-28*

We are not quite there yet, but we are close. These things were revealed to John and left for us on record. John was the youngest disciple Jesus had chosen to follow him. Jesus trusted this disciple with his earthly mother, Mary, to take her into his household for the rest of her days. This is the same disciple Jesus rebuked Peter on his behalf and said, "What is it to you if I should say for him to tarry until I come." John was the only one of the chosen Apostles who was not martyred. Instead, he was sent into exile to the

Island of Patmos. While there, he had several visits from angels, and ultimately, he was visited by Jesus himself. Jesus instructed John to write a book about what he saw and told him not to try to figure it out but to write down what he saw.

The Book of Revelation is important and unique simply because it is not inspired but revealed. We read what John saw, best described by his era and times. We are witnesses to what John saw being fulfilled right before our eyes in our generation. It's fascinating to note that despite appearing crazy at the time, John wrote the Bible's most revered and feared book. We are truly blessed to be able to read it today and gain valuable insights from it..mysteries never revealed to any other generation to see so many things to come to pass. John saw the woman being persecuted and hated in the universe but loved by her God and chosen for one of the most revered assignments of all times…to give birth to The Son of God, who would take away the sins of the world. For this reason, the woman has been pursued by the devil on so many levels throughout the ages.

Stop bringing the devil into your house and around your children. You are called, ordained, and anointed by God to destroy the works of the devil, not to use your gifts to empower him and his kingdom. The outcome of his actions is causing frustration in your life. He has caused you to be depressed, has molested and raped your children, and has exploited them for sex and pleasure, and abused them consistently when you are not around. He has put fear into them, convincing them that you will not believe them over him. Now, their house is not a home just because of his presence. They know they are being tolerated, not celebrated because love is absent. They have learned to survive at an early age. Satan wants to be your children's stepdaddy and your luster-lover. He understands that you, as a woman, have the power to give birth out of your spirit and body to destroy his offspring. This means in the flesh and spirit. So his strategy is to get in your mind, into your heart, and get in your body. He has to get into your life by any means because he needs to protect his interests. He knows you have the power and authority to destroy him and his offspring, even if you do not know how powerful you are.

The Devil is doomed and grooming as many people as he can to follow him to destruction. He'll pay you to destroy you, just as he did Judas. Don't be overly confident in your titles and positions; stay with God, do His will, not yours, and humble yourself. If he got a disciple/apostle/bishop to sell God out for money, then you are no different if you are in it for the wrong reasons. Judas thought he was getting away with stealing from the ministry, and greed took him over and presented him with the ultimate payday. The enemy is too selfish to go down by himself and will take you down with him in shame. Everything he's tempting you with is temporary—you can't keep it!

Eternity is too long to get it wrong.

Jesus told them, "The secret of the kingdom of God has been given to you. But to those on the outside, everything is said in parables so that " 'they may be ever seeing but never perceiving, and ever hearing but never understanding; otherwise, they might turn and be forgiven!'"Mark 4:11-12 NIV

"Can anyone hide himself in secret places So that I cannot see him?" says the LORD. "Do I not fill heaven and earth?" says the LORD. Jeremiah 23:24

"For God will bring every act to judgment, every hidden and secret thing, whether good or evil." Ecclesiastes 12:14 AMP

Don't be deceived by the enemy to make you think you can outthink or outsmart God. Jesus said all things hidden will be revealed.
Jesus said, "So have no fear of them, for nothing is covered that will not be revealed, or hidden that will not be known. What I tell you in the dark, say in the light, and what you hear whispered, proclaim on the housetops. And do not fear those who kill the body but cannot kill the soul. Rather, fear him, who can destroy both soul and body in hell. Matthew 10:26-28 ESV

Jesus did not come to this world to start a new religion;

He came to teach and demonstrate to us the kingdom and save us from sin. Sin is the enemy, the disease. We did not know about the kingdom until he taught us. No one had come from the kingdom to demonstrate how it functioned. No one until Jesus exposed the devil and his works. Every religion and spin-off of Jesus are mere copycats and counterfeits. Jesus is the real deal; he is the truth. All of these denominations and doctrines are distractions from the real work needed to be done in this world. Jese is Lord, love it or hate it! We are in the end times. Please make no mistake about this: we are in denial, trying to dance over the diabolical state we are in as humanity. This happened in Noah's day, when people would rather be drunk than be sober, trying to avoid the truth. We seek peace when there is no peace without defeating the adversary of peace. We say we want peace, but we work for the same devil who started this war in the first place. He will never grant us peace; we have to take it by taking him down, getting him out of our households, marriages, relationships, away from our children, out of our churches, and our families.

Listen to what Jesus had to say about peace, ***"Do not think that I have come to bring peace on the earth; I have not come to bring peace, but a sword [of division between belief and unbelief].***

For I have come to SET A MAN AGAINST HIS FATHER, AND A DAUGHTER AGAINST HER MOTHER, AND A DAUGHTER-IN-LAW AGAINST HER MOTHER-IN-LAW; and A MAN'S ENEMIES WILL BE THE

MEMBERS OF HIS [own] HOUSEHOLD [when one believes and another does not]. " He who loves father or mother more than Me is not worthy of Me, and he who loves son or daughter more than Me is not worthy of Me.

And he who does not take his cross [expressing a willingness to endure whatever may come] and follow Me [believing in Me, conforming to My example in living and, if need be, suffering or perhaps dying because of faith in Me] is not worthy of Me. Whoever finds his life [in this world] will [eventually] lose it [through death], and whoever loses his life [in this world] for My sake will find it [that is, life with Me for all eternity], Matthew 10:34-39 AMP

How can you make anyone in the kingdom of darkness love you? You are the enemy unless you abandon Jesus, your mission, and eject the Holy Spirit; it's that easy. All you have to do is defile yourself with the devil and his lustful and evil ways. This is when people inherit more demons and begin to do things that they had never done before because satan wants insurance that you never make it back to God again. But God has sent me who knows this devil and has consistently fought against him to get free. I was a backslider or one who left God for the pleasures of this world, but it was a trick. I am compelled to warn about the dangers of straying from faith. Imagine someone who was once fervently praying for their loved ones but suddenly stopped talking about God or engaging in spiritual practices. This is when the enemy, who had previously been ousted from their soul, sees an opportunity to return. It's a constant battle; the devil will stop at nothing to regain control. You will never truly belong, even if you try to fit in with your old friends and family. God has marked your soul, and the devil will do everything within his power to undermine that. He may even bring in reinforcements to help him achieve his goals. So, if you find yourself struggling to prove that you're not a child of God, remember that this is precisely what the devil wants. He's been practicing his tricks for centuries, and none are new. Stay strong in your faith, and don't let him win.

The darkness is constantly trying to overcome your light. Your loved ones may not share your faith, but they have always looked up to you as a source of hope during difficult times. However, they're now questioning your values, wondering how you could engage in immoral activities. The truth is, you carry two marks on your soul. One is from God stating you are His property, and the other is a blemish or stain of sin that only the blood of Jesus can wash away. You find yourself in a precarious situation, positioned between two kingdoms that neither trust you. The people under your protection are at risk due to your decision to turn away from God and ally yourself with His enemy, who is also your enemy. However, you cannot see the truth as the enemy disguises himself with tempting pleasures and desires.

* * *

Look how Jesus exposed Satan, *"When the unclean spirit comes out of a person, it roams through waterless places in search [of a place] of rest; and not finding any, it says, 'I will go back to my house (person) from which I came.' And when it comes, it finds the place swept and put in order. Then it goes and brings seven other spirits more evil than itself, and they go in [the person] and live there, and the last state of that person becomes worse than the first."*

It is believed that those who do not have the spirit of God in them, for instance, family members, will eventually oppose you as they lack the fear of God. Even friends who are not saved may turn against you, leaving you confused and wondering what went wrong. The reason behind this is that you have changed kingdoms and lords, and Satan is no longer your lord. Hence, a war begins, as the devil is a sore loser and will do everything in his power to put pressure on you to come back to him. He may send ex-partners or old friends who pretend to have missed you or want to reunite. However, you should not fall for their traps, as they will turn on you if they do not have the Holy Spirit in them and Jesus is not their Lord. The devil cannot love, so it is essential to understand that. When you reject their offer and refuse to go back, you may see the demonic presence in them, and they may not react positively. They may even use famous lines such as "You have changed" or "I miss the old you" to lure you back, but you should know that these are scripts given to demons from Satan.

* * *

If you left God and are reading this word and want to return home, the Father loves you and disrupted my entire life to write this to you. If you ask Him for forgiveness and confess your love for Him more than yourself or this world, He will beat down every devil and demon that holds you in bondage. Pray along with me as your confession, "Father, forgive me for my sins against you. I repent of my sins, meaning with your help, I will never turn back to that life of dirt and grime. I give my life to you; do with me, Lord, as you see fit. Deliver me from these adversaries. My life belongs to you, Lord, in Jesus' name. Lord God, I pray for those who have believed your word and what was read in this book. I ask for their total restoration and vindication from the enemies of God. Lord, let them feel your love and power of your Holy Spirit; give them the peace that only you can provide with the understanding that we are more than conquerors through Jesus Christ our Lord. We thank you, Father, for never turning your back on us, no matter how bad we had gotten. Have your way, oh Lord; I give you my mind, heart, body, and soul to do with me as you please, Father; I am yours…Amen.

My dear friend, I speak to you as a fellow believer in Jesus Christ and a warrior fighting for God. I have faced off against devils and demons, and through the authority of Christ, I have emerged victorious every time. These evil beings prey upon our weaknesses, our thirst for more, and our fear. But do not be afraid, for Christ has already defeated everything you will ever face. You are capable of so much more than you realize. Do not keep secrets with the devil; expose him and shame him. Remember, he wants to humiliate you and all of us. When you belong to God, the devil will never accept you; he will only tolerate you. Expect him and his demons to harass you, tempting you to do things that degrade you, but hold onto your faith in God and never let go. I know firsthand how the devil can try to destroy you through fleeting pleasures that you can never truly satisfy. Don't be fooled by the momentary rush, for shame is sure to follow. Stay strong, my friend, and remember that God is always with you.

Jesus said, "So do not be afraid of them, for nothing is hidden that will not be revealed [at the judgment], or kept secret that will not be made known [at the judgment]. Matthew 10:26 AMP

Throughout history, individuals have come to this world with a mission to expose the enemy and go to war. John the Baptist and Jesus were two such individuals. Their message challenged the status quo and threatened those in power. This is why King Herod resorted to killing babies, and the religious leaders fought against the followers of John and Jesus. Jesus stirred up the nest of the serpent and his offspring, who had infiltrated humanity and blended into our society. They were hiding in marriages, fathers and mothers, sons and daughters, priests and pastors. The message of John and Jesus was a call to action against the enemy within, a call to recognize and expose the forces that seek to control and manipulate us.

It's no secret that divorces, abuses, and divisions plague our society. But have you ever wondered why? According to Jesus, when you give your life to the Lord and accept Him as your Savior, all hell breaks loose. When you receive God's Spirit, the devil knows that you have left his kingdom and entered the kingdom of God, and he will do everything in his power to get you back. He will use the cares of this world - bills, cars, clothes, and even distractions like men and women - to try and win you over. His ultimate goal is to make you God's enemy and claim your soul. But don't let him win. Stay strong in your faith, and remember that you can overcome any obstacle with God on your side.

Look at what Jesus said, "He who is not with Me [believing in Me as Lord and Savior] is against Me [there is no impartial position]; and he who does not gather with Me [assisting in My ministry], scatters. Luke 11:23 AMP

The idea that attending church is a haven from the devil is a misconception. The devil is not afraid of you going to church but instead of the spirit of God dwelling within you. Many pastors and leaders who preach do not possess the Holy Spirit and are incapable of demonstrating the power of the word. They despise God and the Holy Spirit and will tell you that the acts of the Holy Spirit were only for those in the past. However, the book of Acts is not about the acts of the apostles but the acts of the Holy Spirit. It is a continuation of God's work in every generation, not just in the past. To expose a false prophet, all you need is the Holy Spirit within you and a knowledge of the book of Acts and the acts of the Holy Spirit. They cannot fake how they feel about the Holy Spirit; they will show who they are if you challenge them on the works of the Holy Spirit and why they don't have access to this authority and power.

Wake up for real children of the kingdom! If God is dead, then there's no more Holy Spirit, but we know God is not dead, so why should the acts of the Holy Spirit be a thing of the past? He is right here and right now waiting on a generation who believes in God again and is not consumed with religious services and dogma. There is a book of Acts in this generation, and submitting to God the Father and Jesus as the Way is a good start. The book of Acts talks about the people of The Way. What way? Where are they now? The first church must come back before the Anti-Christ reveals himself. The Holy Spirit was not sent to give us goosebumps or speak in tongues; He was sent to give us POWER! Power for what? To blend in with the world or to try to be accepted and liked by the world? No!

Stop trying to get the world to like you if you are from

God's kingdom. Satan hates you; when are we, as believers, going to get that message? Asking the devil to like you on social media is like showing yourself naked to a rapist and asking him not to touch you, and when he does, afterward, asking him do he still like you? When did he like you? We have the nerve to be hurt and shocked when the world turns on the church…because they never liked you; they hate you and always will. Look at the history of good versus evil. We do not have the authority to rewrite the laws of the universe given by God himself. As believers, we must stop seeking approval from the world. Satan hates us, and we need to acknowledge that. Let's not be shocked when the world turns on the church because they never liked us in the first place.

We are in the end times, *"Now concerning the coming of our Lord Jesus Christ and our being gathered together to him, we ask you, brothers, not to be quickly shaken in mind or alarmed, either by a spirit or a spoken word, or a letter seeming to be from us to the effect that the day of the Lord has come. Let no one deceive you in any way. For that day will not come unless the rebellion comes first (a great falling away from the truth), and the man of lawlessness (Anti-Christ) is revealed, the son of destruction, who opposes and exalts himself against every so-called god or object of worship (Lucifer) so that he takes his seat in the temple of God, proclaiming himself to be God.   2 Thessalonians 2:1-4 ESV.*

* * *

People make a mockery of the coming of Jesus out of ignorance; let me update you on this: It is for this generation to know that there is a personal return and a corporate return, just like taxes. We all will pay something; our souls are our returns. When we are born, our souls are assigned to a body, like an assigned social security number. We live and are required to give an account of how we use our bodies in life. We live a lifetime in time, whatever that may be, and then we must return to eternity to be processed. We will see Jesus one way or another. If you are saved and one of His and do not see Him as part of the Rapture (corporate return), you will see Him immediately when you take your last breath (personal return). For the Believer, death is not a punishment but a reward; it will be the best time you've ever experienced; words cannot explain how this feels.

This is why we judge ourselves in this world according to God's word while we are here; then, we do not have to pay or be judged later. It's like owing the IRS payment versus the IRS owing you and making a payment. God is giving out payments (rewards) to His people on that day and the souls that owe Him; that's another story. If you die in your sins, you will see Him when He sends his officers (holy angels) to get you from jail (hell) to come to court and stand before Him for judgment. Your friends and family who didn't make it wish they could come back to tell you they are not Resting In Peace. Hell is not the final destination; the Lake of Fire is. Hell is jail, where you are waiting on your court date. Hell has different parts, just like any other jail, with officers. If there is a Supreme Court in heaven, God the judge, then there must be jail, prison, death row, life without the possibility of parole, and or execution. Didn't they kill Jesus? He said, "My kingdom is not of this world."

What makes people think they can get away with murder? Only the devil can spin that lie. Why do we deceive ourselves into believing there is no justice in Jesus's world (kingdom)? Do you genuinely think that the courts in this world could find God guilty of crimes he did not commit and get away with no punishment, and he definitely did not deserve death? You want to believe all of those who conspired in His death are Resting In Peace. This is a fantasy of no accountability. Satan and his followers are going down, and he wants us and our children to go down with him. We have the power to crush this serpent's head… It is prophesied.

Satan has a reason for coming after you and your seed. This prophecy manifests God's power and grand design, culminating in the triumph of good over evil. The prophecy regarding the power bestowed upon a woman and her seed to crush the head of the serpent and his seed is considered a declaration of war, indicating an ultimate conflict between good and evil. This prophecy tells us there is an ultimate victory of the woman and her seed over evil.

* * *

For those who are not called to preach but are called to be the best woman they can be, don't allow anyone or anything to stop you from your purpose and destiny. If you are a woman and know that you are a real woman, then respect and represent her. Know that if God made you a woman, He made you a game changer. There's no greater influence in this world than you besides God Himself. Bring the good to this troubling world that only you can. You have been ordained to have God's glory and favor to work alongside your anointing. The enemy knows this and has been abusing you while recruiting you at the same time to work for his kingdom, with the understanding that you have the power to turn things around. It's a war going on in the world, and we fight the fight everywhere and every day in politics, relationships, families, marriages, the churches, amongst leaders, our careers, our finances, and above all, a war in our minds. Fight like you've never fought before.

We must be warriors for Christ and the right things. Warriors for your rights as a woman and a woman of God. Whatever you are supposed to do, then fight to do it! We are fighting the fight of faith because we cannot literally see what we are fighting, but the fight is real, and so are the defeats and or victories.

On that day, you will be surprised at who this weak devil is who you allowed to lead you and destroy your life if you don't get to know God and the gift given in the sum of Jesus Christ.

* * *

I am a warrior of Christ and the kingdom. This is why I can write these things because I have fought this devil and know about the enemy. I am looking forward to the day when I crossover to eternity and judgment, where I will be allowed to see eye to eye and fight this cowardly devil who has been hiding behind anyone and anything, manipulating circumstances, and not taking responsibility for the evils he has caused and the lives he deceived and destroyed.

Know this: the enemy is seeking to destroy you because of what God said about you. That Word over your life as a woman. If you don't believe this, then you do not believe God. The enemy is after your faith! This is a faith fight, and "without faith, it is impossible to please God." Know who and what you are up against; know your enemy (no matter what disguise he comes in) and how it's your faith in God, His Word, and what He gives you to speak and do that will crush his head and his offspring.

God said to the devil, "You and the woman will be at war as long you exist," and then he came for her and her seed...***This Is War!***

The Letters

Chapter 15

Paul's conversion is considered proof of the immense power of Divine Grace. Despite his efforts to completely eradicate Christianity, he was transformed into a believer. This event indicates that there is no fall so deep in which grace cannot descend and no height so lofty that grace cannot lift the sinner to it. Moreover, it shows that God can use even a hostile persecutor to accomplish His divine purpose. It cannot be proven that Paul had a clear and coherent theological framework before arriving on the road to Damascus. Instead, his conversion and realization of the importance of the resurrection of Jesus caused him to reevaluate everything he had ever believed in. This included his identity, understanding of Second Temple Judaism, and his perception of who God truly was.

Paul's conversion had a transformative effect on him, leading him to perceive a clear contrast between pursuing righteousness under the law (which he had sought in his earlier life) and righteousness based on the death of Christ. He describes this contrast in his Epistle to the Galatians, among other writings. According to Paul's testimony in Galatians 1 and the accounts in Acts (Acts 9, 22, 26), it appears that Paul was not only converted from first-century Judaism to a faith centered on Jesus Christ but also commissioned as an Apostle to the Gentiles. This is because it is mentioned explicitly that Paul was tasked to be a witness to the Gentiles. It is worth noting that in Paul's mind, conversion and commissioning amounted to the same thing.

"For you have heard of my previous way of life in Judaism. I was known for intensely persecuting the church of God and trying to destroy it. I was advancing in Judaism beyond many of my peers and was extremely zealous for the traditions of my fathers."—Galatians 1:13–14, NIV.

Before his conversion, Paul was known as Saul and was described as "a Pharisee of Pharisees" who "intensely persecuted" the followers of Jesus. In his Epistle to the Galatians, Paul explained that the gospel he preached was not of human origin. He did not receive it from any man or taught it. Instead, he received it by revelation from Jesus Christ. Paul also talked about his previous way of life in Judaism, where he persecuted the church of God and tried to destroy it. However, when God revealed His Son in him, he was called by his grace to preach him among the Gentiles. Paul's immediate response was not to consult any human being.

The Acts of the Apostles discusses Paul's conversion

experience at three different points in the text, in far more detail than in the accounts in Paul's letters. The Book of Acts says that Paul was on his way from Jerusalem to Syrian Damascus with a mandate issued by the High Priest to seek out and arrest followers of Jesus, to return them to Jerusalem as prisoners for questioning and possible execution. The journey is interrupted when Paul sees a blinding light and communicates directly with a divine voice.

The account continues with a description of Ananias of Damascus receiving a divine revelation instructing him to visit Saul at the house of Judas on the Street Called Straight and there to lay hands on him to restore his sight (the home of Judas is traditionally believed to have been near the west end of the street). Ananias is initially reluctant, having heard about Saul's persecution, but obeys the divine command: ***"Then Ananias went to the house and entered it. Placing his hands on Saul, he said, "Brother Saul, the Lord—Jesus, who appeared to you on the road as you were coming here—has sent me so that you may see again and be filled with the Holy Spirit." Immediately, something like scales fell from Saul's eyes, and he could see again. He got up and was baptized, and after taking some food, he regained his strength.— Acts 9:13–19, NIV***

Acts' third discussion of Paul's conversion occurs when Paul addresses King Agrippa, defending himself against the accusations of antinomianism that have been made against him. This account is briefer than the others. The speech here is again tailored for its audience, emphasizing what a Roman ruler would understand: the need to obey a heavenly vision and reassuring Agrippa that Christians were not a secret society. Our Lord blessed Saul with His grace, which enlightened his understanding, moved his heart, and prepared his will to obey all he commanded. Amid his sinful ways, Saul was called by grace to stop, and his heart was utterly transformed. The once bitter enemy of Jesus Christ became an apostle, filled with love, and the persecutor of the Christian faith became its indefatigable defender and advocate. St. Paul was able to recognize the work of grace in his transformation and said of himself: ***"By the grace of God, I am what I am, and His grace in me has not been in vain. I have labored more abundantly than they all, yet not I, but the grace of God with me"*** **(1 Cor. 15:10).**

No one can speak for you. When you have a personal experience with God, it becomes your testament of truth. There may be times when people don't believe you about your encounter with God, but others out there have also had their own spiritual encounter with God. They are your spiritual family. Your spirit, as well as theirs, bears witness that Jesus Christ is the real deal. The Apostle Paul knew much about human nature — the good, the bad, and the ugly. Perhaps it was because he had lived the life of a controlling narcissist and remembered what it was like to have no gratitude in his heart. Before encountering the risen Jesus Christ on the road to Damascus, Paul (or more precisely Saul as he was known at the time) was significant, in charge, and very much in control of his world. He was clearly the authority and had little patience for others who would upstage his glorious character.

The love of God's son, Jesus Christ, had a profound impact on the life of a man who was once notorious for persecuting the church. This man, named Paul, transformed from someone who chased after wealth and power to a person who lived by faith. He moved away from his past, filled with hatred towards anything and anyone beyond his control, to someone who willingly relinquished control out of love for God. Paul became one of God's most notable and productive evangelists from being a disgrace to God. In Philippians 4:12, Paul wrote that he learned an essential secret to living a fulfilling life - the ability to embrace life in both good times and bad times. According to Paul, this secret lies in focusing one's heart and mind on Christ and not worldly things such as money, power, control, fame, and fortune.

However, Paul's secret to happiness and blessings goes beyond confessing faith in Jesus Christ. Paul lived a life of prayerful appreciation and gratitude, as illustrated in 1 Thessalonians 16-18 when he instructed believers to "rejoice always, pray without ceasing, give thanks in all circumstances, for this is the will of God in Christ Jesus for you." Thus, Paul's secret to a fulfilling life is to maintain constant gratitude, prayer, and joy, regardless of one's circumstances. Rather than living lives of spiritual blessing and sacred service in Christ's name, many languish as Saul did. We crave control, power, dominance, and material gain over service, sacrifice, and love. Punitive judgment takes the place of grace. Disdain for differences takes the place of love. Partisan priority takes the place of faithful service. Paul was a person who understood the significance of being grateful, even when things were not going his way. He faced beatings, imprisonment, and disruptions to his daily life without responding with anger or hatred towards the forces working against him. Instead, he chose to find the greater good and the faithful path of resistance by responding with prayerful reflection to his time's political and social challenges. As Christians, we could learn from Paul's example and strive to be more like him rather than the person he was before, Saul.

The Books of the Letters Written by Paul the Apostle were written to the early church, which was nascent and formative. The church needed instructions and guidance as it moved from the Law to Christ, a challenging transition. Becoming a public example of believers in the movement was a new adventure that required careful consideration. They didn't want to be wrong and risk destroying a belief system passed down for generations. The stakes were high, and the question of who is right and wrong loomed large. The Pharisees believed in the Mosaic Law so fervently that they were willing to kill for it. They were convinced that

Jesus of Nazareth's gospel of the kingdom and his claim to be the son of God were false. In this context, imagine Paul being called by God to bring the message of salvation through the grace of God through Jesus Christ. Preserving the Mosaic Law, which was the Pharisees' most sacred belief, and including grace through Jesus Christ as the much-awaited Messiah who had come and gone was a delicate balancing act.

It's important to understand that Paul was sincere and serious about his salvation. He was very protective of reserving the holiness brought to them as a chosen people.

Although Paul was not one of the original 12 Apostles of Jesus, he was one of the most prolific contributors to the New Testament. Of the 27 books in the New Testament, 13 or 14 are traditionally attributed to Paul. These Pauline epistles are accepted as being entirely authentic and dictated by Paul himself.

The Letter of Paul to the Romans: The sixth book of the New Testament, the Letter of Paul to the Romans, was written by Paul while he was in Corinth about 57 CE. It was addressed to the Christian church in Rome, whose congregation he hoped to visit for the first time on his way to Spain. The epistle is the longest and doctrinally most significant of St. Paul's writings and is more of a theological treatise than a letter. In it, he acknowledges the unique religious heritage of the Jews (before his conversion, Paul was a Jewish Pharisee). Still, he asserts that righteousness no longer comes through the Mosaic Law but through Christ.

The Pharisees and Sadducees were the religious leaders who had great power and influence over the Jews as a people. The people looked to them as the holiness of God and the ones chosen to know the way to God. These are the very same leaders who manipulated the circumstances which were responsible for the death of Jesus. They were the direct cause. They made it known privately and publicly that Jesus was an enemy of God, his people, Moses, and their belief system, and his influence was a direct threat to the way they lived. So, these leaders concluded that Jesus must go…he must be put to death. The Romans would carry out the crucifixion, but the Pharisees had their hand on the trigger. They believed Jesus to be a false prophet and were now reserved at making such claims. They hated the influence that Jesus had on the people, and they felt like those were their people. They thought that killing Jesus would solve their problems, and by doing so, they could regain control of the Israelite people and get on with business as usual and temple services.

Paul's birth name was Saul (of Tarsus). He was a very educated man believed to have spoken several languages. Saul was a devout Israelite, loyal and dedicated to the God of Israel. Saul is entrusted with the most notable task of destroying this new movement and phenomenon, Jesus of Nazareth and his followers. Saul was the man! He was focused, wasn't married, had no children, and appeared to have no interest in a personal life…the temple was his life. He served his religious leaders as his way of serving God. Saul was on a mission to destroy this movement called, The Way," those who were followers of Jesus of Nazareth. Saul and his crew were on a direct assignment to punish, kill, abuse, torture, stone, beat, and destroy these people in hopes of deterring them from joining this movement. His reputation had preceded him, and the disciples of Jesus were terrified of him. He had made a name for himself. To the church, Saul was considered to be enemy number one.

He had proven that he had no regard for anyone following Jesus and his disciples. One of the most disturbing things about these followers of Jesus of Nazareth was they had women and children as a part of this movement. The religious leaders viewed this as a cult, very threatening and damaging to their way of life. The women's place was in the home with their children, not being witnesses of this false teacher and prophet. Now, women are allowed to be in worship with men. The Sanhedrin was outraged…something had to be done. They thought they had put a stop to this Jesus of Nazareth. Saul is given this assignment to put an end to this cult, and he is serious about eradicating these people. They are considered traitors to God and the Law of Moses by which they lived.

* * *

During the early days of the Christians, the church was not a physical building but rather a community of believers who followed Jesus and his teachings. They were willing to risk their lives for their freedom and way of life. However, they faced great persecution from religious leaders who saw them as criminals and lawbreakers. They had to be mobile and ready to disperse at a moment's notice to avoid persecution. They would go from house to house, taking turns where the next worship service and teaching would be held. They were constantly on the lookout and had to "watch and pray" to avoid being caught. Despite the persecution and killings, the movement continued to grow, and today, we still follow their teachings. According to the Book of Acts, Saul was traveling to Damascus, where there was a gathering of Jesus's followers known for their congregation and fellowship. This event took place around 4-7 years after the crucifixion of Jesus, indicating that the church was gaining some momentum during that time. It is worth noting that Saul's conversion occurred on the road to Damascus, a significant event in the history of the Christian movement.

Paul is aware that this conversion is historic and brand new, meaning there are no manuals or guidelines to follow. He realizes that he is saved and forgiven by grace, even though he has committed terrible acts against God's people. However, he was only following orders from the Sanhedrin, Pharisees, and Scribes, who were regarded as the oracles of God and the holy men of Israel. Despite their misguided beliefs, he now understands that he was wrong and that God has opened his eyes to the truth. After Jesus revealed himself to Paul, he could no longer continue his mission to fight against the people and believers of the Way. As a result, he no longer feels like the person he was before, as he has been saved by grace. Paul is the apostle chosen by God, while Saul was the self-righteous tyrant fueled by hate and the law.

Paul has a lot to learn quickly and has no reliable human teacher. The Holy Spirit becomes his teacher. Paul is separated from everything familiar; does this sound biblically familiar? All leaders are taken through a process of separation from the familiar. This man has recently become a chosen vessel for the Lord, and He told him that he will suffer many things for His Namesake. This is where we would lose probably 99% of today's apostles. Satan has deceived them into thinking being an apostle means prestige, popularity, acceptance, and prosperity, which could not be further from the truth. Today's apostles love money and want to be rock stars, wanting people to worship them; at the same time, people are suffering and dying; what a waste. This is a disgrace compared to what Jesus, his disciples, and apostles stood for and died for. Why don't you do something openly ungodly as a profession? This way, you're not a hypocrite pretending to be a servant of God and his people. God did not call you; Satan did, and God is calling you out.

* * *

God would not trust any apostle without him first suffering for His name and being set apart. His faith has to be tried against almost everything you thought was right and of God. God can choose no person who loves money or attention for this office because he will abuse the office for selfish gain. True apostles are not chasers of flesh and every kind of doctrine, neither thirsty for the world nor its material things. Those whom Jesus Christ chooses as apostles are granted access to the divine things of the kingdom that cannot be purchased with money, nor should they be tempted to sell them. Apostles are called to establish order and structure rather than selling their bodies to the highest bidder under the guise of "speaking engagements, revivals, and conferences."

It is high time for apostles to take the reins and bring order to the chaos that has consumed us. We must resist the temptation to bow down to the devil in pursuit of recognition, riches, or power. Our weakness as a church lies in the diluted and polluted messages we preach, falsely believing that praise alone satisfies God. But know this: everything gained from the devil will be tested by fire. Let us wait on God and resist the devil's schemes to gain actual open doors, blessings, and everlasting glory.

If God has chosen you, where is your authority over the devil? Where are your Acts of the Holy Spirit that you do not charge money to do? Where are the testimonies of isolation, wilderness, fights with devils and demons, hell, and dimensions of principalities? How about rejection, loss, misunderstanding, sacrifices, suffering, not having many trustworthy friends, and being challenged not to be their deliverer but to wait on God no matter what people say? To be the target of everything undesirable for the call. A true apostle of Jesus Christ will choose God over money and his life.

The apostle Paul went through so much for years, walking in his calling when the other apostles didn't accept or believe him. First, he was the church's number one active enemy and assassin. Two: He had not walked with Jesus with the original 12 disciples turned apostles. He had no physical proof that Jesus had come to him. All he had was his testimony. The church was afraid of him, and rightfully so; he was treacherous. Paul was given three years to learn from the Lord Jesus directly and spiritually; he did not walk with Jesus when he was on the earth. Peter did not meet with Paul until after the three years. By this time, Paul had his doctrine from what he learned in the three years of isolation from religion. Consider that Paul, the apostle, was roughly 30 years old at his conversion. Before his conversion, he had spent three decades taught and trained in the Law of Moses and other religious teachings. These teachings were deeply ingrained in him, and he lived his life according to them.

However, after his conversion, he received teachings

from Jesus and the Holy Spirit for three years. According to his account, he realized that he was a product of the grace and love of Jesus Christ. He knew he was not worthy of being an apostle according to the standards of the law and religion. Despite this, Jesus chose Saul, who later became Paul, to be an apostle. With 30 years of the law versus three years of revelation, he began preaching and guiding new converts, many of whom were Gentiles. He was well-versed in the law but had also experienced grace himself.

However, he faced a challenge in that if he were to teach the law, he would be seen as a hypocrite due to his past actions, such as breaking the law by interacting with Gentiles. Therefore, he had to establish order and set a standard for the church. Paul was an on-the-job learner and did his best to guide the church while staying true to his newfound faith in Jesus Christ. The task of maintaining order in the early Christian community was a challenging one for Paul. As a newly converted apostle, he faced the daunting task of managing a growing network of churches across different regions and cultures. Complicating matters further, was the fact that many of these churches were composed of Gentile converts, who had little knowledge of the Jewish laws and customs that had previously governed religious life.

Paul was keenly aware that he needed to establish a clear set of guidelines that would help to maintain order within the church without imposing the strictures of the

Jewish faith on the Gentile converts. He recognized that the church needed to be distinct from the world in its deeds and appearance, but he also knew that this needed to be achieved in a way that was sensitive to the needs and beliefs of all members of the community. As the churches continued to grow and expand, Paul worked tirelessly to find a way to balance these competing demands. He drew on his deep knowledge of the Jewish faith and his own experiences as a Christian convert to develop a set of principles that would guide the churches in their daily activities and interactions with the broader world. Through his tireless efforts, Paul helped to establish a new order that would ultimately shape the course of Christian history.

- Paul's contributions to the New Testament are recognized by his letters to the church by names or regions, such as;
    - Letter of Paul to the Romans
    - Letters of Paul to the Corinthians, First and Second
    - Letter of Paul to the Galatians
    - Letter of Paul to the Ephesians
    - Letter of Paul to the Philippians
    - Letter of Paul to the Colossians
    - Letter of Paul to the Thessalonians
    - Letters of Paul to Timothy, First and Second
    - Letter of Paul to Titus
    - Letter of Paul to Philemon

* * *

It is widely believed that Apostle Paul wrote neither of the two Letters of Paul to Timothy. Using different words for the same things, repeated unusual phrases, and other linguistic peculiarities provide compelling evidence against their authenticity. Scholars contend that both epistles were likely penned by members of the Pauline school a generation after the apostle's death. The letters were probably written between 80 and 100 CE and should be considered "trito-Pauline."

The letter to Titus is challenged as well, given many of the similarities in content and style to the two letters of Paul to Timothy; this work may also be a trito-Pauline epistle, written a generation after the death of Paul. The three letters together are often called Pastoral Letters, as they were written to instruct and admonish the recipients in their pastoral office rather than address congregations' specific problems like many of the other Pauline epistles.

It's important to delve into the historical and cultural context of Paul's letters to truly understand his stance on women's roles in the church. While he once wrote that women should remain silent and not have authority over men, later accounts show him accepting and honoring women for their teaching and contributions to the faith. It's important to remember that these letters were written to specific people and situations and cannot be viewed as universal truths. Furthermore, it's worth noting that Paul struggled to reconcile the old and new ways of thinking and wrote to devout Israelites under the Law of Moses. He had to be wise and sensitive to cultural nuances to address each situation and people effectively, given that he grew up in the law. Paul had one of the most supernatural and phenomenal encounters with Christ that ultimately changed his life forever, and it's essential to recognize that this experience cannot be the norm or expected of every believer. Therefore, it's crucial to consider all these factors before making any assumptions about Paul's teachings.

We must consider one's upbringing. I grew up in the Pentecostal, Holiness, and Apostolic Faith denominations, which had a strict upbringing. Men were prohibited from wearing shorts or short-sleeved shirts that showed their arms. They were not allowed to wear jewelry except for a watch or wedding ring if they were married. Long hair, braids, movie theaters, and televisions were also not allowed. Women had even more restrictions, including no pants, makeup, hair color, no cutting of the hair, earrings, or braids. The rules varied depending on which of the three denominations you were affiliated with. Later on, preachers would ask us to donate to their Christian and television ministries; they were wearing jewelry and makeup on almost everything and pulpits everywhere, which was confusing considering the strict upbringing we had. Did God change His mind, or was it the mind of men in power and authority?

* * *

I wonder what happened from the 1960s to the present day. I once heard preachers tell the women in the congregation that wearing pants, makeup, or jewelry would send them to hell. This was their doctrine. I'm not mocking the teachings, but was it God or His heart? Were these preachers evil? Did they not want people to live full lives, or were they following a law or scriptures without full understanding? Did you know that when light bulbs were first introduced as a more convenient alternative to kerosene lamps and candles, some Christian pastors condemned them as "the works of the devil" and advised their congregants not to bring them into their homes? This is a clear example of ignorance leading to superstition, with an attempt to explain new technology through the concept of the devil. It's hard to imagine church services and life without electricity now. What's ironic is that Jesus himself said, "You are the lights of the world," yet some Christians believed that electric light was the devil's creation.

Did you know that in Israelite and Hebrew cultures, only the Priests were allowed to handle the Tora, the word of God? And that anyone outside of the seed of Abraham was considered a heathen, a dog? It's fascinating to think that even today, some people call each other dogs a sign of endearment, but in that culture, it was derogatory. Furthermore, it was a sin punishable by death for any Gentile or non-Abrahamic person to preach the gospel or God's word, call God's name, or read scripture. These cultural traditions highlight the strict adherence to religious practices and the deep-seated prejudices and exclusions within the community. So here's my letter: Apostle Paul was not talking to you and the entire world; some letters were written specifically to particular persons. We desperately need revival, and Paul loved the Lord too much to be an adversary and a stumbling block to the gospel being preached. People are dying with no hope while celebrity preachers are on the golf course, at nail salons, massage, and spas, on yachts, getting fitted for designer clothes, at the car dealership, looking at a bigger house, I have no problem with those things and if I did… who cares right? But to stop a woman from answering her call to preach while you are hooking up with mistresses and misters, doing drugs, getting drunk, and sowing your oats all over the world.

This is what I have a problem with. We are short of non-hypocritical preachers who have a consecrated prayer life. Men of the cloth and power have taken prayer out of the church… don't talk to me about them taking prayer out of the schools. We need prayer more than production… someone's been deceived. Our churches have good production; we know how to put on a good show, but we can't live holy. Sounds familiar, of course; the devil can't live holy, either. Don't tell me a woman can't preach. We need to see prayer warriors and preachers who are faithful, dedicated, and who can say no to the devil and "The lust of the eye, the lust of the flesh, and the pride of life."

* * *

I stand against those who deny women the right to preach while indulging in the oldest sins of the flesh. I advocate for dedicated women who serve God wholeheartedly, understanding that one day they will answer to Him for their lives. These women desire to please God but are hindered by man-made restrictions. It's time to stop using them for your purposes and telling them they cannot preach. The truth is that God made the woman and will use her to His glory. If you are guilty of using a woman to gratify your desires, then it's time to stop and repent. God did not call you to manipulate or abuse anyone.

He anointed these women to preach the Kingdom's Gospel and save lives. And if they are doing that, they are following in the footsteps of Jesus. Don't be like Eve in the Garden of Eden, who made foolish decisions that led to her and her husband's downfall. Instead, listen to the voice of God and embrace the truth. Jesus prayed for you in the Garden of Gethsemane, submitted to God's will, and died for you to set you free from bondage and sex slavery, especially in the church. So, let's honor God and His sacrifice of His son, Jesus, by empowering women to preach and to fulfill their God-given destinies.

It is a sin to make a woman feel condemned for preaching the Gospel of the Kingdom and Jesus Christ, especially when she has been anointed and called by God.

This is not what the Apostle Paul intended to endorse through his letters. Paul's unwavering commitment towards the salvation and deliverance of people from the clutches of the enemy is unparalleled. His dedication to the growth of the kingdom is beyond reproach, and he would never do anything that could hinder or deflect it. This man loved Jesus too much for this foolishness, and he proved it and was playing no games, so why are you?

Can A Woman Preach? She already is…

Note from The Author

When a person has everything yet still feels incomplete, they often take risks in search of fulfillment. But in doing so, they may lose what they already have. Many try to hold onto their current life while seeking something more, only to find themselves trapped in confusion and loss.

As believers, one of our greatest struggles is that we do not fully understand our enemy. But make no mistake—he knows everything about us. He studies our weaknesses, crafts deceptive strategies, and sets traps to sever our connection with God. His greatest downfall was his failure with God, and humanity became his replacement. But before he waged war against all of humankind, he targeted one figure in particular—the woman.

The woman was the first to capture his attention after his fall from grace. In her, he saw beauty, divine glory, and the miraculous ability to create life. But instead of revering her, he envied her. His jealousy turned into hatred, and from that hatred, he sought to destroy her. This is why, throughout history, women have been blamed for the world's evils, scorned, and silenced. But the truth is, she was set up—targeted with cunning precision to make her stumble, in hopes that her fall would bring down humanity and betray God's plan.

Yet, despite his relentless attacks, the woman has always risen. And yes, she can preach. She can lead. She can teach the Word of God with power and authority because she was never meant to be silenced—she was meant to be a voice.

"Beware, for the Devil and his followers have fallen to the earth with great wrath."
Lucifer was the first to be "mad as hell," and from his rage, Satan emerged. Out of Satan came the Devil. His mission is clear—to keep us bound in deception and fear. But we have a choice.

It is imperative that while you are still on this earth, you ask yourself: **Whose side are you on?** Will you let the enemy steal your purpose, silence your voice, and keep you from the calling God has placed on your life? Or will you rise, take charge, and walk boldly in the truth?

You cannot serve two masters. Choose today whom you will follow.

* * *

Note from the Author

As Believers, we desperately need to come together in prayer. We must find a way to unify with the love of Jesus Christ. Imagine the power of an entire nation praying at the same time to the same God. Think about the impact we could have in our relationships, homes, communities, schools, and even work if we started our days with prayer. Just 7 minutes of giving God our undivided attention. I believe this is the offering our Lord desires from us, not money. He wants our hearts...

Prayer Challenge

"My Father's House Shall Be Called A House Of Prayer."
7 MINUTES WITH GOD PRAYER CHALLENGE
A place where we are laying down our phones and devices…yes, you heard me correctly, our smart phones and devices for just Seven (7) DEDICATED minutes with God.
Calling on all Prayer Warriors!
We have traded praying for great production. We are in troubling times. The world and the church are falling apart; we must admit that we owe God an apology and must repent.
Wherever you are in this world, as believers let's agree to pray everyday
@ 7:00 a.m.
Whatever your time zone
INFO@KINGDOMRIGHTS2.ORG
LET'S PRAY!

Stay Connected

<u>Books:</u>

We are excited to announce that Joseph Brice has published three (3) additional books:

* God The Woman & Their Enemy: (Available in English and Spanish)

* Why I Satan Hate The Woman

* Resurrection

- These books are available in Hardback, Paperback, Ebook, and Audio.

- Available on Amazon, Barnes and Noble, Apple Books, Google Books, and Walmart Ebook

- Also available on our own Kingdom Store @kingdomrights2.org

* * *

Available NOW!   On Apple Podcast, Audible, Amazon Music, Spotify, Pandora, iHeart Radio, SiriusXM, and Google Podcast.

Kingdom Podcast: See the Link Below

When It's All Said And Done

https://KingdomRights.sermon.net/main/main/22177375

Seven Minutes with God Podcast: See the Link Below

Can A Woman Preach?

https://KingdomRights.sermon.net/22180281

ALL options are available on your Apple and Android App Store and Our own Kingdom Rights app.   Look for our Logo.

Kingdom Rights Website: Kingdomrights2.org